Practitioner's Guide to Quality and Process Improvement

Practitioner's Guide to Quality and Process Improvement

Adedeji B. Badiru PhD

Associate Professor
School of Industrial Engineering
University of Oklahoma
USA, and
Senior Member
Institute of Industrial Engineers

and

Babatunde J. Ayeni PhD

Statistical Specialist
3M Information Technology, Statistical Consulting Department
St Paul
Minnesota
USA

CHAPMAN & HALL

London · Glasgow · New York · Tokyo · Melbourne · Madras

Published by Chapman & Hall, 2–6 Boundary Row, London SE1 8HN

Chapman & Hall, 2–6 Boundary Row, London SE1 8HN, UK

Blackie Academic & Professional, Wester Cleddens Road, Bishopbriggs, Glasgow G64 2NZ, UK

Chapman & Hall Inc., 29 West 35th Street, New York NY10001, USA

Chapman & Hall Japan, Thomson Publishing Japan, Hirakawacho Nemoto Building, 6F, 1–7–11 Hirakawa-cho, Chiyoda-ku, Tokyo 102, Japan

Chapman & Hall Australia, Thomas Nelson Australia, 102 Dodds Street, South Melbourne, Victoria 3205, Australia

Chapman & Hall India, R. Seshadri, 32 Second Main Road, CIT East, Madras 600 035, India

First edition 1993

© 1993 Adedeji B. Badiru and Babatunde J. Ayeni

Typeset in 10/12pt Times by Columns Design and Production Services Ltd., Reading, Berks
Printed in Great Britain by TJ Press (Padstow) Ltd, Cornwall

ISBN 0 412 48280 0

A catalogue record for this book is available from the British Library.

Library of Congress Cataloging-in-Publication data

Badiru, Adedeji Bodunde, 1952–
   Practitioner's guide to quality and process improvement / Adedeji B. Badiru and Babatunde J. Ayeni.
      p. cm.
   Includes bibliographical references and index.
   ISBN 0–412–48280–0
   1. Quality control – Statistical methods   2. Process control – Statistical methods.   I. Ayeni, Babatunde J.   II. Title.
   TS156.B33   1993
   658.5'62'015195 – dc20   103900   93–3335
                                                                CIP

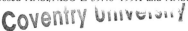

To our wives, Flora Ayeni and Iswat Badiru, without whose support (night and day) we could not have completed this book

Contents

Preface   xi
Acknowledgments   xiii

1 The quality revolution   1
   1.1   Systems definition of quality   2
   1.2   Total quality management   4
   1.3   Just in time   6
   1.4   Move toward globalization   7
   1.5   Japanese influence on quality movement   8
   1.6   European influence on quality movement   9
   1.7   International standard for quality: ISO 9000   10
   1.8   Malcolm Baldrige award   12
   1.9   Deming's contributions   18
   1.10 Taguchi's contributions   22
   1.11 Juran's contributions   24
   1.12 Ishikawa's contributions   25
   1.13 Feigenbaum's contributions   26
   1.14 Crosby's contributions   26
   1.15 Motorola's six sigma approach   28
   1.16 Quality and competitive edge   28
   1.17 Case study: quality and productivity
         improvement in Taiwan   30

2 Fundamentals of quality improvement   36
   2.1   Components of quality improvement   36
   2.2   Customer involvement   37
   2.3   Vendor involvement and certification   39
   2.4   Employee involvement   41
   2.5   Quality of manufactured goods   42
   2.6   Quality of service   44
   2.7   Employee motivation and quality of work   45
   2.8   MBO versus Deming philosophy   48
   2.9   Management support   49
   2.10 Preparing for change to quality improvement   50
   2.11 Strategic quality planning   50

2.12 Prevention versus detection and correction   51
2.13 Benchmarking for quality improvement   52
2.14 Triple C approach to quality improvement   61
2.15 Quality improvement group meetings   64
2.16 Continuous process improvement   69
2.17 Continuous measurable improvement   72
2.18 Quality function deployment   72
2.19 Quality–productivity improvement relationship   73
2.20 Quality evaluation using the analytic hierarchy process   74

3 Fundamentals of process improvement   84
3.1 Defining a process   84
3.2 Barriers to quality and process improvement   87
3.3 Improving quality through process improvement   89
3.4 Process improvement feasibility study   90
3.5 Product redesign and process improvement   90
3.6 Quality–value breakeven analysis   92
3.7 Importance of ergonomics in process improvement   99
3.8 Learning curves and process improvement   101
3.9 Learn–forget models   110
3.10 Process technology transfer   116
3.11 Process conversion strategies   118
3.12 Fuzzy set modeling for process improvement   120
3.13 Fuzzy quality model   123
3.14 Managerial aspects of process improvement   128

4 Project management approach to quality and process improvement   130
4.1 Importance of project management   131
4.2 Project management steps for quality improvement   132
4.3 Project implementation model   136
4.4 Selling the project plan   138
4.5 Quality policy   139
4.6 Project leadership   140
4.7 Project organization   141
4.8 Selecting a project manager   145
4.9 Work breakdown structure   146
4.10 Project planning   147
4.11 Project scheduling   148
4.12 Project control   166
4.13 Project decision model   171
4.14 Resolving project conflicts   173

5 Process management and control   175
   5.1   Process formulation   175
   5.2   Key quality characteristics   176
   5.3   Process flow diagram   177
   5.4   Monitoring a process   178
   5.5   Diagnosing a process   184
   5.6   Case study for vendor selection   214

6 Statistical tools for quality improvement   222
   6.1   Statistical process control   222
   6.2   Trend analysis   234
   6.3   Process capability   238
   6.4   Design of experiments   256

7 Additional statistical techniques   268
   7.1   Factorial designs   268
   7.2   Experimental run   271
   7.3   Experimenting with two factors: 2^2 275
   7.4 2^3 factorial design   280
   7.5   Fractional factorial experiments   283
   7.6   A 2^4 factorial design   284
   7.7   Saturated designs   288
   7.8   Response surface methodology   290
   7.9   Central composite designs   298
   7.10 Time series analysis   302
   7.11 Exponentially weighted moving average   306
   7.12 Systems approach to process adjustment   314
   7.13 ARIMA modeling of process data   314
   7.14 Minimum variance control (MVC)   316

Appendix A   Glossary and acronyms   318
Appendix B   Process conversion factors   328
Appendix C   Statistical tables   333
Bibliography   338
Index   350

Preface

Quality and process improvement is now a major concern of business and industry establishments all over the world. A good indicator of the increasing interest in quality is the number of quality-related awards that have been instituted in various parts of the world in the past few years. To implement their quality improvement programs, many organizations need simple guidelines that can be followed in practical terms. This book is designed to offer such a guideline. The book presents techniques through which quality and process improvement can be achieved in any business, service, or manufacturing organization. The book shows the steps to improving quality, increasing productivity, reducing product development costs, and meeting the challenges of competition.

The primary audience for the book consists of practitioners in all functional areas of business and industry. Examples of the relevant functional areas include industrial and systems engineers, process engineers, designers, R&D managers, plant managers, production supervisors, manufacturing engineers, and quality engineers. The book should also appeal to academic institutions and professional training organizations as a reference material.

The book presents both the managerial and technical aspects of quality and process improvement. Chapter 1 presents a detailed discussion of the quality revolution currently sweeping the world. The national quality drives in Japan, Europe, and the US are discussed. The individuals who pioneered world-famous quality concepts are also discussed. The chapter concludes with a case study of quality and productivity improvement in Taiwan. Chapter 2 presents the fundamentals of quality improvement. Topics covered in the chapter include customer, vendor, and employee involvement processes, management support, strategic planning for quality improvement, and benchmarking for quality improvement.

Chapter 3 presents the fundamentals of process improvement. Topics covered in this chapter include process improvement feasibility study, product redesign, quality-value breakeven analysis, tooling for process improvement, learning curves, fuzzy modeling for process improvement, and managerial aspects of process improvement. Chapter 4 covers the project management approach to quality and process improvement. Topics discussed include project management steps for quality improvement, quality policy, work breakdown structure, project control, and resolving project conflicts. Chapter 5 covers process management and control. Topics covered include process formulation, quality characteristics, monitoring a process, run charts, process variation, and vendor selection. Chapters 6 and 7 present a comprehensive coverage of statistical tools for quality improvement. Topics covered include statistical process control, control charts, trend analysis, process capability analysis, factorial designs, design of experiments, and time series analysis. An extensive bibliography is included for further reference by interested readers.

Adedeji B. Badiru PhD
Babatunde J. Ayeni PhD

Acknowledgments

We thank all our friends and colleagues who extended their moral support and encouragement throughout the preparation of this book. We thank Mark Hammond, senior editor at Chapman & Hall, for his aggressive and prompt pursuit of this project. Without his total commitment, this work would not have been possible. We also thank the entire staff of Chapman & Hall for their excellent job throughout the production process. We thank our families for bearing with us during the writing of this book. We also thank our colleagues at 3M who reviewed the earlier draft of this book.

The quality revolution

1

Good quality is everybody's responsibility; bad quality is everybody's fault
Badiru, 1990

This chapter presents an overview of the revolution that has occurred in quality management in the past few years. Quality is now on the mind of every entrepreneur. Even public agencies that have traditionally been viewed as not caring about the quality of their products and services are now aggressively pursuing quality improvement standards. Worldwide business competition has helped to fuel the drive towards quality improvement. So prevalent has the notion of quality become that parents are being urged to spend 'quality time' with their children.

Customers and consumers are so sophisticated now that they will no longer simply accept whatever is offered in the market. In the past, consumers were expected to make do with the inherent quality of the available product, no matter how low it may be. This has changed drastically in the past few years. For a product to satisfy the sophisticated taste of the modern consumer, it must exhibit a high level of quality. Only high quality products and services can survive the prevailing market competition. The premise of this book is that quality improvement must be approached from an integrated point of view. Thus, the systems approach to quality improvement is a concept that is presented throughout the book.

There are two aspects of quality and process improvement: the qualitative aspects and the quantitative aspects. It is recommended that the qualitative aspects precede the quantitative aspects. So important are the qualitative aspects that we have devoted most of the first four chapters to the fundamental qualitative considerations. The last two chapters are devoted to quantitative analyses needed to pave the way for quality and process improvement.

Sections presented in this book are, by design, brief and concise to facilitate ease of assimilation for practical implementations. The need of the practitioner is kept in mind throughout the discussions. Simple illustrative examples are presented for the cases where mathematical or theoretical approaches are discussed. An extensive bibliography is presented at the end of the book for the reader's further reference.

1.1 SYSTEMS DEFINITION OF QUALITY

Quality is a universal language
Badiru (1990) points out that 'good quality is everybody's responsibility while bad quality is everybody's fault.' What is quality? Several definitions have been offered for quality in recent years. No matter which definition one adopts, the bottom line is that quality is a measure of customer satisfaction. Quality refers to the combination of characteristics of a product, process, or service that determines the product's ability to satisfy specific needs.

The quality of a product or service should be defined in terms of how the user perceives the product or service. A product that is viewed as being of high quality for one purpose or at one given time frame may not be considered to be of high quality for another purpose or in another time frame. The goal of an organization should be to strive continually to provide higher quality products and services based on the prevailing customer needs.

An integrated systems approach to quality management facilitates an awareness of the importance of quality throughout an organization. A systems approach considers all the interactions necessary between the various elements of the organization, including people and machines. A system is a collection of interrelated elements working together synergistically to achieve a common goal. We offer the following systems-oriented definition of quality:

> Quality refers to an equilibrium level of functionality possessed by a product or service based on the producer's capability and the customer's needs.

The producer's capability is defined by the aggregate capabilities of the people, machines, and other production facilities available to the producer. The customer's needs are defined by a combination of what the customer wants, what the customer needs, and what the customer favors. Each component of the producer's capability and the customer's needs may be viewed as a subsystem of the overall quality management system.

The supporting cooperative actions of subsystems in a quality management system serve to counterbalance the weaknesses at certain points in the system. The individual capabilities of the subsystems complement each other. Thus, the overall effectiveness of the system can be higher than the sum of the individual outputs from the subsystems. The customer and the producer must work together to define what constitutes an acceptable quality level. Figure 1.1 illustrates how the customer's input is vital to the pursuit of quality improvement.

Organizations that consistently deliver high quality products and services in a timely fashion succeed because of the efforts they commit to quality management. Quality is not just a matter of having high quality raw material, it is also a matter of the people and equipment handling the raw material. Total quality management should cover the systems integration of all the functions in a product life cycle including:

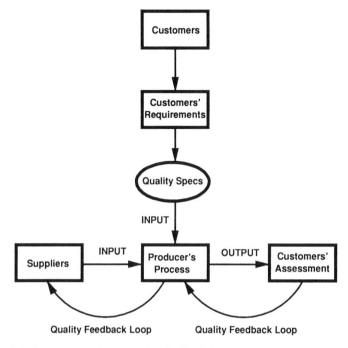

Figure 1.1 Customer–producer quality feedback loop.

1. Design;
2. Planning;
3. Production;
4. Distribution;
5. Field service.

Each of these functions needs to be integrated with respect to quality objectives. It is only then that the quality of output at each stage of organizational effort will be preserved throughout the subsequent stages. The design stage, in particular, should consider future operating environments and the capability of the available manufacturing processes. For example, the lack of proper communication between design and manufacturing groups has been the root of major quality problems in many manufacturing companies. The prevailing self-serving views of functional departments in industry continue to make it difficult for those departments to achieve cooperative communication and interaction. Sole point performance measurement approaches currently used by managers create disruptive competition rather than cooperation among departments in the same organization.

The global view provided by a systems approach ensures that all the factors which can influence product quality are considered. Such factors may include the business activities of purchasing, budgeting, and customer service. These non-manufacturing functions are often ignored in conventional quality control efforts; but they, none the less, can affect product quality just as much as any physical manufacturing function.

1.2 TOTAL QUALITY MANAGEMENT

Total quality management (TQM) is a concept that has emerged as a way to achieve a systems approach to quality management. Total quality management refers to a total commitment to quality. Total, in this sense, refers to an overall integrated approach to all aspects of quality, considering all the people, all the hardware, all the software, and all the organizational resources. This requires the total participation of everyone. Quality is required from all the people at all times! A colleague once remarked that, 'If you could say TQM, CPI, JIT, TQC, SPC, etc. fast enough, you could get promoted to the next higher level.' Figure 1.2 presents a model of components integration in a total quality management system. The model recommends the integration of the various subsystems with respect to quality objectives.

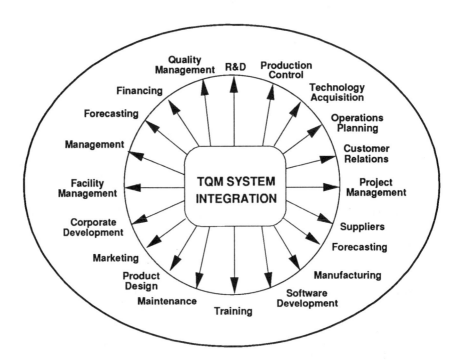

Figure 1.2 Systems integration of quality functions.

In non-TQM organizations, a variety of systems and subsystems exists without an effective interaction. Such disjointed subsystems may include the following:

- management system;
- manufacturing system;
- design and engineering system;
- management information system;
- financial information system;
- marketing information system;
- inventory information system;
- personnel information system;
- production information system.

Some of these subsystems may even have different and conflicting priorities within the same organization. In order to achieve the benefits of TQM, management must ensure that quality objectives are prioritized, integrated, and applied uniformly and consistently throughout the organization with a global systems objective. An organization should pursue a total commitment to quality.

1.2.1 Characteristics of a TQM system

As in the classical definition of a system, a TQM system has some unique characteristics that an organization should understand and promote. These characteristics are:

1. interaction with the environment;
2. possession of an objective;
3. self-regulation capability;
4. self-adjustment capability.

With respect to quality management, interaction with the environment may be defined in terms of what the market environment (the customer) wants. The objective of the quality management system is to achieve an acceptable level of quality. The self-regulation characteristic relates to the system's ability to maintain the stipulated quality level once it is achieved. The self-adjustment characteristic relates to the system's ability to make amendment should the quality level deviate significantly from the required level. The acceptable quality level itself should not be stagnant. It should be reviewed periodically and upgraded as market desires shift.

1.2.2 Justification and benefits of TQM

Manufacturing and service organizations are now being characterized by an increased demand for higher quality products and services. There is an increasing pressure for more effective use of the few resources that are available. Technology and quality management have emerged to play a major role in the success or failure of enterprises. To manage operations successfully, managers will need to view the quality management function on the basis of systems requirements. Specific operations within an organization should be viewed as components of a large system that must be integrated to achieve the overall quality objective of the organization. TQM facilitates an appreciation for integration of advanced technology, a revision of the corporate culture, upgrade of production infrastructure and, most importantly, the utilization of human resources. It is the people aspects of managing quality that make TQM essential. TQM is not in effect in an organization if it does not affect all the people and all the products all the time. TQM offers the following advantages:

- higher productivity;
- better employee relations;
- cooperative regulation of efforts;
- higher potential for profitability;
- interaction with subsystem environments;
- uniformity and consistency of quality objectives;
- specification of the interrelationships of subsystems;
- systematic solution of quality problems in an organization;
- coordinated adjustment of functions to solve quality problems;
- dynamic integration of activities into an effective total system;
- increased probability, frequency and consistency of making good products.

Lehr (1989), retired chairman of the board and CEO of 3M Company, pointed out that 'lack of quality is one of the most obvious symptoms of real organizational problems.' Mishne (1988) suggested that a new attitude toward quality be instituted in all organizations. Such a new attitude can be fostered by TQM.

1.3 JUST IN TIME

If we don't have time to do it right, right now, when would we have time to do it? Doing things at the right time is the premise of just in time (JIT), a concept that complements the ideas of TQM. JIT is a materials control strategy that schedules supplies as required for work without buffer stock or excess inventory. JIT calls for getting the right materials in the right quantity at the right time. JIT links a series of work requirements, analyzing demands for the next work to be done. JIT has been called by various names including the following:

- ZIPS (zero inventory production system);
- MAN (material as needed);
- MIPS (minimum inventory production system);

- stockless production;
- continuous flow manufacturing;
- Kanban;
- Toyota system;
- Ohno system (after Taiichi Ohno, a Toyota vice-president and mastermind of the system).

What is worth doing is worth doing right, promptly. The major benefits of JIT can be summarized as follows:

- fast feedback about process performance;
- reduction in lot size;
- more consistent output rates;
- less inventory in system;
- less material waste;
- fewer rework labor hours;
- less indirect cost in the following areas:
  (a) interest charge on idle inventory
  (b) inventory holding cost
  (c) inventory accounting cost
  (d) control cost for physical inventory.

1.4 MOVE TOWARD GLOBALIZATION

Momentous changes around the world are having profound effects on international trade. The changes in eastern Europe, the advancements in western Europe, the reunification of Germany, the breakup of the former Soviet Union, economic advancements in Japan, Korea, Singapore, Malaysia, Taiwan and China, and the emergence of Africa as a viable market will all affect international trade in the coming years. The quality of product will be one common basis for trade communication. Companies and countries must recognize the trend and refocus their efforts. Some of the key aspects of globalization are:

- transition of some countries from being trade partners to being trade competitors;
- reduction of production cycle time to keep up with the multilateral introduction of products around the world;
- increased efforts to cope with the reduction in the life span of products from years to months;
- increased responsiveness to the needs of a mixed work force;
- the need to eradicate cultural barriers;
- relaxation and expansion of trade boundaries;
- integration of operations and services, and consolidation of efforts;
- more effective and responsive communication media;

- increased pressure for multinational cooperation;
- need for multicompany and multiproduct coordination.

1.5 JAPANESE INFLUENCE ON QUALITY MOVEMENT

The emergence of Japan as an economic leader has had a profound effect on the quality revolution. The Japanese approaches, as evidenced by the works of Akao and Asaka (1990), Mizuno (1988), Taguchi (1990), Deming (1982), Kume (1988), Osada (1991), Imai (1990), Ishikawa (1986), Feigenbaum (1983), Crosby (1984), and Juran (1989), have provided the impetus for new approaches to quality. Japanese quality improvement and management models are now widely adopted all over the world. The key to the success of Japan in the world market lies in the multilateral approaches used for quality management. In a Japanese production environment, quality is viewed as a bottom-up, top-down, and lateral integration of functions.

As long ago as 1961, Juran pointed out that the Japanese attention to quality would be the impetus that would take them to the top of the world market (Juran, 1961). In the late 1970s, western companies began to recognize and accept the fact that Japanese success in the world marketplace was as a result of the high quality products offered by Japan. Awareness of the Japanese approach to quality led American industry to begin to focus on the quality management and statistical techniques now being disseminated through numerous publications.

Dr W. Edwards Deming provided the catalyst for the quality movement that started in Japan. The Japanese enthusiastically adopted and methodically implemented Deming's philosophies to improve the quality of their products. Western companies that originally ignored Deming's philosophies before Deming exported them to Japan are now scrambling to find out how Japan turned the philosophies into pragmatic production approaches. Japan's success has established the yardstick by which all quality improvement endeavours will be measured throughout the world.

The Japanese approach to quality is simple, straightforward, and effective. It is the simplicity of the approach that makes it understandable and workable in any organization. The approach covers the basics listed below:

- avenues for identifying, analyzing, and correcting problems are put in place;
- significant emphasis is placed on training;
- each employee is given the basic tools needed for quality improvement efforts;
- attitude of pride in workmanship is encouraged throughout the organization;
- each employee is empowered to preside over the quality issues affecting his or her job;
- each employee exhibits a sense of responsibility for the products and services he or she generates.

Most of the basic tools that the Japanese use to study and improve quality originated from western organizations. But the Japanese have found an effective way to make practical uses of these tools, even while the developers are still debating their merits. The drive and motivation for quality improvement is one of Japan's major exports to the rest of the world.

1.6 EUROPEAN INFLUENCE ON QUALITY MOVEMENT

Just as the Japanese influence of quality revolution has been widely recognized, the European influence has also been widely acclaimed. The advent of the European Community (EC) has brought on the adoption of national and international quality standards. The 1957 Treaty of Rome established four areas of European cooperation: continental trade; regional research and technology development; economic and monetary union; and working conditions and environment. Twelve countries make up the EC: Britain, France, Germany, Italy, Ireland, Belgium, Holland, Luxembourg, Spain, Portugal, Denmark, and Greece. The Single European Act of February of 1986 amended the Treaty of Rome to facilitate progress with the unification program.

The Single Europe Act (SEA) of 1992 unified over 350 million Europeans into a single market. The main purpose of unification is to ensure that products manufactured in one EC country will be admitted to the markets of all other member countries. The unified Europe will be the largest and fastest growing marketplace for the next several decades. Every government and every individual in the EC member countries, as well as those outside the EC, will be affected by widespread changes in many economic domains including regulations on quality standards. In the EC, labour, capital, goods, and services may cross borders freely.

The objectives of the EC are achieved by establishing and adhering to standards. Standards written by different European countries pertaining to the same area will be unified into one integrated standard. The EC has agreements with EFTA (the European Free Trade Association of Austria, Finland, Iceland, Norway, Sweden, and Switzerland) for the adoption of standards. Many European companies are now requiring their suppliers, both within and outside the EC, to comply with the prevailing quality standards. Due to the removal of trade barriers in Europe, companies want to be assured that their suppliers deliver high quality products and services.

Instead of negotiating quality requirements with each customer, companies will be required to submit to auditing by licensed quality system auditors in order to be registered as complying suppliers. Most companies that expect to export their products to Europe are now planning to conform to the quality standards. These standards are now being required for doing business in the international marketplace. Thus, the European quality requirements have fueled the race for better quality all over the world. In terms of sheer numbers, the

European influence cannot be ignored. The statistics below attest to this fact:

- a combined population of 355 million (larger than that of the US);
- a combined GNP of $5 trillion (compared to $4 trillion for the US);
- the addition of 1.8 million new jobs;
- an estimated increase of $260 billion in goods and services;
- potential for attracting technical manpower away from developing and developed countries.

1.7 INTERNATIONAL STANDARD FOR QUALITY: ISO 9000

The striving for better quality worldwide has led to the need for unified international quality standards. The International Organization for Standardization (ISO) in Geneva, Switzerland, in responding to this need, has prepared the quality standard known as ISO 9000. The ISO is a special international agency for standardization composed of the national standards bodies of 91 countries.

What is ISO 9000?

ISO 9000 is a set of five individual but related international standards on quality management and quality assurance. The standards were developed to help companies effectively document the quality system elements required to maintain an efficient quality system. The standards were originally published in 1987. They are not specific to any particular industry, product, or service. The five individual standards that make up the ISO 9000 series are explained below.

ISO 9000

Title: *Quality Management and Quality Assurance Standards: Guidelines for use.* This is the road map that provides guidelines for selecting and using 9001, 9002, 9003, and 9004. A supplementary publication, ISO 8402, provides quality related definitions.

ISO 9001

Title: *Quality Systems: Model for quality assurance in design/development, production, installation and servicing.* This is the most comprehensive standard. It presents a model for quality assurance for design, manufacturing, installation and servicing systems.

ISO 9002

Title: *Quality Systems: Model for quality assurance in production and installation.* This presents a model for quality assurance in production and installation.

ISO 9003

Title: *Quality Systems: Model for quality assurance in final inspection and test.* This presents a model for quality assurance in final inspection and test.

ISO 9004

Title: *Quality Management and Quality Systems Elements: Guidelines.* This provides guidelines to users in the process of developing in-house quality systems.

Purpose of ISO 9000

The ISO 9000 standards help in determining capable suppliers with effective quality assurance systems. The standards help reduce buyers' quality costs through confidence and assurance in suppliers' quality practices. Compliance with an ISO 9000 standard provides a means for contractual agreement between the buyer and the supplier. Companies that are certified and registered as meeting the ISO standards will be perceived as viable suppliers to their customers. Those that are not will be perceived as providing less desirable products and services.

The standards are designed to address a variety of quality management scenarios. For example, if a supplier has only a manufacturing facility with no design or development function, then ISO 9002 would be used to evaluate the quality system. Each country has its own quality system standards that relate to the ISO 9000 standards. Each individual company is encouraged to register formally for compliance with the standards. In fact, a request for a supplier's ISO 9000 registration number has become an important element when companies make their selection of suppliers.

The ISO 9000 series standards define the minimum requirements a supplier must meet to assure its customers that they are receiving high quality products. This has had a major impact on companies around the world. Through the ISO standards, suppliers can now be evaluated consistently and uniformly. The ISO 9000 series has been adopted in the US by the American National Standards Institute (ANSI) and the American Society for Quality Control (ASQC) as ANSI/ASQC Q90 standards. The European equivalent of ISO 9000, named EN 290000 series, also has world impact.

ISO 9000 audit and registration process

The implementation of ISO 9000 is carried out through a third-party process. The third party, usually a local standards organization, for example, Underwriters Laboratory (UL), acts as an independent body in evaluating a supplier's quality system. Some of the key elements that the third-party auditors check for in a company are as follows.

- A check of whether the company has a documentation process. Does the documentation provide adequate guidelines for workers?
- A check of whether everyone in the company is following the documented process. Is everyone aware of updates and changes to the documentation?

- A check of how materials are selected. Are appropriate materials selected for specific processes?
- A check of how in-house inspections of suppliers' deliveries are carried out. Is the company getting what it wants from suppliers?
- A check of the calibration and metrology processes. Are calibrations done properly? Are measurements being made accurately?
- A check of the procedure for taking corrective actions. Are avenues available for identifying, reporting, and correcting problems?
- A check of the internal self-auditing process. Are problems overlooked when they are identified? Is there a formal process review policy? Is the company defensive about obvious quality problems?

A successful ISO 9000 audit is a prerequisite for ISO 9000 registration. Thus, registration affirms that a company is meeting acceptable quality standards. Even after registration, the auditors come back periodically to make sure that the standards continue to be met. Good quality documentation helps each employee to know exactly what is expected of him or her with respect to the quality of products and services. This awareness can positively affect morale and provide the impetus for further personal commitment to quality.

1.8 MALCOLM BALDRIGE AWARD

Quality and process improvement is now a major concern of business and industry establishments all over the world. A good indicator of the increasing interest in quality is the Malcolm Baldrige national quality award, which has become the most coveted prize in US industry. The award, set up in 1988 by the US Department of Commerce in memory of the late commerce secretary, Malcolm Baldrige, is designed to honor the companies that have shown the greatest commitment to quality improvement and management. The award originated from the Malcolm Baldrige National Quality Improvement Act signed by President Ronald Reagan on August 20, 1987. The awards are given in three categories: manufacturing, service, and small business. No more than two awards per category can be awarded per year. The awards are managed by the US National Institute of Standards and Technology, an agency of the US Commerce Department's Technology Administration. The private sector is also actively involved in the award process.

The US Commerce Department reported that in 1988, 12 000 requests for application materials were received and 66 companies submitted applications. In 1989, 65 000 requests for application materials for the award were received and 40 companies applied. In 1990, 180 000 companies requested application materials and 97 applied. For 1991, over 250 000 application materials were requested and 106 companies applied. Figure 1.3 presents a summary of the application trend for the award. Figure 1.4 presents a breakdown of the awards for manufacturing, service, and small business categories.

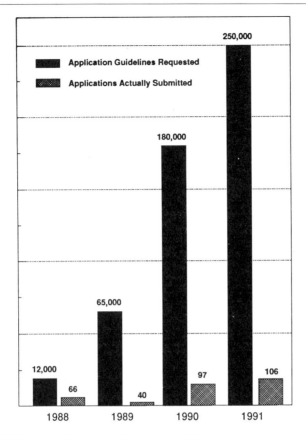

Figure 1.3 Baldrige applications and awards statistics.

The dramatic increase in interest in the award is a clear indication that companies are becoming more and more quality conscious. Companies applying for the Baldrige quality award spend hundreds of hours and thousands of dollars in preparing their applications. For example, it is reported that Xerox spent more than $1 million on preparing its 75-page application in 1989. Table 1.1 lists the winners in the first four years of the award. Table 1.2 shows the award categories.

The design of the Baldrige award framework accommodates several broad-based requirements. Specifically, it has the following characteristics:

- it defines what constitutes quality;
- it is presently the highest level of national recognition a company can receive in the US;
- it commends companies that improve the quality of their goods and services, thus enhancing productivity and lowering costs;

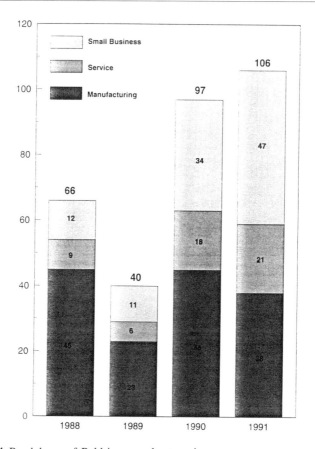

Figure 1.4 Breakdown of Baldrige award categories.

- it is an avenue for companies, large and small, in manufacturing or services, to examine their own approaches to quality;
- it serves as a diagnostic standard against which companies can measure their own progress;
- it measures both the qualitative and quantitative aspects of quality;
- its philosophy complements existing quality improvement philosophies, such as TQM and Deming's 14 points.

Many states in the US have established their own state-level versions of the Baldrige award. For example, the Minnesota quality award (MQA), developed along the lines of the framework of the Baldrige award, has received national acclaim in the US because of its integrative model. The MQA model consists of four major categories: Driver, Systems, Measurement, and Goal. The model is presented in Figure 1.5. The driver is the driving force that facilitates, promotes, and serves as a champion of quality improvement efforts.

Table 1.1 Previous winners of Baldrige award (compiled from various sources)

Year	Company	Product	1990 Sales
1988	Globe Metallurgical, Cleveland, Ohio	Metal alloys	$100 million
	Motorola, Schaumburg, Illinois	Radio equipment, cellular phones, microprocessors	$11 billion
	Westinghouse, Commercial Nuclear Fuel Division, Pittsburgh, Pennsylvania	Fuel rods for nuclear power plants	$350 million
1989	Milliken, Spartanburg, South Carolina	Fabrics and carpeting	$2 billion
	Xeros Business Products and Systems Group, Rochester, New York	Copiers, printers, work stations, software	$14 billion
1990	Cadillac, General Motors, Detroit, Michigan	Luxury cars	$8 billion
	IBM, AS/400 Unit, Rochester, Minnesota	Intermediate computers	$14 billion
	Federal Express, Memphis, Tennessee	Parcel shipment	$7 billion
	Wallace Company, Houston, Texas	Distributes pipes, valves, etc. for oil and chemical companies	$90 million
1991	Solectron Corporation, San Jose, California	Electronics	$265 million
	Zytec Corporation, Eden Prairie, Minnesota	Electronics	$56 million
	Marlow Industries, Dallas, Texas	Electronics	$11 million

Table 1.2 Baldrige award categories

Business Category	1988	1989	1990	1991
Manufacturing	2	2	2	2
Service	0	0	1	0
Small Business	1	0	1	1
Total Awards	3	2	4	3

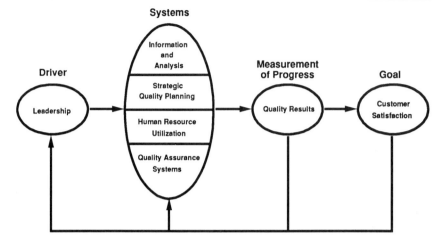

Figure 1.5 Minnesota quality award model.

The publicity, interests, and efforts generated by the Baldrige award have significantly heightened the awareness of quality in many organizations. Many organizations that do not even plan to apply for the award for several years to come are already committing time and efforts to quality improvement now. To emphasize results rather than mere commitment to quality improvement, the requirements for the Baldrige award for 1992 were modified. Companies applying for the award in the future must demonstrate areas where they have been successful in achieving quality improvement. The award candidates must not only indicate the extent of their quality efforts, but also must prove that the efforts really work. Applicants must provide details on their quality management system, and show achievements and improvements in the following seven areas:

- leadership;
- information and analysis;
- strategic quality planning;
- human resources development and management;
- management of process quality;
- quality and operational results;
- customer focus and satisfaction.

The developments in Europe have somewhat, if temporarily, distracted some companies from the Baldrige award. Fewer companies applied for the award in 1992 compared to the preceding years. In 1991, 106 companies applied for the award. By comparison, only 90 applied in 1992. However, it is expected that interest will pick up once again after the market directions in Europe pass the transient stages. The major reasons for the 1992 decline in the Baldrige applications are discussed below.

Diversion due to ISO 9000

Many companies are now preoccupied with keeping or expanding their markets in Europe. They are more concerned with the immediate requirements and long-term benefits of ISO 9000, rather than the short-term reward of the Baldrige award.

Competition from other awards

Several new awards have now been instituted. More than ten states in the US now have their own quality awards patterned after the Baldrige award. Numerous companies have also established company-wide awards that promote healthy competition between divisions of the same company. For example, the International Quality Europe Award, which highlights Europe's prevailing focus on quality, has been attracting applications from every corner of the world. For example, two of the awards for the 1991 competition, held in Madrid, Spain, went to two Nigerian companies: Obokun Bola Dare Nigeria Limited and South Coast Development Company Limited. Some US companies that would have applied for the Baldrige award are opting for the international awards instead.

Apprehension about level of readiness

Some organizations do not believe that they are yet ready to compete successfully for the award. Many giant companies, including AT&T, competed and lost in 1991. Such an example has discouraged many companies from applying before they think they are ready.

High cost of application

The Baldrige award application can be very costly. In a weak economy, companies are more cautious about the type of projects they can engage in. The application fee alone ranges from $1200 for small businesses to $4000 for large companies. In addition, the application process requires a lot of time and effort, and involves several hidden costs. As was mentioned earlier, Xerox Corporation, a 1989 winner, and Corning, a 1989 finalist, revealed that they spent hundreds of thousands of dollars and a large number of labor hours on their applications.

Skepticism about the quality impact of the award

Some critics of the Baldrige award note that it does not reflect outstanding product quality. They cite the case of Cadillac, a 1990 winner. Despite winning the award, Cadillac is not in the top ranks of most surveys of automobile quality. The criticisms helped motivate the new requirements for the award emphasizing actual results rather than mere preparations.

Despite the criticisms, there is no doubt that the Baldrige award has contributed to the reshaping of the attitude of companies towards quality. In just a few years, the Malcolm Baldrige National Quality Award has become an important agent for transforming company attitudes towards quality from complacency to renewed enthusiasm.

1.9 DEMING'S CONTRIBUTIONS

Dr W. Edwards Deming has promoted several concepts and philosophies relating to quality improvement all over the world. His most notable teachings are known as 'Deming philosophy', 'Deming's 14 points', and 'Deming's PDCA cycle'. These teachings are discussed briefly in the following three sections.

1.9.1 Deming's philosophy

The basic element of Deming's philosophy is that management must develop the proper theory and provide the appropriate tools to manage quality. He advocates building quality into a product so as to achieve lower costs, improved productivity, and better customer satisfaction. He admonishes the practice of 100% inspection. Instead, he favors the use of statistical methods for tracking and reporting product quality.

1.9.2 Deming's 14 points

The 14 points presented by Deming (1982) as an approach to quality improvement have been widely acclaimed. The points are listed below.

1. Create constancy of purpose for improvement of product and service. The aim should be to become competitive and stay in business to provide jobs.
2. Adopt the new philosophy. The time is ripe for changes and new leadership in management approaches.
3. Cease dependence on inspection to achieve quality. Eliminate the need for inspection on a mass basis by building quality into the product in the first place.
4. End the practice of awarding business on the basis of price tag alone. Instead, minimize total cost by using a single supplier for any one item to facilitate a long-term relationship of loyalty and trust.
5. Improve constantly and forever the system of production and service in order to improve quality and productivity, and, consequently, decrease costs.

6. Institute training on the job.
7. Institute leadership. The goal of supervision should be to help people and machines and gadgets do a better job. Supervision of management and production workers should be reviewed.
8. Drive out fear so that everyone can work effectively for the company.
9. Break down barriers between departments. Those who are involved in research, design, sales, and production must work together as a team.
10. Eliminate slogans, exhortations, and targets for the work force requiring zero defects and new levels of productivity. Exhortations only create adversarial relationships. The majority of causes of low quality and low productivity can be found in the production system itself rather than within the control of the work force.
11. (a) Eliminate work quotas on the factory floor.
    (b) Eliminate management by objective. Eliminate management by numbers and numerical goals. Substitute leadership.
12. (a) Remove barriers that rob the hourly worker of his or her right to pride of workmanship. The responsibility of supervisors must be changed from sheer numbers to quality.
    (b) Remove barriers that rob people in management and in engineering of their right to pride of workmanship. This requires the elimination of annual rating or merit systems.
13. Institute a vigorous program of education and self-improvement for everyone.
14. Put everybody in the company to work to accomplish the transformation. The transformation is everybody's job.

1.9.3 Deming's PDCA cycle

Deming's PDCA (Plan–Do–Check–Act) cycle is another well-known philosophy that has characterized the increased interest in quality. Although it is popularly known as Deming's cycle, it was actually first introduced by W. A. Shewhart as Shewhart's cycle. Deming introduced the Shewhart cycle to Japan in the early 1950s. It was the Japanese who implemented it as Deming's cycle. That name has since been popularized more than the original name. Deming recommends using the PDCA cycle as a means to implement point 14 in Deming's 14 points. The cycle recommends continuing efforts to achieve continuous improvement in product quality. Figure 1.6 presents a graphical representation of the cycle. The steps in the PDCA cycle are explained below.

Step 1: Plan

This step involves a determination of what is to be achieved and how it will be achieved. Appropriate questions for this step are: What is the specific objective? Who are members of the team? When is the plan to take effect? When is the

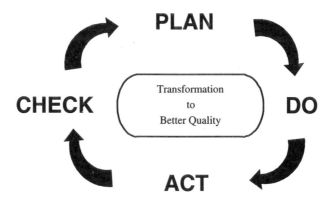

Figure 1.6 Deming's PDCA cycle.

plan expected to end? What will be needed to carry out the plan? What data are already available? What data will need to be collected? What statistical tools are needed to interpret results?

With a clear documentation of the plan, the possibility of misunderstanding and misconception can be reduced. A key aspect of the plan should be to attempt to match the process output with the customer's needs.

Step 2: Do

A plan is just a plan until it is implemented. In this step, activities are actually performed in accordance with the established plan. The techniques of activity scheduling using CPM (critical path method) and PERT (program evaluation and review technique) could be useful at this step. The interrelationships between activities should be determined and reviewed based on the desired goals. The 'do' step facilitates actual experimentation with new ideas. It permits the plan to be implemented on a small scale to evaluate its effectiveness. For example, a small group of customers or a limited segment of the market may be used to test the performance of a new product. The result of the pilot experiment can then determine how the plan may be carried out on a larger scale.

Step 3: Check

No improvement can be achieved without a review of the current performance level. In this step, a check of the result of the plan is made. Appropriate questions for this purpose are: How well does the plan satisfy the specified objectives? What level of deviation was observed? Is the deviation acceptable? Can the prevailing deficiency be overcome? Can the trial run be extended to a full run? Can the plan be replicated for other processes?

An important aspect of the 'check' step is a determination of what measurements to take to facilitate the evaluation process. The appropriate variables must be measured to ensure that accurate conclusions are reached.

Step 4: Act

Planning, doing, and checking are the precursors for action. In this step, actions must be taken based on the results of Step 3. If the results are negative, steps should be taken to identify the mistakes made so that they can be avoided in the future. If the results are positive, steps should be taken to determine how similar results can be achieved in the other processes. By planning to achieve the good results on a larger scale, the PDCA cycle is repeated. Thus, the quality improvement effort becomes permanent.

Quality improvement can be likened to a journey with no ending point. Deming's PDCA cycle requires that quality improvement be approached as a never-ending cycle. Continuous interaction between functional departments is important to provide products and services that satisfy customers. The Toyota people in Japan refer to this continuous process as *Kaizen*. *Kaizen* means the search for a better way.

1.9.4 Deming prize

Deming is credited with the resuscitation of Japan's economy after the Second World War. Many authors give Deming credit for laying the foundation for Japan's current dominant status in world trade. In recognition of his contributions to the advancement of quality control, the Japanese Union of Scientists and Engineers honoured Deming in 1951 by establishing the Deming prizes. The research and education prize goes to individuals who have made significant contributions to the foundations of quality improvement. The applications prize goes to organizations that have demonstrated outstanding results in quality improvement. The prizes are awarded annually, and are open to companies and individuals throughout the world. In 1989, Florida Power and Light Company became the first western company to win the Deming prize. To date, there have been over 140 winners of the Deming prize. The evaluation for the Deming prize is based on the ten major factors listed below.

1. **Policy**: Management's total plan for quality control. This covers various aspects from setting objectives, to implementation and integration into long-range relationships.
2. **Organization**: Defining responsibilities, delegating power, use of staff, and feedback from performance auditing.
3. **Education**: Educational plan and scope. The plan should include the training of vendors, implementation, and response to employee suggestions.

4. **Information**: Assembly, dissemination, analysis, and use of all forms of information.
5. **Analysis**: Problem selection, analysis, and use of results.
6. **Standards**: How standards are established, revised, and used.
7. **Control**: Control systems and control points for quality and feedback from quality circles.
8. **Quality assurance**: The basic quality-assurance system, quality audits, and evaluations expanded to cover everything from new product development to process capabilities, to safety and product liability prevention.
9. **Effects**: Measuring visible and invisible effects, such as quality, serviceability, delivery, cost, profit, safety, and environmental effects.
10. **Future planning**: Relationship of total quality promotion in long-range plans.

1.10 TAGUCHI'S CONTRIBUTIONS

Genichi Taguchi's approach to quality improvement involves the development of new techniques and the modification of existing statistical approaches. Taguchi's techniques have introduced significant changes to the way experiments are conducted for quality improvement. There is an increasing interest in the Taguchi method in business and industry. Taguchi's philosophy relates to the following two points:

1. quality losses must be defined as the deviation from a specified target;
2. quality should be defined into the product right from the beginning.

The classical approach to quality control has been to produce products that are within specifications (specs). Thus, the old thinking is that if an item falls within specs, there is no need for improvement. But the Taguchi method suggests that this traditional view of quality is wrong since there is some level of loss associated with a product, based on whether it falls within or outside the specification limits.

Taguchi loss function

Taguchi defines quality as the losses a product imparts to the society from the time the product is shipped. He describes this phenomenon as the loss function. The function indicates that the more a product deviates from a target level, the higher the loss it impacts on society. Loss, in this concept, can be defined to consist of several components. Examples are as follows.

- Opportunity cost of not having the service of the product due to its quality problems. The loss of service implies that something that should have been done to serve the society could not be done.

- Time lost in the attempt to find what is wrong with the product. The problem identification effort takes away some of the time that could have been productively used to serve the society. Thus, the society incurs a loss.
- Time lost in the attempt to find a solution to the quality problem.
- Time lost waiting for the solution to be implemented.
- Decrease in productivity due to the reduced effectiveness of the product. The decreased productivity deprives the society of a certain level of service and, thereby, constitutes a loss.
- Actual cost of correcting the quality problem. This is, perhaps, the only loss that is most easily recognized. But there are other subtle losses that the Taguchi method can point out.
- Actual losses (e.g. loss of life) due to a failure of the product resulting from its low quality. For example, a low quality tire on a high quality automobile creates a potential for catastrophe and an ensuing loss.

Figure 1.7 depicts Taguchi's view of the loss function. As the product deviates from the target level eastward or westward, its loss increases. Note that a product that is just inside the upper specification limit exhibits a loss that is almost equal to the loss created by a product that is just outside the limit. The implication then is that the society should be as concerned about Item A as it is concerned about Item B with regard to quality loss.

In Figure 1.7, a parabolic function is used to illustrate the quality function. In actuality, the specific form of the function may not be known. The actual function may follow a triangular function, a step-wise function, or any other functional form. The higher the capability of a process, the lower the loss the product imparts on the customer. Capability, in this sense, refers to the ability

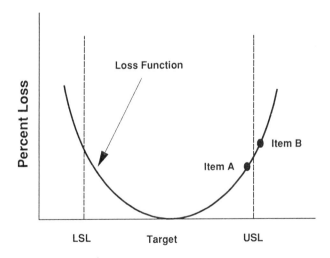

Figure 1.7 Taguchi's quality loss function.

of the process to produce close to the target level. More will be discussed on process capability in subsequent chapters. It can be concluded that a reduction of the process variation around the target facilitates continuous process improvement, reduced quality loss, and better customer satisfaction.

In addition to the concepts and philosophies that Taguchi introduced, he also developed a procedure for performing quality-related experimental designs more effectively. He introduced a collection of fractional factorial experiment matrices that can be adopted for different experimental situations. The matrices, called orthogonal arrays (OAs), will be discussed in more detail in Chapter 6. The availability of the Taguchi method has contributed to the quality revolution. Companies that, hitherto, would not have undertaken quality improvement projects are now doing so because effective tools are now available.

1.11 JURAN'S CONTRIBUTIONS

Dr Joseph M. Juran, like Deming, spearheaded the quality management movement in Japan. Juran is a leading authority and author on quality control. The popular Pareto chart was developed by Juran. He named the chart in honor of the Italian economist, Vilfredo Pareto (1848–1923). In 1897, Pareto studied the distribution of wealth in Italy. He presented a formula which showed that the distribution of wealth was uneven. Pareto found that 80% of the wealth was controlled by only 20% of the population. His 80/20 split, often referred to as the Pareto distribution, has been proved true in other areas apart from wealth distribution.

Juran applied Pareto's approach to classify problems of quality into the two categories of the 'vital few' and the 'trivial many'. Juran contends that over 80% of quality defects are caused by a few factors. He suggests that management should focus on and control these few factors. Juran also urges management continually to pursue improvements by using the trilogy of quality: planning, control, and improvement. He recommends that a combination of hands-on management and training be used in the pursuit of excellence in quality. Through his many publications, Juran has made significant contributions to training in the area of quality management. The Juran Institute has offered numerous quality improvement training programs that have attracted practitioners from all over the world.

1.11.1 Juran's ten steps to quality improvement

The Juran Institute teaches a project-by-project, problem-solving, team-oriented approach to quality improvement. The approach requires the active participation of upper management. Juran's ten steps to quality improvement are listed below.

1. Build awareness of the need and opportunity for improvement.
2. Set goals for improvement.
3. Organize to reach the goals:
   (a) establish a quality council;
   (b) identify problems;
   (c) select projects;
   (d) appoint teams;
   (e) designate facilitators.
4. Provide training.
5. Carry out projects to solve problems.
6. Report progress.
7. Give recognition.
8. Communicate results.
9. Keep score.
10. Maintain momentum by making annual improvement part of the regular systems and processes of the company.

1.12 ISHIKAWA'S CONTRIBUTIONS

Dr Kaoru Ishikawa has made significant contribution to the quality revolution by introducing several simple and practical quality management tools. He is credited with developing the concept of quality circles. Ishikawa, a professor at the University of Tokyo, introduced the fishbone diagram sometimes referred to as the Ishikawa diagram. This is a cause-and-effect diagram that highlights how each factor affects the overall quality of a product. In 1953, Ishikawa used the diagram to summarize the opinions of engineers at a plant in the form of cause-and-effect relationships as the engineers discussed a quality problem. This is widely known as the origin of the fishbone diagram. Having proven its practicality, the diagram quickly became widely used in Japanese companies. It is now used not only for studying the quality characteristics of a product, but also for studying any process. It was included in the Japanese Industrial Standards (JIS) terminology of quality control with the following definition:

'Cause-and-effect diagram: A diagram which shows the relationship between a quality characteristic and its factors.'

Ishikawa recommends company-wide quality control in which all employees jointly manage the quality control efforts. This is in contrast to cases where the quality control function is left only to a few quality control specialists. Ishikawa's concepts involve the following:

- the identification of the quality aspects that the customer desires and is willing to pay for;
- the movement from an inspection-based quality control program to a

process-oriented program, which integrates customers' needs;

- the use of basic statistical tools to pinpoint underlying sources of quality problems;
- the elimination of the underlying sources of quality problems so that the problems do not recur;
- the establishment of voluntary quality control circles to create a participative environment for quality improvement;
- the administration of a company-wide quality control program that includes vertical and horizontal quality responsibility.

1.13 FEIGENBAUM'S CONTRIBUTIONS

Dr Armand V. Feigenbaum introduced the concept of total quality control (TQC) in 1951 with the publication of a book entitled *Total Quality Control*. Until that time, quality control involved mostly correcting quality problems rather than preventing them. TQC advanced the concept of quality control in all areas of production, including design and sales. TQC advocates making quality a responsibility of everybody in an organization. In the Japanese model, the quality responsibility lies with the foremen and workers instead of with the quality control department. Feigenbaum recommends that more time and effort should be directed at correcting quality problems at the source and less on quality inspections. Thus, he suggests paying more attention to prevention costs compared to failure costs.

1.14 CROSBY'S CONTRIBUTIONS

Phillip B. Crosby became prominent in the quality area after the publication of his book *Quality is Free* in 1979. At that time, he was a corporate vice-president and the director of quality at ITT. He is now a world-famous quality management consultant. Crosby pointed out that companies incur significant cost by not doing the job right the first time. He identified the hidden costs of poor quality as consisting of the following:

- lost sales;
- increased labor cost;
- increased machine hours;
- increased machine failures;
- increased warranty costs;
- increased downtime;
- delivery delays.

The hidden costs above do not include the traceable costs of scrap. Crosby recommends continuous process improvement as a means of achieving the goal of zero defects. He pointed out that the cost of building quality into a product can be overcome by the benefits provided by savings in rework and scrap. Crosby summarized his quality improvement concepts as follows.

- The system should emphasize prevention rather than checking and inspection. Inspection is wasteful.
- Prevention involves identifying areas where errors can occur, and once identified, the process should be modified to eliminate the causes permanently.
- The ultimate goal in quality management is to reach zero defects.
- The cost of quality is the cost of doing things wrong.
- The price of non-conformance can be as high as 25 to 35% of a company's operating costs.
- Prevention costs include the cost of quality-related education, training, preventive maintenance, process change, and process design.

With the publication of his other famous book, *Quality Without Tears*, in 1984, Crosby introduced his own version of the steps to a quality improvement program.

1.14.1 Crosby's 14 steps to quality improvement

1. Make it clear that management is committed to quality.
2. Form quality improvement teams with representatives from each department.
3. Determine where current and potential quality problems lie.
4. Evaluate the quality awareness and personal concern of all employees.
5. Raise the quality awareness and personal concern of all employees.
6. Take actions to correct problems identified through previous steps.
7. Establish a committee for the zero defects programs.
8. Train supervisors actively to carry out their part of the quality improvement program.
9. Hold a 'zero defects day' to let all employees realize that there has been a change.
10. Encourage individuals to establish improvement goals for themselves and their groups.
11. Encourage employees to communicate to management the obstacles they face in attaining their improvement goals.
12. Recognize and appreciate those who participate.
13. Establish quality councils to communicate on a regular basis.
14. Do it all over again to emphasize that the quality improvement program never ends.

1.15 MOTOROLA'S SIX SIGMA APPROACH

The six sigma approach introduced by Motorola's Government Electronics Group has caught on quickly in industry. Many major companies are now embracing the approach as the key to high quality manufacturing. Six sigma means six standard deviations from a statistical performance average. The six sigma approach allows for no more than 3.4 defects per million parts in manufactured goods or 3.4 mistakes per million activities in a service operation. To appreciate the effect of the six sigma approach, consider a process that is 99% perfect. That process will produce 10 000 defects per million parts. With six sigma, the process will need to be 99.99966% perfect in order to produce only 3.4 defects per million. Thus, six sigma is an approach that pushes the limit of perfection. The approach uses statistical methods to find problems that cause defects. For example, the total yield (number of nondefective units) from a process is determined by a combination of the performance levels of all the steps making up the process.

If a process consists of 20 steps and each step is 98 per cent perfect, then the performance of the overall process will be:

$$(0.98)^{20} = 0.667608 \text{ (i.e. } 66.7608\%)$$

Thus, the process will produce 332 392 defects per million parts. If each step of the process is pushed to the six sigma limit, then the process performance will be:

$$(0.9999966)^{20} = 0.999932 \text{ (i.e. } 99.9932\%)$$

Thus, the six sigma process will produce only 68 defects per million parts. This is a significant improvement over the original process performance.

In many cases, it is not realistic to expect to achieve the six sigma level of production. But the approach helps to set a quality standard and provides a mechanism for striving to reach the goal. In effect, the six sigma process means changing the way people do things so as to minimize the potential for defects.

1.16 QUALITY AND COMPETITIVE EDGE

Quality is the ultimate weapon. Higher product quality is required for a company to become more competitive, both locally and in international trade. Higher quality is the basis for achieving a competitive edge. Important decisions must be made regarding the quality of products and services. With the increasing global pressures of quality requirements, the traditional concept of quality control must be expanded to the concept of total quality management. Traditional quality control attempts to meet a specified quality standard, typically through product inspections. By contrast, quality management addresses the broader issues of eliminating quality problems and improving

Figure 1.8 Ingredients of competitive quality.

product quality through all facets of the organization. Figure 1.8 shows the ingredients of competitive quality.

The overall quality management effort should address both the quality assurance functions and the quality control functions. Quality assurance is concerned with the functions of anticipating and preventing quality problems. Quality assurance encompasses all the actions necessary to ensure that the product or service generated by a project will conform to quality requirements. Quality assurance personnel serve as the liaison between the customer and the project. They evaluate and outline project quality specifications with respect to customer requirements. Quality control is concerned with the operational techniques for detecting, recording, and taking actions to eliminate quality problems. Quality management involves an integrated management of all the functions that can impact the quality of a product. In summary:

'Quality assurance sets the standards for product quality while quality control implements or enforces those standards. Quality management oversees and integrates all functions that can influence quality.'

Under the notion of quality management, quality control inspections serve only as an aid in detecting quality problems and providing signals for needed improvements. Quality inspections will not necessarily lead to better quality products. In fact, strict quality inspection policies take a pessimistic view at a production process in which products with poor quality characteristics are expected. Thus, inspections are performed to locate those defective products. In the emerging competitive markets, efforts must be made to prevent quality problems rather than designing mechanisms to detect problems. Proper attention must be given to all the crucial factors in a process. We have adapted a popular nursery rhyme to emphasize the importance of a bottom-up approach to improving quality. The nursery rhyme goes as follows:

> For the want of a nail, the horse shoe was lost;
> For the loss of the horse shoe, the horse was lost;
> For the loss of the horse, the rider was lost;
> For the loss of the rider, the message was lost;
> For the loss of the message, the battle was lost;
> For the loss of the battle, the war was lost;
> For the loss of the war, the kingdom was lost.
> All for the want of a nail!

The rhyme gives credence to the fact that it is the little problems which are neglected that lead to much bigger problems. Our adaptation of the rhyme for quality improvement goes as follows:

> For the want of quality, the product value was lost;
> For the loss of value, the product was lost;
> For the loss of the product, the customer was lost;
> For the loss of the customer, the business was lost;
> For the loss of the business, the competition was lost;
> For the loss of the competition, the enterprise failed.
> All for the want of QUALITY!

1.17 CASE STUDY: QUALITY AND PRODUCTIVITY IMPROVEMENT IN TAIWAN

This case study (Badiru and Chen, 1992) discusses how industrial engineers played direct roles in the transformation of Taiwan from an agricultural economy to an industrial giant. The case study is based on a visit to the China Productivity Center (CPC) in Taipei, Taiwan, Republic of China (ROC). The case study presents a first-hand account of how industrial engineering techniques and practices were directly responsible for many of the productivity gains that Taiwan has experienced in recent years. Through integrated industrial development programs, the small island of Taiwan has achieved a giant status in the world market. Taiwan now has one of the highest external reserves in the world. The case of Taiwan is certainly an inspiring lesson for other developing countries with a vision of industrial development.

China Productivity Center

The China Productivity Center (CPC) is the avenue through which most of the techniques for business and industrial productivity and quality improvement have been passed on to Taiwan's small and large scale industries. The center, headquartered in Taipei, Taiwan, was established by government statute in 1955. It now has several regional offices around the country. The current state of industrial development in Taiwan is by careful design dating back to the establishment of CPC. There is a direct link between the growth of CPC and the economic development of Taiwan. The center is now 50% funded by the government. The other 50% of its operating budget is raised entirely through productivity-related services rendered to private industry. It is organized and run as a private non-profit institution. Its primary charter is to help improve business and industrial productivity and quality in Taiwan. It specializes in providing training classes for workers, supervisors, managers, and top executives. Every year, the center invites international experts to give lectures and conduct seminars on various topics, ranging from product design, use of computer software, and joint venture strategies to project management. The center has enjoyed significant achievements over the past three and a half decades. Of the several achievements, those listed below stand out in terms of direct contribution to industrial development, productivity and quality improvement.

- Establishment of the *Productivity Magazine* in 1957. The magazine, which was renamed *Strategy Productivity Magazine* in 1990, is dedicated to the dissemination of the latest productivity and quality issues and techniques to local industry.
- Helping to launch the Enterprise Management Development Association in 1963. This association provides business and industrial management strategies to Taiwan industry.
- Helping to establish the industrial engineering department at Tung Hai University in September 1963. This is one of the earliest fully-fledged industrial engineering academic programs.
- Participating in the establishment of the Metals Industry Development Center in 1963.
- Assisting in the establishment of the Chinese Society for Quality Control in 1964.
- Assisting in establishing the ROC Industrial Design Association in 1967.
- Participating in the establishment of the ROC Industrial Safety and Hygiene Association in 1970.
- Establishing the Low-Cost Automation Technology Promotion Department in 1979. This department was later renamed Industrial Automation Promotion Department.
- Launching of a five-year national productivity enhancement program under the auspices of the Ministry of Economic Affairs in 1984.
- Launching of a five-year national product quality enhancement project under the auspices of the Ministry of Economic Affairs in 1988. In 1990, the average savings from quality improvement projects were US $792 000 per participating company.

- Implementation of a three-year medium and small enterprise technology acquisition program in July 1989.

Leadership

The continuing success of CPC is based on solid leadership and unrelenting effort to improve productivity and quality. The current president of the center is Dr Casper T. Y. Shih. Dr Shih was recruited by the government of Taiwan from General Electric in Canada to head the factory automation task force in 1983. The automation task force later became an integral part of CPC. The goal of the task force is to facilitate the injection of automation technology into Taiwan industry through free consultation, government subsidized low-cost loans, and other support services. Prior to going to Canada, Dr Shih worked in Japan, where he was credited with developing the special welding techniques that were used in the construction of Japan's bullet train railway. So, he came into the productivity improvement effort with an established industrial reputation. Dr Shih was the 1991 chairman of the Asia Productivity Organization (APO), which includes Taiwan, Japan, Korea, India, Indonesia, Pakistan, Vietnam, and other Asian countries (USSR is an observer–member of APO).

Even though he does not have formal industrial engineering training (he earned his doctorate in materials science from Tokyo University), Dr Shih is familiar with and fully appreciates the potential contributions of industrial engineers. He introduced many new concepts and ways of doing things in Taiwan industry. Some industry leaders call him the 'industrial megastar'. He admonishes the short-term views of entrepreneurs and advocates long-term strategic plans for productivity and quality improvement. He encourages industry to continue to find better ways of achieving their goals with his proclamation that 'winners always have an answer and losers always have an excuse.' In his leadership vision, he predicts that, by the year 2000, the Pacific Rim will match North America's total GNP and exceed that of western Europe. He suggests that the '21st century is the Pacific century', and the countries ringing the Pacific (including Taiwan) will continue to experience tremendous economic growth. He believes that while the first 30 years of the next century will be dominated by the Japanese, the 70 years that will follow will be dominated by the Chinese in terms of economic activity. A major responsibility of CPC is to develop and disseminate the strategies needed to achieve and sustain the projected world economic leadership.

Role played by industrial engineers

Industrial engineering played a very significant role in the early success of CPC. To achieve what Shih and CPC have achieved, a lot of trust was needed on the part of industrial entrepreneurs. As Dr Shih pointed out, trust is a prerequisite for innovation. To get industries to implement his productivity ideas, Shih had to convince them that the techniques could work for them. One of his first approaches as the head of the factory automation task force was the strategy of rationalization and conversion. Prior to 1983, few or none of the basic industrial engineering tools were in regular use in many companies. There were limited quality control efforts. Consistent production control was nonexistent. Poor plant layout severely limited industrial productivity.

In 1983, Dr Shih employed scores of industrial engineering students and deployed them strategically to various companies on summer vacation assignments with specific instructions on how to introduce industrial engineering techniques in the companies. He instructed the industrial engineers to ensure that there were significant gains resulting from the techniques they introduced and to document all the benefits achieved properly. The documented improvements provided the rationalization for the need for new techniques to improve productivity. Once the rationalization was achieved, it was easy to get the companies to convert to industrial engineering approaches. The higher the number of companies that adopt industrial engineering techniques, the better off the overall economic outlook of the nation. Figure 1.9 illustrates the quality and productivity improvement process responsible for Taiwan's emergence as an industrial and economic leader.

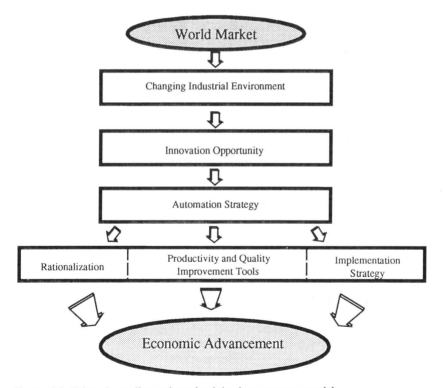

Figure 1.9 Taiwan's quality and productivity improvement model.

The services of the industrial engineering students were funded by CPC and offered free to the companies as a part of government support for industrial development. The students were supervised and guided by fully qualified industrial engineers. The free service of the students removed whatever initial apprehension the companies might have had in hiring the students. The techniques included in the students' repertoire were basic industrial engineering tools such as quality control, plant layout, production planning, activity scheduling, and work measurement. The idea was that if the companies had an opportunity to try these techniques, they would become aware of their potential benefits and would, thereafter, embrace the techniques as a part of their regular modes of operation. The approach worked so successfully that most of the companies went on to hire industrial engineers on their regular staff. With the prevailing poor layouts and inefficient practices, the industrial engineering students were able to achieve significant improvements. When other companies that did not even participate in the summer programs saw the gains that were being achieved, they also created industrial engineering positions.

Rationalization before automation

Now, industrial engineering is well known and respected among Taiwan industries. Once the companies began to trust the efforts of CPC, they began to avail themselves of the other productivity and quality programs offered by the center. The goal of the strategy is to get companies introduced to a new idea that will benefit them individually and, in turn, benefit the overall economic development of Taiwan. It is believed that the good reputation and goodwill that CPC enjoys today is due to that initial industrial engineering experiment. It was reported that companies were so impressed by the improvements brought by industrial engineers that they referred to them as industrial doctors. Under the guidance of industrial engineers, many companies in Taiwan now routinely adopt FMS, robotics, CAD/CAM, TQM, SPC, APC, Taguchi method, PERT/CPM, and expert systems. With minimum investment, many companies were able to increase output. The efforts of industrial engineers helped to prepare companies for the proper attitude towards automation (i.e. rationalization for automation) before actual implementation.

The same strategy of conversion is still in use today. When CPC brings in an international expert now, it makes his initial consultation and services available free to the relevant companies. The expert may conduct seminars or study specific industrial problems and offer expert advice. This, at least, gets a new concept or technique introduced to the companies. If the companies like what they see, they will then adopt the idea and be willing to pay consultation fees to CPC for further help and implementation of the new techniques. It is from such further paid service that CPC raises the balance of its operating budget.

National drive

The push for industrial productivity and quality improvement is fully supported by the Taiwan government through the activities of the Ministry of Economic Affairs. In 1989, after 40 years of hard work, Taiwan created a trade quota of US$118 billion. This made Taiwan the world's 13th largest trading nation. The economic development of Taiwan is essentially driven by gains in small and medium-sized enterprises. About 95% of Taiwan industry is in the small-scale privately-owned sector. The government has set aside a portion of Taiwan's huge external reserve for construction projects and industrial development. It has been said that behind the post-war reconstruction in Kuwait, Taiwan will have the next largest collection of construction projects within the next few years. The prevailing efforts in industrial development in Taiwan also rival those of any developed country. Joint venture partners will do well to study the Taiwanese corporate culture and approach to industrial development in order to maximize the potential for success.

Looking to the future

Through the China Productivity Center and other similar organizations, several productivity improvement programs are available to Taiwan industry. With the available services, small businesses can get help both for the financial aspects of their operations, and the technological and managerial aspects. The emerging industrial initiative in Taiwan now is to supplement the prevailing strategy of original-equipment manufacturing (OEM) with original-design manufacturing (ODM) and original-brand manufacturing (OBM). This means that, in the near future, products will not only be Made-in-Taiwan, but also Designed-in-Taiwan, and Created-in-Taiwan.

2 | Fundamentals of quality improvement

There is always room for more improvement
Somasundaram and Badiru, 1992

Quality improvement requires that we should not be satisfied with the current quality level, regardless of how satisfactory it may be. Efforts should be made continuously to improve quality. Even when it appears that the limit of quality has been reached, new technologies and new techniques may make it possible to achieve further improvement. Using the TQM approach, the overall business environment should be surveyed for areas where further improvements can be achieved. The combination of minor improvements made here and there can lead to a much larger gain in quality improvement. Old bad habits and hype should be abandoned in favour of real quality improvements. Short-term goals of quality improvement should be extended to long-term and permanent improvement strategies. Writing and speaking about quality improvement is not enough. Something tangible must be done about it. Priorities must be reorganized so that quality is first. Quantity and schedule, while very important, should not be allowed to pre-empt quality.

2.1 COMPONENTS OF QUALITY IMPROVEMENT

Little bits of quality make up high quality
Management must recognize that quality improvement consists of numerous prerequisite factors. These factors must be identified in each specific quality improvement endeavour. As a minimum, management must play a leadership role and do the following.

- Recognize that quality takes time. Rush jobs lead to poor results.
- Recognize that quality comes from care.
- Know the customers and get them involved very early.
- Simplify the quality improvement approach. Complicated approaches confuse and discourage participants. Deming's PDCA cycle, for example, is a simple model to implement.

- Recognize that incremental improvements are easier to achieve than one giant improvement.
- Start at the elementary levels of the quality system.
- Use the divide and conquer approach in organizing quality functions.

2.2 CUSTOMER INVOLVEMENT

Customer involvement is the best alliance there is in the marketplace
The absence of defects is no longer a sufficient definition of quality. Thus, the process of improving quality requires that associated operations be understood, improved, and well managed. Figure 2.1 presents a flowchart of a quality improvement process. The business mission and overall quality objectives must be integrated with customer needs with respect to organizational capabilities. There must be a feedback mechanism through which changes in customers' needs are conveyed to drive the mission of the business further. Getting closer to the customer and employee empowerment are two of the basic requirements for achieving quality improvement.

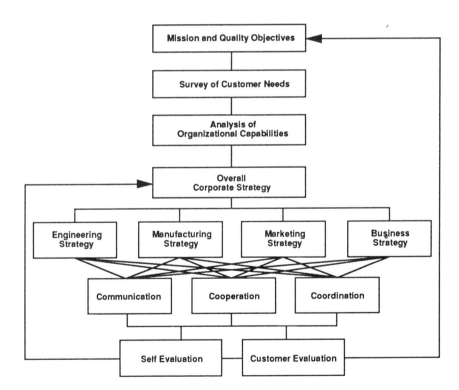

Figure 2.1 Flowchart to quality improvement.

2.2.1 Business versus customer definitions of quality

Quality (beauty) is in the mind (eye) of the customer (beholder). The customer is the producer's spokesperson

When pursuing quality improvement, the business and customer definitions of quality must be matched. What the customer wants should be what the producer is willing to provide. A business definition of quality may indicate that quality is the level of product appeal and functionality needed to make a product acceptable and profitable in the marketplace. By comparison, a customer definition of quality may indicate that quality is the level of product capability required to satisfy the customer's use and requirements. The customer may not care whether or not the business is profitable in the provision of the product, whereas the business has to worry about both its profitability requirements and its customers' satisfaction.

The business and customer views should be a two-way affair. If the business is profitable, it will be in a better position to provide better products to meet new customer needs. If the customers are satisfied, they will be more willing to embrace the products offered by the business and, thereby, create further profit potential for the business. As Badiru (1991) pointed out in his *Ode to systems integration*, 'one hand washes the other.' One system component must brace the other. Quality systems integration requires that the business looks out for the customer while the customer looks out for the survival of the business. For, if there is no business, there will be no product. If there is no product, customers' needs cannot be met. A model of the business–customer integration loop is presented in Figure 2.2.

The problem in the conflicting views of business and customers was pointed out by John Akers, CEO of IBM, when he was quoted in the *Wall Street Journal* as saying, 'I am sick and tired of visiting plants to hear nothing but

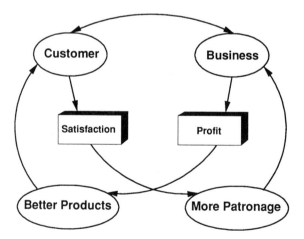

Figure 2.2 Business–customer integration loop.

great things about quality and cycle time, and then to visit customers who tell me of problems.' His statement emphasizes the need to correct the conflict between business and customer definitions and views of quality. To enhance the responsiveness to the customer, manufacturers should let customer needs determine product choices.

2.2.2 User training and instructions

User training is an important aspect of quality improvement. If a user is given proper training and instructions, the chances of misusing a product will be reduced. To solidify customer involvement in quality improvement, user training is required at the customer end of the transaction. A product that is used and cared for in accordance with the producer's instructions will more likely carry a higher perception of quality. The more time the producer has to spend attending to quality 'problems' that result from the misuse of a product, the less time will be available to pursue real improvements.

Consequently, efforts must be made to ensure that products are used correctly. For certain types of products, this cannot be achieved through written instructions only. There must be a combination of instructions and formal training, however short it may be. User training should be the joint responsibility of the user, the customer organization, and the producer. Each has a benefit to be derived from proper product use. In this sense, the customer is defined as the organization which employs the user. By the correct use of a product, the user (an individual) will minimize the chances of frustration with the product. The elimination of frustration will enable him or her to participate more actively in quality improvement efforts. By the correct use of a product, the customer (an organization) will have more time to devote to real quality improvement issues. By the correct use of a product, the producer will enjoy more favorable perception of the quality of the product, thus having more time and goodwill to attend to critical quality issues. Since it is impossible to design a product for all kinds of potential abuses, it will actually be cheaper for the producer to participate in user training programs.

2.3 VENDOR INVOLVEMENT AND CERTIFICATION

To be involved is to be committed. A vendor must be committed to the producer; the producer must be committed to the vendor
Just as customers are expected to be involved in quality improvement, so also should vendors be expected to be involved. Customer requirements should be relayed to vendors so that the goods and services they supply to the production process will satisfy what is required to meet customer requirements. Selected vendors may be certified, based on their previous records of supplying high quality products. A comprehensive program of vendor–producer commitment

should hold both external vendors and internal production facilities jointly responsible for high quality product. The importance of vendor involvement and certification is evidenced by the following advantages:

- vendor and producer have a joint understanding of customer requirements;
- skepticism about a vendor's supply is removed;
- excessive inspection of a vendor's supply is avoided;
- cost of inspecting a vendor's supply is reduced;
- vendors reduce their costs by reducing scrap, rework, and returns;
- vendor morale is improved by the feeling of participation in the producer's mission.

To facilitate vendor involvement, the producer may assign a liaison to work directly with the vendor in ensuring that the joint quality objectives are achieved. In some cases, the liaison will actually spend time in the vendor's plant. This physical presence helps to solidify the vendor–producer relationship. Also, the technical and managerial capability of the producer can be made available to the vendor for the purpose of source quality improvement. Many large companies have arrangements whereby a team of technical staff is assigned to train and help vendors with their quality improvement efforts.

Vendor rating system

A formal system for vendor rating can be useful in encouraging vendor involvement. Vendors that have been certified as supplying high quality products will enjoy favorable prestige in an organization. Presented below is a vendor rating system developed by the authors. The system is based on the opinion poll of a team of individuals.

Requirements

1. Form a vendor quality rating team of individuals who are familiar with the company's operations and the vendor's products.
2. Determine the set of vendors to be included in the rating process.
3. Inform the vendors of the rating process.
4. Each member of the rating team should participate in the rating process.
5. Each member will submit an anonymous evaluation of each vendor, based on specified quality criteria.
6. Develop a weighted evaluation of the vendors to arrive at overall relative weights.

Steps

1. Let T be the total points available to vendors.
2. $T = 100(n)$, where n = number of individuals in the rating team.

3. Rate the performance of each vendor on the basis of specified quality criteria on a scale of 0 to 100.
4. Let x_{ij} be the rating for vendor i by team member j.
5. Organize the ratings by team member j as shown below:

Rating for Vendor 1: x_{1j}
Rating for Vendor 2: x_{2j}

.   .
.   .
.   .

Rating for Vendor n: x_{nj}
_____

Total Rating Points $100n$
_____

6. Tabulate the team ratings as shown below and calculate the overall weighted score for each vendor i from the expression below:

$$w_i = \frac{1}{n} \sum_{j=1}^{n} x_{ij}$$

	Rating by Member $j=1$	Rating by Member $j=2$	. . . . . .	Rating by Member n	w_i
Rating for Vendor $i=1$					
Rating for Vendor $i=2$					
. . .					
. . .					
Rating for Vendor n					

For the case of multiple vendors for the same item, the relative weights, w_i, may be used to determine what fraction of the total supply should be obtained from each vendor. The fraction is calculated as follows:

$$F_i = (w_i)(\text{Size of total supply}),$$

where F_i is the fraction of the total supply that should go to vendor i. The size of the supply may be expressed in terms of monetary currency or product units.

2.4 EMPLOYEE INVOLVEMENT

Employees are the custodians of quality
Employees make quality improvement possible. Grass roots commitment to quality must be pursued even at the lowest employee level. It has been widely reported that the quality achievements experienced by Japan were due largely to

the individual and collective commitment of employees (Ebrahimpour and Withers, 1992). With the support of management, employees must play active roles in quality improvement efforts. An organization should do the following in order to increase employee involvement in quality improvement:

- establish quality awareness programs;
- listen to employees;
- find out what each employee needs in order to do a better job;
- encourage everyone (from the custodian to the CEO) to speak the language of quality;
- build a participative model through quality circles;
- watch for the subtle quality danger signals of employees;
- be specific about the role of employees in quality improvement;
- create avenues for employee inputs and feedbacks on quality;
- make employees feel like a part of the quality decision team;
- recognize employee contributions;
- follow up on employee ideas quickly and forthrightly.

The total employee involvement (TEI) concept has emerged in recent times as one approach to achieving quality improvement. TEI is a management practice that emphasizes the significance of employee contribution to quality improvement in the work place. The concept provides a practical approach to giving everyone the power to be a manager of a process and be responsible for the continuous improvement of that process. This empowerment facilitates goal-oriented actions by all employees. Total employee involvement gets everyone working together synergistically to pursue a common goal of quality improvement. More job-control power should be given to employees without overstepping management's authority. First, employees should be trained on how best to perform their jobs. Then they should be given the right tools to perform the jobs. Finally, let them control their own approaches to making use of the training and tools available. Total employee involvement encourages a feeling of job ownership that can help maximize the contribution of each employee.

2.5 QUALITY OF MANUFACTURED GOODS

Quality is manufactured; not acquired

The quality of a manufactured product is determined by several elements, including the design, the production equipment, the infrastructure that supports the production, and the operators that are involved in the production. Product proliferation has been one way by which manufacturers attempt to increase market share and revenue. Unfortunately, the increase in the number of product choices is achieved at the expense of quality. Product complexity, in terms of design, production, and marketing, places a big demand on a company's operations and resources. The company must accommodate both low and high volumes for different product lines, short and long lead times, standard and custom products, stock and order products, and fixed versus variable production setups. In addition, the company must provide support services such as customer service, marketing, and personnel training. Product fragmentation is another source of complexity to both the manufacturer and the consumer. Most consumers are familiar with the introduction of several new products labeled as 'new improved.' While there may be no question about the newness of the products, the improved aspect is often questionable. In order to improve product quality, product complexity and fragmentation must be controlled.

2.5.1 Managing product complexity

Product complexity adversely affects quality
The rate at which new products are introduced far exceeds the rate at which consumers can assimilate the changes. A product's complexity, inherent quality, and compatibility will ultimately influence a customer's perception of the overall quality of the product. To evaluate how a product might meet the needs of the customer, the following questions should be addressed.

- What is the purpose of the product?
- What are the characteristics of the users?
- What skill level is required to use the product?
- What customer support services will be provided?
- Will the producer furnish all the product components?
- What, if any, product components will users need to buy separately?
- Where will the product be used?
- What communication facilities are available?

Product planning

In some cases, a redesign of the product may be necessary to meet customers' quality needs. Product planning is the process of determining which products to offer in a competitive market. From the design and blueprint specification stage to the actual production stage, the needs of the customer should be kept in mind. Product planning requires that new designs are added as new products when justified, while old products are modified or discontinued as appropriate. In general, product planning should address the following three essential elements.

1. *Product characteristics*: This covers product plans, market analysis, specifications, drawings, tests, design review, prototypes, cost procedures, and value engineering.
2. *Product configuration*: This should cover drawing release procedures, design review process, change order procedures, inspection, production level,

technical supervision, quality control procedures, and product assurance (reliability and maintainability).

3. *Coordination of one product with other products*: This involves integrating the activities involved in the production of one product with other product schedules with respect to quality requirements, resource allocation, and production capabilities.

The product planning should be an iterative process that is continuously reviewed and revised, based on the prevailing customer needs. Some of the specific items of focus in product planning are as follows.

1. *Materials and supplies*: The generation of reports showing materials and supplies that will be required by a product.
2. *Labor*: The analysis of labor hours required to accomplish good quality work on a product.
3. *Overhead allocation*: The distribution of production overhead based on the current mix of products.
4. *Product tracking*: The tracking of the status of a product with respect to production and quality standards.
5. *Job transfer*: The routing of a job from one product center to another with respect to the preservation of quality.

2.6 QUALITY OF SERVICE

Service with a smile sets the stage for quality

A service is often an intangible solution that is provided to a client. Interpersonal skills play a more significant role in the quality of services than they do in the quality of manufactured products. Quality alone is not enough, better customer relations should also be pursued. The service provider must ensure that those directly providing services to the client have the proper tools adequately to discharge their duties. The personal needs and recognition of these individuals are essential to achieving improvement in the quality of services. Quality of service has several dimensions.

- *Reliability*: This deals with the consistency, accuracy, and dependability of service.
- *Promptness*: This involves the timeliness, responsiveness, and willingness to provide service.
- *Competence*: This refers to the adequacy of the skill and knowledge required to deliver service.
- *Access*: This involves the receptiveness of the service provider to customer requests.
- *Courtesy*: This deals with the empathy, respect, consideration, and politeness with which a service is provided.

- *Communication*: This refers to the ability to listen to the customer, keep the customer informed, and accept customer feedback.
- *Comprehension*: This refers to the readiness of the service provider to learn, know, and understand the customer and his or her needs.
- *Credibility*: This refers to the honesty, believability, and reputation of the service provider with respect to the delivery of service.
- *Tools*: This refers to the collection of tangible and physical instruments at the disposal of the service provider.

All of the above dimensions come into play in determining the quality of service. An organization must strive to improve in each dimension in order to achieve overall improvement in service quality. A survey of service employees by a company (Inset Systems Company of Brookfield, Connecticut, *The Insetter*, 1992) concerning what 'quality' means in terms of job performance yielded the following responses.

'Providing extremely polite, prompt, and accurate service.'
'Viewing the customer as having done us a favor by buying our product.'
'Knowing as much as possible about products in order to support them better.'
'Researching problems to come up with good, solid solutions.'
'Maintaining good relationships with distributors and dealers to make customers feel comfortable.'
'Giving your all and going out on the limb for the customer.'
'Providing the customers with simple solutions that enable them to do their own work more efficiently.'

2.7 EMPLOYEE MOTIVATION AND QUALITY OF WORK

With the advent of new technologies (e.g. desktop computers), the elements of a service function should be designed to take advantage of the new developments. An objective selection and appropriate assignment of service tasks will alleviate potential motivational problems that can develop in a service environment. Frederick Taylor (1911) stated that management was knowing exactly what you wanted men to do, and seeing to it that it was done in the best and cheapest way. Koontz and O'Donnel (1959) alternatively defined management as the function of getting things done through people, while McGregor (1960) stated that successful management depends significantly on the ability to predict and control human behavior. The level of the quality of service involves some human elements with behavioral implications. In order to get a worker to work effectively, he or she must be motivated. Some workers are inherently self-motivating. On the other hand, there are workers for whom motivation is an external force that must be explicitly activated. McGregor (1960) classified the view of workers into two basic categories of Theory X and Theory Y.

Theory X

Theory X assumes that the worker is essentially uninterested and unmotivated to perform his or her duties. Motivation must be instilled into the worker by the adoption of external motivating agents. A Theory X worker is inherently indolent and requires constant supervision and prodding to get him or her to perform. To motivate a Theory X worker, a mixture of managerial actions, including those listed below, may be needed:

- strict rules to constrain worker behavior;
- incentives to encourage better performance;
- rewards to recognize improved effort;
- threats to job security associated with performance failure.

Theory Y

Theory Y assumes that the worker is basically interested and motivated to perform his or her assigned duties. In effect, the worker views his or her job function positively, and uses self-control and self-direction to pursue stated objectives. Under Theory Y, management is confronted with the task of taking advantage of the worker's positive intuition so that his or her actions coincide with the objectives of the organization. Thus, a Theory Y manager attempts to use the worker's self-direction as the principal instrument for accomplishing work. In general, Theory Y facilitates:

- worker participation in decision-making;
- cordial management–worker relationship;
- worker-designed job methodology;
- worker individualism within acceptable company limits.

Hierarchy of needs

Maslow (1954) presented what is usually known as Maslow's hierarchy of needs. He stressed that the needs of man are ordered in a hierarchical fashion consisting of five categories, as listed below.

1. *Physiological needs*: The needs for the basic things of life; such as food, water, housing, and clothing. This is the level where access to money is most critical.
2. *Safety needs*: The needs for security, stability, and freedom from threat of physical harm.
3. *Social needs*: The needs for social approval, friends, love, affection, and association.
4. *Esteem needs*: The needs for accomplishment, respect, recognition, attention, and appreciation.
5. *Self-actualization needs*: The need for self-fulfillment and self-improvement. This is the desire to grow and learn.

Hierarchical motivation implies that the particular motivation technique utilized for a given worker should depend on where the worker is in Maslow's hierarchy. For example, the needs for esteem take precedence over the physiological needs when the latter are relatively well satisfied. Money, as an example, cannot be expected to be a very successful motivational factor for a worker who is already on the fourth level of the hierarchy of needs. Things that are highly craved in youth tend to assume less importance later in life. Using the hierarchy of needs, the needs of a service employee should be more carefully considered to determine how the quality of service may be improved.

Hygiene factors and motivators

Herzberg (1968) presented another motivation model that deals with two motivational factors: hygiene factors and motivators. He stated that the hygiene factors are necessary but not sufficient conditions for a contented worker. The negative aspects of the factors may lead to an unsatisfied worker, whereas their positive aspects do not necessarily improve the satisfaction of the worker. Below are some examples.

1. *Administrative policies*: Bad policies can quickly lead to worker dissatisfaction while good policies are viewed as something expected.
2. *Supervision*: A bad supervisor can adversely affect worker performance while a good supervisor cannot necessarily improve worker performance.
3. *Working condition*: Bad working conditions distract workers and impede performance, but good working conditions do not automatically generate improved productivity.
4. *Salary*: Low salaries can make a worker unhappy, but a raise will not necessarily lead to a better performance.
5. *Personal life*: Miserable personal life can adversely affect worker performance, but a happy life does not imply that he or she will be a better worker.
6. *Peer, superior, and subordinate relationships*: Good relations are important to keep a worker happy, but extraordinarily good relations do not guarantee that he or she will be more productive.
7. *Status*: Low status can force a worker to perform to his or her 'level', whereas high status does not imply that the worker will rise to a higher performance.

Herzberg suggested that motivators are motivating agents that should be inherent in the work itself. These include the following.

1. *Achievement*: The job design should give consideration to opportunity for worker achievement and avenues to set personal goals to excel.
2. *Recognition*: The mechanism for recognizing superior performance should be incorporated into the job design.

3. *Work content*: The work content should be interesting enough to motivate and stimulate the worker.
4. *Responsibility*: The worker should have some measure of responsibility for how his or her job is performed. Personal responsibility leads to accountability which can positively influence performance.
5. *Professional growth*: The work should offer an opportunity for advancement so that the worker can set his or her own aspiration level for professional growth.

Herzberg's motivation model may be described as a job enrichment process with the basic philosophy that work can be made more interesting in order to induce an individual to work better. Many people regard work as an unpleasant necessity (a necessary evil). Herzberg's model provides the framework under which 'work' can be designed to be a potential motivator whereby workers are anxious to perform and improve their quality of service.

2.8 MBO VERSUS DEMING PHILOSOPHY

Give the worker some room so that he may fill the gap
Management by objective (MBO) is the management concept whereby a worker is allowed to take responsibility for the design and performance of a task under controlled conditions. It gives each worker a chance to set his or her own objectives in achieving organizational goals. The worker can monitor his or her own progress and take corrective actions when needed without management intervention. MBO has the following positive characteristics:

1. it encourages each worker to find better ways of performing his or her job;
2. it avoids over-supervision of self-motivated workers;
3. it helps a worker in becoming better aware of what is expected in his or her job function;
4. it permits timely feedback on worker performance.

However, MBO does have some disadvantages which include possible abuse of the freedom to self-direct and possible disruption of the overall coordination of efforts. Deming advocates the abolishment of MBO, but there are various implementations of MBO. There are probably some MBO approaches that adversely affect quality and, thereby, justify the call by some quality gurus for its abolishment. However, if implemented correctly, MBO can create opportunities for quality improvement.

Management by exception

Management by exception (MBE) is an after-the-fact management approach to control. Contingency plans are not made and there is no rigid monitoring.

Deviations from expectations are considered to be the exception to the rule. When unacceptable deviations from expectations occur, they are investigated, and only then is any action taken. The major advantage of MBE is that it lessens management's workload. However, it is a dangerous concept to follow, especially for high risk products and services. Many of the problems that can develop in quality improvement efforts are such that after-the-fact corrections are expensive or even impossible. As a result, MBE runs counter to the teachings of continuous quality improvement. The irony of MBE is that managers who operate under crisis management are often recognized as superstars because they solve problems whenever they develop. On the other hand, managers who prevent problems may be viewed as inactive because they are rarely seen solving problems.

Management should work toward avoiding quality problems rather than exposing the organization to potentially expensive crisis management actions. An organization that operates under the notion of 'if it ain't broke, don't fix it' will never have the opportunity to achieve quality improvement.

2.9 MANAGEMENT SUPPORT

Quality should not be an occasional concern of management; it should be a steadfast commitment

Management must play an active role in implementing the systems approach to total quality management. Management must discourage the work force from cutting corners when it comes to quality. The idea of making products quicker and cheaper should not supersede the idea of making them better. While making products quicker and cheaper is a major determinant of short-term competitive edge, better products are invariably the determinant for long-term survival. If the systems view is implemented effectively, quicker and cheaper products can very well coexist with better and more profitable products.

Management must not only proclaim the need for better quality, but must also commit the necessary resources for it. Investments made for quality today will lead to higher profits in the future. Management must overcome its naivety about the source of quality problems. Quality problems sometimes have their origins in the most unimaginable sources. Management can support total quality management with a systems viewpoint by doing the following:

- raising the level of awareness about the implications of low and higher quality;
- adopting a supportive quality philosophy;
- backing the philosophy with required resources;
- making total quality management a mandatory requirement throughout the organization;
- instituting periodic quality reporting requirements;

- establishing quality liaisons with clients and suppliers;
- adopting a flexible perception of systems operations;
- playing a visible role in quality management;
- requiring that functional managers document how department level quality decisions affect other units of the organization;
- appreciating the limitations of automation in quality management.

2.10 PREPARING FOR CHANGE TO QUALITY IMPROVEMENT

Changing is the root of advancement. Quality improvement requires change
An organization must be prepared for change. Quality improvement must be instituted into every aspect of everything that the organization does. If employees are better prepared for change, then positive changes can be achieved. The 'pain but no gain' aspects of quality improvement can be avoided if proper preparations have been made for changes. The requirements for getting an organization ready for the drastic changes that may be needed by quality improvement include the following:

- keep everyone informed of the impending changes;
- get all employees involved;
- make employees a part of the decision input mechanism;
- highlight the benefits of improved quality;
- train employees about their new job requirements;
- create an environment for job enrichment;
- allay the fears about potential loss of jobs due to improved quality;
- promote change as a transition to better things;
- make changes in small increments;
- make employees feel that they are owners of the change.

2.11 STRATEGIC QUALITY PLANNING

A plan is the map of the wise
Quality planning determines the nature of actions and responsibilities required to achieve a specified quality goal. Strategic quality planning involves the long-range aspects of quality improvement. Planning forms the basis for all actions. Badiru (1991) presented strategic planning in three distinct hierarchies as discussed below.

Supra level planning

Planning at this level deals with the big picture of how quality improvement fits the overall and long-range organizational goals. Questions faced at this level may concern the potential contributions of quality improvement to the survival of the organization, the use of limited resources, the required interfaces with other projects within and outside the organization, the management support for the quality improvement, company culture, market share, customer expectations, and business stability.

Macro level planning

Planning at this level addresses the overall planning within a defined product boundary. The scope of the improvement effort and its operational interfaces are addressed at macro level planning. Questions faced at the macro level include goal definition, project scope, availability of qualified personnel, resource availability, project policies, communication interfaces, budget requirements, goal interactions, deadline, and conflict resolution strategies.

Micro level planning

This deals with detailed operational plans at the task levels of quality improvement. Definite and explicit tactics for accomplishing specific improvement objectives are developed at the micro level. Factors to be considered at micro level planning include scheduled time, training requirement, tools required, task procedures, reporting requirements, and quality requirements.

2.12 PREVENTION VERSUS DETECTION AND CORRECTION

Prevention is the remedy for a cure. If prevention works, there will be no need to search for a cure

The efforts devoted to preventing quality problems will always yield more benefits than the costs of detecting and correcting quality problems. The detection and correction approach to quality management is a crisis management approach that can actually foment crisis. If quality problems are allowed to develop, even the best detection system may not be able to locate the source of the problem. Even if the problem source is detected, the existing correction system may not be capable of solving the problem. The prudent approach to quality management is the approach that prevents problems from developing. The concept of 'if it ain't broke, don't fix it' should never be applied to quality management issues. Whether the product or service is 'broken' or not, efforts should be made continuously to 'fix' and improve it. Prevention has the following advantages:

- it eliminates the cost and time required to detect problems;
- it keeps employees constantly aware of the importance of good quality;
- it precludes the perils of bad quality;
- it promotes 'fire safety' rather than 'fire fighting';
- it enhances the faith in the production process.

2.13 BENCHMARKING FOR QUALITY IMPROVEMENT

With a good example, every process can excel

Metrics based on an organization's most critical quality issues should be developed. The objective is to equal or surpass the best in the industry. Benchmarking is a process whereby target quality standards are established based on the best examples in the industry. In its simplest term, benchmarking means 'learning from the best.' The premise of benchmarking is that if an organization replicates the best quality examples, it will become one of the best in the industry. A major objective of benchmarking is to identify negative gaps, as shown in Figure 2.3, where other companies surpass an organization. An attempt is then made to close the gaps by improving quality.

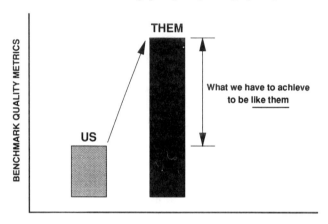

Figure 2.3 Identification of benchmark gaps.

2.13.1 Construction of polar plots for benchmarking

Polar plots can be used as a tool to convey a visual representation of benchmarking gaps. In a conventional polar plot, vectors are drawn from the center of a circle on individual scales based on the outcome ranges for each quality factor. Figure 2.4 shows an example of using a polar plot for quality benchmarking. Two companies are compared in the example: Company A is the benchmark; Company B is the company being compared to the benchmark. The five quality factors used for illustrative purposes in the example are:

1. customer satisfaction;
2. customer interface;
3. employee involvement;
4. management support;
5. saving due to quality awareness.

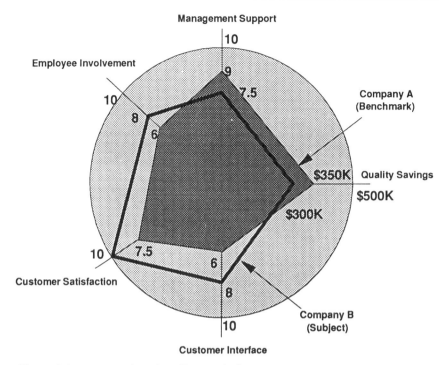

Figure 2.4 Benchmarking of quality standards.

In Figure 2.4, the vector for savings due to quality awareness is on a scale of $0 to $500 000, while the scale for customer service is from 0 to 10. The rating of each company with respect to each quality factor is marked along the respective vectors. The rating points for each company are then connected to form a polyhedron. The polyhedron for the benchmark is shown shaded in the figure. The overall performance of the companies being compared are not proportional to the areas of their respective polyhedrons. However, a quick visual assessment can be made of where the subject company stands with respect to the benchmark. The areas where positive gaps exist should be strengthened, while attempts should be made to improve areas where negative gaps exist.

Badiru (1991) presented a modification of the basic polar plot. The modification involves a procedure which normalizes the areas of the polyhedrons with respect to the total area of the base circle. With this modification, the normalized areas of the polyhedrons are proportional to the respective priority weights of the factors. So, the companies being compared can be ranked on the basis of the areas of the polyhedrons. Steps involved in the modified approach are presented below.

1. Let n be the number of factors involved in the comparison of companies such that $n >= 4$. Number the factors in a preferred order $(1, 2, 3, \ldots, n)$.
2. If the factors are considered to be equally important (i.e. equally weighted), compute the sector angle associated with each attribute as:

$$\theta = \frac{360°}{n}$$

3. Draw a circle with a large enough radius. A radius of 4 cm is usually adequate.
4. Convert the outcome range for each attribute to a standardized scale of 0 to 10 using appropriate transformation relationships.
5. For factor number one, draw a vertical vector up from the center of the circle to the edge of the circle.
6. Measure a clockwise and draw a vector for factor number two. Repeat this step for all factors in the numbered order.
7. For each company, mark its standardized relative performance with respect to each factor along the factor's vector. If a 4 cm radius is used for the base circle, then we have the following linear transformation relationship:
0.0 cm = rating score of 0.0
4.0 cm = rating score of 10.0
8. Connect the points marked for each company to form a polyhedron. Repeat this step for all companies.
9. Compute the area of the base circle as:

$$\begin{aligned} \Omega &= \pi r^2 \\ &= \pi (4\text{cm})^2 \\ &= 16\pi \text{ sq cm} \\ &= 100\pi \text{ squared rating units.} \end{aligned}$$

10. Compute the area of the polyhedron corresponding to each company. This can be done by partitioning each polyhedron into a set of triangles and then calculating the areas of the triangles. To calculate the area of each triangle, note that we will know the lengths of two sides of the triangle and the angle subtended by the two sides. With these three known values, the area of each triangle can be calculate through basic trigonometric formulas.

    For example, the area of each polyhedron may be represented as b_i ($i = 1, 2, \ldots, m$) where m is the number of companies. The area of each triangle in the polyhedron for a given company is then calculated as:

$$\Delta_t = \frac{1}{2} (L_j)(L_{j+1})(\text{Sin } \theta),$$

where:
L_j = standardized rating with respect to factor j
L_{j+1} = standardized rating with respect to factor $j+1$

L_j and L_{j+1} are the two sides that subtend a

Since $n >= 4$, a will be between 0 and 90 degrees and $\sin(a)$ will be strictly increasing over that interval.

The area of the polyhedron for alternative i is then calculated as:

$$\lambda_i = \sum_{t=1}^{n} \Delta_{t(i)}$$

Note that a is constant for a given number of factors and the area of the polyhedron will be a function of the adjacent ratings (L_j and L_{j+1}) only.

11. Compute the standardized area corresponding to each company as:

$$w_i = \frac{\lambda_i}{\Omega}(100\%)$$

12. Compare the subject companies to the benchmark company based on the values of λ_i.

Illustrative example

This example illustrates the use of the modified polar plots for benchmarking analysis. Table 2.1 presents the ranges of possible evaluation ratings within which a company can be rated with respect to each of five attributes. The evaluation rating of a company with respect to attribute j must be between the given range of a_j to b_j. Table 2.2 presents the data for raw evaluation ratings of three companies with respect to the five attributes specified in Table 2.1. The attributes quality level, profit level, and productivity level are quantitative measures that can be objectively determined. The attributes flexibility level and customer satisfaction level are subjective measures that may be rated through surveys or other subjective approaches.

Table 2.1 Ranges of raw evaluation ratings for polar plots

			Evaluation Range	
Attribute (j)	*Description*	*Rank* k_j	*Lower Limit* a_j	*Upper Limit* b_j
I	Quality	1	0.5	9
II	Profit (× $1,000)	2	0	100
III	Productivity	3	1	10
IV	Flexibility	4	0	12
V	Satisfaction	5	0	10

Table 2.2 Raw evaluation ratings for modified polar plots

Alternatives	Attributes				
	I ($j=1$)	II ($j=2$)	III ($j=3$)	IV ($j=4$)	V ($j=5$)
A ($i=1$)	5	50	3	6	10
B ($i=2$)	1	20	1.5	9	2
C ($i=3$)	8	75	4	11	1

The steps in the solution are presented below:

Step 1: $n = 5$. The attributes are numbered in the following order:
Quality: Attribute I
Profit: Attribute II
Productivity: Attribute III
Flexibility: Attribute IV
Satisfaction: Attribute V

Step 2:   The sector angle is computed as:
$$a = 360°/n$$
$$= 72°$$

Step 3:   This step is shown in Figure 2.5.

Step 4:   Let Y_{ij} be the raw evaluation rating of alternative i with respect to attribute j (see Table 2.2).
Let Z_{ij} be the standardized evaluation rating.
The standardized evaluation ratings (between 0.0 and 10.0) shown in Table 2.3 were obtained by using the following linear transformation relationship:

$$Z_{ij} = 10 \left[\frac{(Y_{ij} - a_j)}{(b_j - a_j)} \right].$$

Steps 5, 6, 7, 8: These are shown in Figure 2.5.

Step 9:   The area of the base circle is $\Omega = 100\pi$ squared rating units.
Note that it is computationally more efficient to calculate the areas in terms of rating units rather than centimeters.

Step 10:   Using the expressions presented in step 10, the areas of the triangles making up each of the polyhedrons are computed and summed up.

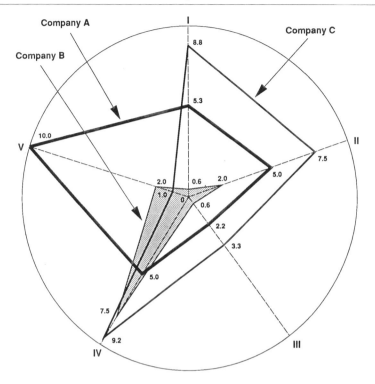

Figure 2.5 Modified polar plot for benchmarking.

Table 2.3 Standardized evaluation ratings for modified polar plots

	Attributes				
Alternatives	I (j=1)	II (j=2)	III (j=3)	IV (j=4)	V (j=5)
A (i=1)	5.3	5.0	2.2	5.0	10.0
B (i=2)	0.6	2.0	0.6	7.5	2.0
C (i=3)	8.8	7.5	3.3	9.2	1.0

The respective areas are:

$$\lambda_A = 72.04 \text{ squared units}$$
$$\lambda_B = 10.98 \text{ squared units}$$
$$\lambda_C = 66.14 \text{ squared units}$$

Step 11: The standardized areas for the three companies are as follows:

$$w_A = 22.93\%$$
$$w_B = 3.50\%$$
$$w_C = 21.05\%$$

Step 12: On the basis of the standardized areas in Step 11, Company A is found to have the best overall performance. This company may then be selected as a benchmark for further analysis.

As an extension to the modification presented above, the sector angle may be a variable indicating relative attribute weighting while the radius represents the evaluation rating of the companies with respect to the weighted attribute. That is, if the attributes are not equally weighted, the sector angles will not all be equal. In that case, the sector angle for each attribute is computed as:

$$\theta_i = p_i \, (360°),$$

where
p_j = relative numeric weight of each of n attributes

$$\sum_{j=1}^{n} p_j = 1.0$$

Assume that the attributes in the preceding example are considered to have unequal weights as shown in Table 2.4.

Table 2.4 Relative weighting of attributes for polar plots

Attribute (i)	Weight p_j	Angle θ_j
I	0.333	119.88
II	0.267	96.12
III	0.200	72.00
IV	0.133	47.88
V	0.067	24.12
	1.000	360.00

The resulting polar plots for weighted sector angles are shown in Figure 2.6. The respective weighted areas for the alternatives are:

$$\lambda_A = 51.56 \text{ squared units}$$
$$\lambda_B = 9.07 \text{ squared units}$$
$$\lambda_C = 60.56 \text{ squared units}$$

The standardized areas for the alternatives are as follows:

$$w_A = 16.41\%$$

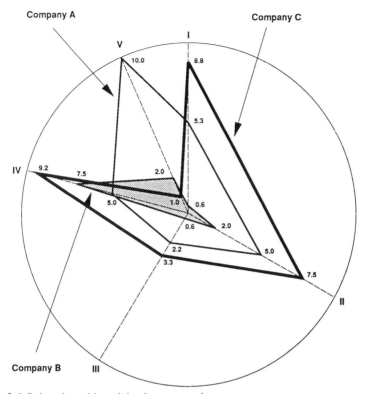

Figure 2.6 Polar plot with weighted sector angles.

$$w_B = 2.89\%$$
$$w_C = 19.28\%$$

Thus, if the given attributes are weighted as shown in Table 2.4, Company C will turn out to be the best. However, it should be noted that the relative weights of the attributes are too skewed, resulting in some sector angles being greater than 90 degrees. It is preferred to have the attribute weights assigned such that all sector angles are less than 90 degrees. This leads to more consistent evaluation since $sin(v)$ is strictly increasing between 0 and 90 degrees.

It should also be noted that the weighted areas for the alternatives are sensitive to the order in which the attributes are drawn in the polar plot. Thus, a preferred order of the attributes must be defined prior to starting the analysis. The preferred order may be based on the desired sequence in which quality improvement goals must be satisfied. For example, it may be desirable to attend to product quality issues before addressing throughput issues. The surface area of the base circle may be interpreted as a measure of global organizational goal with respect to such performance indicators as available capital, market share, capacity utilization, and so on. Thus, the weighted area of the polyhedron associated with an alternative may be viewed as the degree to which that alternative satisfies organizational goals.

A benchmark–feedback model

Benchmarking requires a continuous comparison with the best. Updates must be obtained from companies already benchmarked and new companies to be benchmarked must be selected on a periodic basis. Measurement, analysis, feedback, and modification should be incorporated into the quality improvement program. The benchmark–feedback model presented in Figure 2.7 is useful for establishing a continuous drive towards quality benchmarks.

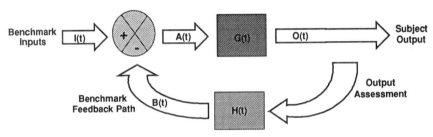

Figure 2.7 Quality benchmark feedback model.

The figure shows the block diagram representation of input–output relationships of the components in a benchmarking environment. In the model, I(t) represents the set of benchmark inputs to the subject company. The inputs may be in terms of data, information, raw material, technical skill, or other basic resources. The index t denotes a time reference. A(t) represents the feedback loop actuator. The actuator facilitates the flow of inputs to the various segments of the company. G(t) represents the forward transfer function which coordinates input information and resources to produce the desired output, O(t). H(t) represents the management control process that monitors the status of improvement and generates the appropriate feedback information, B(t), which is routed to the input transfer junction. The feedback information is necessary to determine what control actions should be taken at the next improvement phase. The primary responsibility of a quality improvement manager should involve ensuring the proper forward and backward flow of information concerning the performance of the company with respect to the benchmarked inputs.

2.14 TRIPLE C APPROACH TO QUALITY IMPROVEMENT

Communication is the prerequisite for cooperation
The triple C concept of project management (Badiru, 1987) may be applied to ensure that communication, cooperation, and coordination functions are carried out to facilitate total quality management. Triple C encourages employee involvement and customer participation. Figure 2.8 presents a pictorial representation of the triple C model.

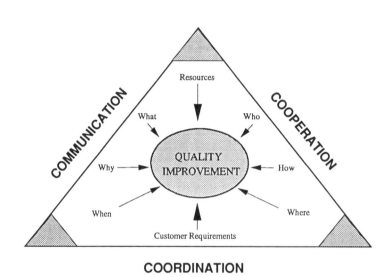

Figure 2.8 Triple C model for quality improvement.

Communication

Every functional group or individual that can influence quality throughout the hierarchies of the organization should be informed and made aware of the quality objectives. Specific details of communication should include:

- the quality objective;
- the scope of the quality objective;
- the plan for achieving the objective;
- the desired personnel interfaces;
- the direct and indirect benefits of higher quality;
- the expected cost of low quality;
- the desired personnel contribution to the quality objective.

The communication channel must be kept open throughout the quality improvement effort. In addition to in-house communication, external communication needs should also be addressed. To facilitate communication, management must do the following:

- exude commitment to quality improvement;
- endorse communication responsibility matrix;
- facilitate multi-channel communication interfaces;
- support internal and external communication needs;
- help resolve organizational and communication conflicts;
- promote both formal and informal communication links.

Cooperation

Not only must the work force be informed and educated about quality, but their cooperation must also be explicitly sought. Merely giving a nod to the quality effort may not be an indication of full cooperation. The justification for the quality objective must be explained to all the groups concerned, including the union, managers, clients, and suppliers. To seek the cooperation of employees, explicit statements must be made about the following:

- what cooperative efforts are needed;
- criticality of cooperation to the quality program;
- rewards of cooperation for quality;
- organizational impact of cooperation;
- implications of low quality.

A documentation of the prevailing level of cooperation is useful for winning further support for quality improvement. Clarification of quality priorities will facilitate personnel cooperation. Relative priorities of multiple projects should be specified so that a quality improvement project that is of high priority to the organization will also be of high priority to all groups within the organization.

Coordination

Having successfully initiated the communication and cooperation functions, the efforts of the groups and individuals (subsystems) in the organization must be carefully coordinated. Coordination facilitates harmonious and systematic integration of the contribution of each subsystem to overall quality objectives. The development of a responsibility matrix may be quite useful in this regard and Table 2.5 presents an example of such a matrix for quality improvement. The matrix consists of columns of 'actors' and rows of specific responsibilities or required actions. The actors can be individuals, groups of people, or functional departments.

Table 2.5 Example of responsibility matrix for quality improvement

RESPONSIBILITIES	ACTORS				
	Management	Marketing	Manufacturing	Person A	Person B
1. Survey of Customer Needs	I	R	I	C	S
2. Funding for Quality Improvement	R	I	I	I	I
3. Design Review	S	C	R	R	I
4. Monitor Progress	R	R	R	R	R
5. Institutionalize Improvement	R	R	R	R	R

Responsibility Codes:

R: Responsible

C: Consult

I: Inform

S: Support

Cells within the responsibility matrix are filled with relationship codes that indicate who is responsible for what and the nature of the responsibility. A code of R indicates that the actor is responsible for the specified action. A code of I indicates that the actor must be informed of what is going on with respect to the action. A code of S indicates that the actor must support the efforts to carry out the action. A code of C indicates that the actor must be consulted on issues related to carrying out the action. The matrix can be as large as needed to cover the scope of the quality improvement effort. Since quality improvement is supposed to be everybody's responsibility, it is recommended that no cell in a responsibility matrix be left blank. Everybody should at least be informed of the ongoing efforts.

The responsibility matrix helps to avoid overlooking critical communication and functional requirements, as well as obligations in the quality management effort. It can help resolve questions such as:

- functional responsibilities for specific quality functions;
- quality performance measurement standards;
- information transfer and feedback loop;
- who will do what;
- who will inform whom of what;
- whose approval is needed for what;
- who is responsible for which results;
- what personnel interfaces are involved;
- what support is needed from whom and when.

Quality circles

Quality circles is a participative technique that should play a significant role in implementing the systems approach to total quality management. The concepts of quality circles and the triple C approach can be combined to achieve the following benefits:

- improved product quality;
- higher employee productivity;
- increased job satisfaction;
- consistent platform for cooperation;
- employee development;
- more visible constructive interaction between departments;
- increased awareness of organizational efforts to improve quality.

2.15 QUALITY IMPROVEMENT GROUP MEETINGS

Several quality minds are better than one
Quality improvement efforts are complex and require several interfaces. No one

person has all the information to make all quality-related decisions accurately. As a result, quality improvement decisions should be made by a group of people, when appropriate. Decisions can be made through linear responsibility. In this case, one person makes the final decision based on inputs from other people. Alternatively, decisions can be made through shared responsibility. In this case, a group of people share the responsibility for making decisions. The major advantages of group decision-making for quality improvement are as follows.

1. *Ability to share experience, knowledge, and resources*: Many heads are better than one. A group will possess greater collective ability to solve a quality problem.
2. *Increased credibility*: Decisions made by a group of people often carry more weight in an organization.
3. *Improved morale*: Personnel morale can be positively influenced because many people have the opportunity to participate in the decision-making process.
4. *Better rationalization*: The opportunity to observe other people's views can lead to an improvement in an individual's reasoning process.

Group decision-making is done by a number of different approaches including brainstorming, delphi method, nominal group technique, and multivoting. Some of these approaches are discussed below.

Brainstorming

Brainstorming is a way of generating many new ideas. In brainstorming, the decision group comes together to discuss alternative ways of solving a decision problem. The members of the brainstorming group may be from different departments, may have different backgrounds and training, and may not even know one another. The diversity of the constituents helps to create a stimulating environment for generating many different ideas. The technique encourages free outward expression of new ideas, no matter how far-fetched the ideas might appear. No criticism of any new idea is permitted during the brainstorming session. A major concern in brainstorming is that extroverts may take control of the discussions. For this reason, an experienced and respected leader is needed to manage the brainstorming discussions. The group leader establishes the procedure for proposing ideas, keeps the discussions in line with the group's mission, discourages disruptive statements, and encourages the participation of all members.

After the group runs out of ideas, open discussions are held to weed out the unsuitable ones. It is expected that even the rejected ideas may stimulate the generation of other ideas, which may eventually lead to other favored ideas. Some guidelines for improving the brainstorming session are:

- focus on a specific decision problem;
- keep ideas relevant to the intended decision;
- be receptive to all new ideas;
- evaluate the ideas on a relative basis after exhausting new ideas;
- maintain an atmosphere conducive to cooperative discussions;
- maintain a record of the ideas generated.

Delphi method

The traditional approach to group decision-making is to obtain the opinion of experienced participants through open discussions. An attempt is then made to reach a consensus among the participants. However, open group discussions are often biased because of the influence of, or even subtle intimidation from, dominant individuals. Even when the threat of a dominant individual is not present, opinions may still be swayed by group pressure. This is often called the 'bandwagon effect' of group decision-making.

The delphi method attempts to overcome these difficulties by requiring individuals to present their opinions anonymously through an intermediary. This method differs from other interactive group methods because it eliminates face-to-face confrontations. It was originally developed for forecasting applications, but it has been modified in various ways for application to different types of decision-making. The method can be quite useful for project management decisions. It is particularly effective when decisions must be based on a broad set of factors. The delphi method is implemented through the following steps.

1. *Problem definition*: A decision problem that is considered significant to the organization or project is identified and clearly described.
2. *Group selection*: An appropriate group of experts or experienced individuals is formed to address the particular decision problem. Both internal and external experts may be involved in the delphi process. A leading individual is appointed to serve as the administrator of the decision process. The group may operate through the mail or gather together in a room. In either case, all opinions are expressed anonymously on paper. If the group meets in the same room, care should be taken to provide enough room so that each member does not have the feeling that someone may accidentally or deliberately spy on his or her responses.
3. *Initial opinion poll*: The technique is initiated by describing the problem to be addressed in unambiguous terms. The group members are requested to submit a list of major areas of concern in their specialty areas as they relate to the decision problem.
4. *Questionnaire design and distribution*: Questionnaires are prepared to address the areas of concern related to the decision problem. The written responses to the questionnaires are collected and organized by the

administrator. The administrator aggregates the responses in a statistical format. For example, the average, mode, and median of the responses may be computed. This analysis is distributed to the decision group. Each member can then see how his or her responses compare with the anonymous views of the other members.

5. *Iterative balloting*: Additional questionnaires based on the previous responses are passed to the members. The members submit their responses again. They may choose either to alter or not alter their previous responses.

6. *Silent discussions and consensus*: The iterative balloting may involve anonymous written discussions of why some responses are correct or incorrect. The process is continued until a consensus is reached. A consensus may be declared after five or six iterations of the balloting or when a specified percentage (e.g. 80%) of the group agrees on the questionnaires. If a consensus cannot be declared on a particular point, it may be displayed to the whole group with a note that it does not represent a consensus.

In addition to its use in technological forecasting, the delphi method has been widely used in other general decision-making. Its major characteristics of anonymity of responses, statistical summary of responses, and controlled procedure make it a reliable mechanism for obtaining numeric data from subjective opinion. The major limitations of the delphi method are as follows.

1. Its effectiveness may be limited in cultures where strict hierarchy, seniority, and age influence decision-making processes.

2. Some experts may not readily accept the contribution of non-experts to the group decision-making process.

3. Since opinions are expressed anonymously, some members may take the liberty to make ludicrous statements. However, if the group composition is carefully reviewed, this problem may be avoided.

Nominal group technique

Nominal group technique is a silent version of brainstorming. It is a method of reaching consensus without the dangers of verbal confrontation. It is normally used to assign priorities to a list of items. Rather than asking people to state their ideas out loud, the team leader asks each member to write down his or her ideas. Typically, between a minimum of five and a maximum of ten ideas would be requested. A single list of ideas is then developed to be presented to the whole group to see. The group then iteratively discusses the ideas and eliminates some of them until a final decision is reached. Thus, the nominal group technique is easier to control. Unlike brainstorming, where members may get into shouting matches, it permits members silently to present their views. In addition, it allows introverted members to contribute to the decision without the pressure of having to speak out too often.

In all of the group decision-making techniques, an important aspect that can enhance and expedite the decision-making process is to require that members review all pertinent data before coming to the group meeting. This will ensure that the decision process is not impeded by trivial preliminary discussions. Some disadvantages of group decision making are:

1. peer pressure in a group situation may influence a member's opinion or discussions;
2. in a large group, some members may not get to participate effectively in the discussions;
3. a member's relative reputation in the group may influence how well his or her opinion is rated;
4. a member with a dominant personality may overwhelm the other members in the discussions;
5. the limited time available to the group may create a time pressure that forces some members to present their opinions without fully evaluating the ramifications of the available data;
6. it is often difficult to get all members of a decision group together at the same time.

Despite these disadvantages, group decision-making definitely has many advantages to nullify the shortcomings. The advantages as presented earlier will have varying levels of effect from one organization to another. The triple C principle described in section 2.14 may also be used to improve the success of decision teams. Team work can be enhanced in group decision-making by following the guidelines below:

1. identify in advance the questions to be addressed;
2. restrict discussions to only one topic per meeting;
3. avoid comments or discussions during the recording of ideas;
4. provide for clarification of meanings instead of arguing points;
5. get a willing group of people together;
6. set an achievable goal for the group;
7. determine the limitations of the group;
8. develop a set of guiding rules for the group;
9. create an atmosphere conducive to group synergism;
10. for major decisions and long-term group activities, arrange for team training which allows the group to learn the decision rules and responsibilities together.

Multivoting

Multivoting is a structured series of votes used to help teams assign priorities in a list of many items and reduce the list to a manageable few (usually three to five). Multivoting may be used at team meetings whenever a brainstorming session has generated a list of items that is too lengthy for all to be addressed at once. The procedure for multivoting is presented below.

1. Take a first vote. Each person votes for as many items as desired, but only once per item.
2. Circle the items receiving a relatively higher number of votes than the others.
3. Take a second vote. Each person votes for a number of items equal to one-half the total number of circled items, but only one vote per item. For example, if six items were circled during the first vote, then each person gets to vote for three items during the second voting.
4. Repeat steps 2 and 3 until the list is reduced to three to five items, which can then be further analyzed as desired. Note: never multivote down to only one item.

The group decision-making approaches above can be adopted to facilitate the following:

- to establish quality improvement procedures and responsibilities;
- to define required activities for improvement;
- to evaluate customer needs;
- to identify improvement opportunities;
- to prioritize improvement opportunities;
- to evaluate progress made towards improvement goals.

2.16 CONTINUOUS PROCESS IMPROVEMENT

Strive to improve so that improvement may thrive for you
Continuous process improvement (CPI) is an approach to obtaining a steady flow of improvement in any process. The term is frequently applied to product quality management functions. However, the approach is also applicable to any goal-oriented process. Continuous process improvement is a proven method of improving business, management, or technical processes. The method is based on the following key points:

- early detection of problems;
- identification of opportunities;
- prioritization of opportunities;
- establishment of a conducive decision-making team;
- comprehensive evaluation of procedures;
- review of methods of improvement;
- establishment of long-term improvement goals;
- continuous implementation of improvement actions;
- company-wide adoption of CPI concept.

A steering committee is typically set up to guide the improvement efforts. The typical functions of the steering committee with respect to continuous process improvement include the following:

- determination of organizational goals and objectives;
- communication with the personnel;
- team organization;
- allocation or recommendation of resource requirements;
- administration of the CPI procedures;
- education and guidance for company-wide involvement.

To illustrate the benefits of CPI, we may consider the two graphical representations in Figures 2.9 and 2.10. The first figure represents the conventional approach to process improvement, while the second figure represents the approach of continuous process improvement.

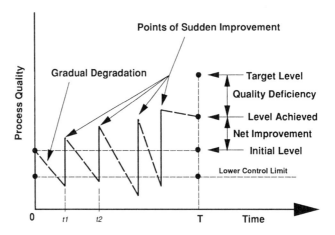

Figure 2.9 Traditional approach to improvement.

In Figure 2.9, the process starts with a certain level of quality. A certain quality level is specified as the target to be achieved by time T. If neglected, the process quality gradually degrades until it falls below the lower control limit at time t_1. At that time, a sudden effort (or innovation) is needed to improve the quality. If neglected once again, the quality goes through another gradual decline until it again falls below the lower control limit at time t_2. Again, a sudden effort is needed to improve the quality. This cycle of degradation–innovation may be repeated several times before time T is reached. At time T, a final attempt is made suddenly to boost the process quality to the target level. But unfortunately, it may be too late to achieve the target quality level. There are many disadvantages to this approach. They are:

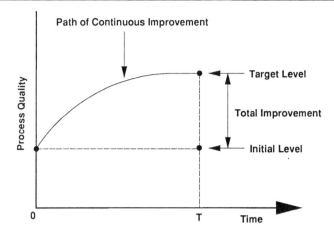

Figure 2.10 Continuous process improvement model.

1. high cost of implementation;
2. frequent disruption of the process;
3. too much focus on short-term benefits;
4. need for sudden innovations;
5. opportunity cost during the degradation phase;
6. negative effect on personnel morale;
7. loss of customer trust;
8. need for frequent and strict monitoring;
9. quality control approach rather than quality management approach.

In Figure 2.10, the process starts with the same initial quality level and it is continuously improved in a determined pursuit of the target quality level. As opportunities to improve occur, they are immediately implemented. The rate of improvement is not necessarily constant over the planning horizon. Hence, the path of improvement is shown as a curve rather than a straight line. The important aspect of CPI is that each subsequent quality level is at least as good as the one preceding it. As has been mentioned previously, the concept of CPI is applicable to any process. A familiar example is a process whereby students perform better in a test by studying continuously and keeping up with the class, rather than trying to study everything the night before the test. The major advantages of CPI include:

1. lower cost of achieving quality objectives;
2. better customer satisfaction;
3. dedication to higher quality products;
4. consistent pace with process technology;
5. conducive environment for personnel involvement;
6. ability to keep ahead of the competition;
7. unambiguous expression of what is expected from the process.

2.17 CONTINUOUS MEASURABLE IMPROVEMENT

Measurable improvement is the yardstick to further improvement
A concept related to the CPI concept is the continuous measurable improvement (CMI) approach. Continuous measurable improvement is a process through which employees are given the authority to determine how best their jobs can be performed and measured. Since the employees are continually in contact with the job, they have the best view of the performance of the process, and they have the most reliable criteria for measuring the improvements achieved in the process. Under CMI, employees are directly involved in designing the job functions. For example, instead of just bringing in external experts to design a new production line, CMI requires that management get the people (employees) who are going to be using the line involved in the design process. This provides valuable employee insights into the design mechanism and paves the way for the success of the design. Readers are referred to Lillrank and Kano (1989) for further details on continuous process improvement and related topics.

2.18 QUALITY FUNCTION DEPLOYMENT

Quality deployment spreads the responsibility for improvement
Quality function deployment (QFD) is a planning approach through which an organization evaluates product performance requirements desired by the customer. The effectiveness of QFD comes from translating customer needs and expectations directly into engineering, manufacturing, and service requirements for an organization. Instead of internally setting product characteristics and then hoping that the customer likes what is produced, QFD ensures that what the customer really wants is produced right from the beginning. Some of the advantages of QFD include:

- improved product quality;
- reduction of material waste;
- reduction of cost of rework;
- reduction in product design cycle;
- reduction in product delivery lead time.

The implementation of quality function deployment is facilitated by the following guidelines:

1. conduct a credible marketing research;
2. establish a communication liaison with the customer;
3. make the customer aware of the capability and limitation of the production facility;
4. establish cooperation between design, manufacturing, and marketing departments;

5. give feedback to the customer on product design and performance;
6. strive for a trusting relationship with the customer.

The QFD process calls for an active participation of design, engineering, manufacturing, sales, marketing, and quality assurance groups within the organization. In addition, external contact points must be included.

Pitfall of ambiguous customer surveys

Question not posed is question not answered
When conducting customer surveys for the purposes of QFD, the questions posed must be explicit and unambiguous. Direct references should be made to the features of the product being surveyed so that useful information may be obtained from customers. For example, in an open-ended survey of customers about the important factors in an airline flight, customers may make reference to such things as quality of food, friendliness of flight attendants, ease of the check-in process, and other obvious factors that they can directly perceive. However, no one may mention anything about the reliability of the airplane's engines, which appear to be the most crucial aspect of flying. QFD surveys must 'lead' the respondents in the pertinent direction.

2.19 QUALITY–PRODUCTIVITY IMPROVEMENT RELATIONSHIP

Quality inbreeding is good breeding
Productivity measures the rate of output based on the rate of input. Productivity can be improved through quality improvement. When quality is improved, less time will be spent on quality troubleshooting. The time that would have, otherwise, been spent on correcting quality problems can be devoted to productivity improvement. Deming's philosophy attempts to change the view that increasing productivity will increase profits. The pressure to raise productivity often leads to producing lower quality products. The higher the defective rate, the lower the number of good units that can be shipped to the customer, consequently, productivity in terms of actual profitable units will fall. The total production cost will also increase. The fact of real life production is that productivity is a function of quality, as shown by the equation below:

$$p = f(q) + e.$$

where:
p = productivity
f = functional relationship
q = quality
e = error allowance

An effective way to improve productivity is to increase both the production process and product quality. Quality and productivity are directly related and are not separable. Improvement in one results in improvement in the other. With an improved process, scarce resources can be transferred from the production of defective units to the production of more good units. This approach, in the long run, will lead to improved productivity and profitability for the organization. The benefits of increasing quality to improve productivity can be summarized as follows:

- production of fewer defective units leads to improved productivity;
- improved quality motivates employees to perform better;
- better quality helps to reduce total production cost;
- production of more good units leads to a more profitable operation;
- improved quality benefits customers, whereas the benefits of improved productivity may be limited to the company only;
- competitiveness is enhanced by better quality.

2.20 QUALITY EVALUATION USING THE ANALYTIC HIERARCHY PROCESS

Analytic hierarchy process (AHP) is an effective method for evaluating quality issues to determine the most crucial areas for improvement. The AHP technique, developed by Saaty (1980), has been used extensively throughout the world for various types of decision analysis. It has significant potential for application in quality evaluation for improvement. AHP is a practical approach to solving complex decision problems involving the comparisons of attributes or alternatives. Golden *et al.* (1989), Vargas (1990), and Zahedi (1986) presented discussions of the technique and its various applications. Based on the previous successful applications of the technique, it can be applied to the evaluation of product characteristics relevant to quality improvement.

In general, AHP enables decision makers to represent the hierarchical interaction of many factors, attributes, characteristics, or alternatives. For example, in quality improvement programs, AHP can be used to identify which product characteristic is the most important for improvement in order better to satisfy customer needs. The general approach to using AHP for quality evaluation may be summarized as follows:

1. specify the overall goal of the quality evaluation process;
2. determine the available alternatives for achieving the goal;
3. determine the quality characteristics to be evaluated in meeting the goal;
4. develop the hierarchical structure for the evaluation problem based on the characteristics, the alternatives, and the overall goal;
5. determine the relative importance of each quality characteristic by using iterative pair-wise comparisons;

6. determine the indicators of consistency in making pair-wise comparisons of the characteristics;
7. revise the pair-wise comparison weights if a consistency ratio is not acceptable;
8. determine the relative weights of the alternatives with respect to each quality characteristic by replicating steps 5, 6, and 7 for the alternatives;
9. determine the overall priority score of each alternative;
10. make a final decision based on the results.

The hierarchy should be constructed so that elements at the same level are of the same class and must be capable of being related to some elements at the next higher level. In a typical hierarchy, the top level reflects the overall objective or focus of the decision problem. Criteria, factors, or attributes on which the final objective is dependent are listed at intermediate levels in the hierarchy. The lowest level in the hierarchy contains the competing alternatives through which the final objective might be achieved. After the hierarchy has been constructed, the decision maker must undertake a subjective prioritization procedure to determine the weight of each element at each level of the hierarchy. Pair-wise comparisons are performed at each level to determine the relative importance of each element at that level with respect to each element at the next higher level in the hierarchy. Figure 2.11 (Badiru, 1992) shows a flowchart of the implementation of AHP.

Figure 2.12 presents an example of an evaluation hierarchy for quality improvement. The objective is to improve outgoing product quality. Three possible approaches are available:

Approach 1: Better inspection system
Approach 2: Process improvement
Approach 3: Product redesign

The approaches are to be compared on the basis of factors that the organization considers to be very important. Such factors may be determined, based on a combination of objectives relating to productivity improvement, quality improvement, better customer satisfaction, better employee morale, economic feasibility, strategic importance, and so on. For the purpose of this illustration, the following five factors are used in evaluating the quality improvement approaches:

Factor A: Employee involvement
Factor B: Customer interface
Factor C: Management support
Factor D: Vendor involvement
Factor E: Facility upgrade

The first step in the AHP procedure involves developing relative weights for the five factors with respect to the objective at the next highest level in the

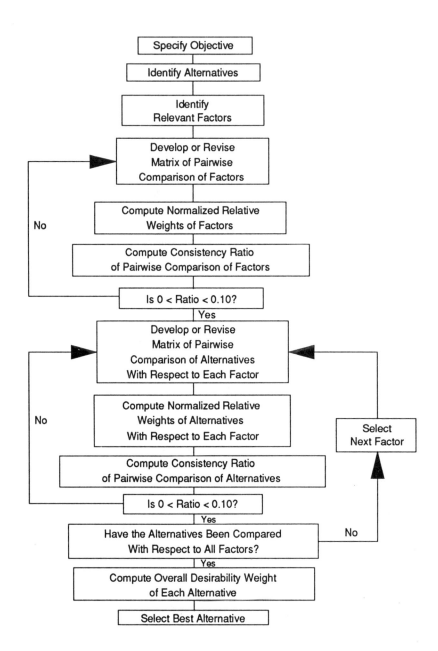

Figure 2.11 Flowchart of AHP methodology.

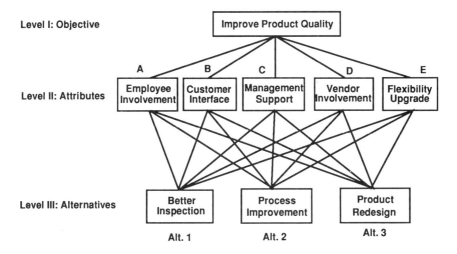

Figure 2.12 AHP for quality improvement approaches.

hierarchy. To come up with the relative weights, the factors are compared pair-wise with respect to their respective contributions to the objective. The pair-wise comparisons are done through subjective evaluations by quality improvement analysts (decision makers). A typical question that may be used to arrive at the pair-wise ratings is the following: 'Do you consider customer interface to be more important than management support in the effort to improve product quality? If so, how much more important is it on a scale of 1 to 9?'

Similar questions will be asked iteratively until each factor has been compared with each of the other factors. In general, the numbers indicating the relative importance of the factors are obtained by using the following weight scales:

Equally important: Degree=1
If factor A is equally important as factor B,
then the importance rating of A over B is 1
Weakly more important: Degree=3
If factor A is weakly more important than factor B,
then the importance rating of A over B is 3
Strongly more important: Degree=5
If factor A is strongly more important than factor B,
then the importance rating of A over B is 5
Very strongly more important: Degree=7
If factor A is very strongly more important than factor B,
then the importance rating of A over B is 7

Absolutely more important: Degree=9
If factor A is absolutely more important than factor B,
then the importance rating of A over B is 9

Intermediate numbers are used as appropriate to indicate intermediate levels of importance. If the comparison order is reversed (e.g. B versus A rather than A versus B), then the reciprocal of the importance rating is entered in the pair-wise comparison table. For example, the following statements are equivalent:

Customer interface is more important than management support with a degree of 6
Management support is more important than customer interface with a degree of 1/6

Because of its fractional rating, the second statement actually implies that management support is less important than customer interface. Table 2.6 shows the tabulation of the pair-wise comparison of the five factors in the illustrative example. Each of the factors listed along the rows of the table is compared against each of the factors listed in the columns. Each number in the body of the table indicates the degree of importance of one factor over the other on a scale of 1 to 9. For example, the table indicates that factor B (Customer interface) is considered to be more important than factor C (Management support) with a degree of 6 with respect to the selection of a quality improvement approach.

Table 2.6 Pair-wise rating for decision factors

Factors	Employee Involvement	Customer Interface	Management Support	Vendor Involvement	Facility Upgrade
Employee Involvement	1	1/3	5	6	5
Customer Interface	3	1	6	7	6
Management Support	1/5	1/6	1	3	1
Vendor Involvement	1/6	1/7	1/3	1	1/4
Facility Upgrade	1/5	1/6	1	4	1

The relative evaluation ratings in Table 2.6 are converted to a matrix of pair-wise comparisons, as shown in Table 2.7. The entries in this table are then normalized to obtain Table 2.8. The normalization is done by dividing each entry in a column by the sum of all the entries in the column. For example, the first cell in Table 2.8 (i.e. 0.219) is obtained by dividing 1.000 by 4.567. Note that the sum of the normalized values in each factor column is one.

Table 2.7 Matrix of pair-wise comparisons of the five factors

Factors	A	B	C	D	E
A	1.000	0.333	5.000	6.000	5.000
B	3.000	1.000	6.000	7.000	6.000
C	0.200	0.167	1.000	3.000	1.000
D	0.167	0.143	0.333	1.000	0.250
E	0.200	0.167	1.000	4.000	1.000
Column Sum	4.567	1.810	13.333	21.000	13.250

Table 2.8 Normalized AHP matrix of paired comparisons

Factors	A	B	C	D	E	Row Sum	Row Average
A	0.219	0.184	0.375	0.286	0.377	1.441	0.288
B	0.656	0.551	0.450	0.333	0.454	2.444	0.489
C	0.044	0.094	0.075	0.143	0.075	0.431	0.086
D	0.037	0.077	0.025	0.048	0.019	0.206	0.041
E	0.044	0.094	0.075	0.190	0.075	0.478	0.096
Column Sum	1.000	1.000	1.000	1.000	1.000		1.000

The last column in Table 2.8 shows the normalized average rating associated with each factor. For example, the first entry in that column (i.e. 0.288) is obtained by dividing 1.441 by 5, since there are five factors. These averages represent the relative weights (between 0.0 and 1.0) of the factors that are being evaluated. The relative weights show that factor B (Customer interface) has the highest importance rating of 0.489. Thus, customer interface is considered to be the most important factor in the selection of an approach to quality improvement. Table 2.9 presents a summary of the relative weights of the factors. Figure 2.13 presents a graphical representation of the relative weights.

Table 2.9 Summary of factor weights

Factors	Weights
Employee Involvement	0.288
Customer Interface	0.489
Management Support	0.086
Vendor Involvement	0.041
Facility Upgrade	0.096

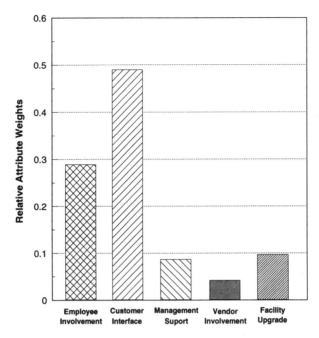

Figure 2.13 Relative weights of five factors.

The relative weights of the factors are denoted as w_i. Thus, if the factors are numbered from 1 to 5, we would have the following:

$$w_1 = 0.288; \quad w_2 = 0.489; \quad w_3 = 0.086; \quad w_4 = 0.041; \quad \text{and } w_5 = 0.096.$$

These factor weights are valid only for the particular goal specified in the AHP model for the problem. If another goal is specified, the factors would need to be reevaluated with respect to that new goal.

Since the pair-wise comparisons of the factors are done based on subjective opinions of the people involved in the quality evaluation process, it is quite possible that there will be some elements of bias and inconsistency in the evaluations. To minimize bias and assure some level of consistency, Saaty (1980) proposed a procedure for calculating the consistency ratio associated with the AHP methodology. The consistency ratio gives a measure of the consistency of the decision maker in comparing factors and alternatives. Consistency refers to the consistency of the transitivity of the weight scales when multiple factors are compared.

It is recommended that the consistency ratio for a matrix of pair-wise comparison should not exceed 10%. The user has the option of modifying the comparison matrix if a consistency ratio exceeds 10% or accepting the potential bias in the ratings and proceeding with the evaluation process. The procedure for calculating the consistency ratios is beyond the scope of our present discussion, but interested readers should refer to the following: Saaty (1977), Saaty (1980), Saaty, Vargas, and Wendell (1983), Saaty and Vargas (1984), and Harker and Vargas (1987). For many applications, most users do not bother to check the consistency ratios if they feel that they have tried to be as consistent as possible in developing the comparison matrices.

After the relative weights of the factors are obtained, the next step is to evaluate the quality improvement approaches on the basis of the factors. In this step, relative evaluation rating is obtained for each approach with respect to each factor. The procedure for the pair-wise comparison of the approaches is similar to the procedure for comparing the factors. Table 2.10 presents the tabulation of the pair-wise comparisons of the three approaches with respect to factor A (Employee involvement). The table shows that Approach 1 and Approach 3 have the same level of importance based on employee involvement. Examples of questions that may be useful in obtaining the pair-wise rating of the approaches are: 'On the basis of employee involvement, is better inspection system more important than process improvement? If so, how much better is it on a scale of 1 to 9?'

Table 2.10 Comparison of approaches on the basis of employee involvement

Approaches	Better Inspection	Process Improvement	Product Redesign
Better Inspection	1	1/3	1
Process Improvement	3	1	2
Product Redesign	1	1/2	1

It should be noted that the comparisons shown in Table 2.10 are valid only when employee involvement is being considered as the basis for selecting an improvement approach. Separate pair-wise comparisons of the approaches must be done whenever another factor is being considered. Consequently, for our example, we would have five separate matrices of pair-wise comparisons of the approaches; one matrix associated with each factor. Table 2.10 is the first one of the five matrices. The other four are not shown. Each matrix is analyzed and normalized by using the same procedure as shown previously for Table 2.6. The normalization of the entries in Table 2.10 yields the following relative weights of the approaches with respect to employee involvement:

Better inspection: 0.21
Process improvement: 0.55
Product redesign: 0.24

Table 2.11 Relative weights of approaches with respect to factors

	Factors				
Approaches	Employee Involvement	Customer Interface	Management Support	Vendor Involvement	Facility Upgrade
Better Inspection	0.21	0.12	0.50	0.63	0.62
Process Improvement	0.55	0.55	0.25	0.30	0.24
Product Redesign	0.24	0.33	0.25	0.07	0.14

Table 2.11 shows a summary of the normalized relative ratings of the three approaches with respect to each of the five factors. The factor weights shown earlier in Table 2.9 are now combined with the system weights contained in Table 2.11 to obtain the overall relative weights of the approaches as shown below:

$$\alpha_j = \sum_i (w_i k_{ij})$$

where:

α_j = *overall* weighted evaluation for Approach j

w_i = relative weight for factor i

k_{ij} = evaluation rating for Approach j with respect to factor i. This is often referred to as the *local* weight.

$w_i k_{ij}$ = a measure representing the *global* weight of approach j with respect to factor i. The sum of the global weights associated with an approach represents the overall weight, α_j, of that approach.

Table 2.12 shows the summary of the final AHP analysis for the example. The three approaches have been evaluated on the basis of all five factors. The question addressed by the AHP approach in this example is to determine which approach should be selected to satisfy the goal of quality improvement based on weighted evaluation of the relevant factors. The summary in Table 2.12 shows that Approach 2 (Process improvement) should be selected since it has the highest weighted rating of 0.484.

Figure 2.14 presents a bar chart of the relative weights of the three approaches. The segments in each bar represent the respective rating of each approach with regard to each of the five factors. The overall weight of an alternative is sometimes referred to as the desirability index. Our illustrative example shows that process improvement is the most desirable of the three approaches that are considered.

Table 2.12 Summary of AHP for quality improvement approaches

	Factors					
	A $i=1$	B $i=2$	C $i=3$	D $i=4$	E $i=5$	
$w_i \in$	0.288	0.489	0.086	0.041	0.096	
System j	k_{ij}					α_j
System 1	0.21	0.12	0.50	0.63	0.62	0.248
System 2	0.55	0.55	0.25	0.30	0.24	0.484
System 3	0.24	0.33	0.25	0.07	0.14	0.268
Column Sum	1.000	1.000	1.000	1.000	1.000	1.000

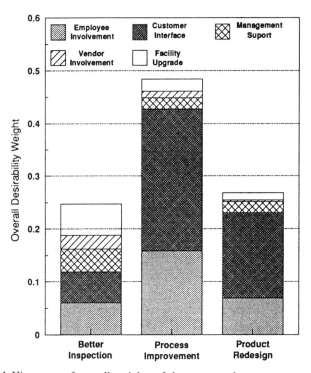

Figure 2.14 Histogram of overall weights of three approaches.

AHP can be very effective for quality and process improvement efforts because of its interactive involvement of the decision makers. For example, it can be used to obtain and organize customer feedback about product quality, customer service, product price, delivery performance, and so on. It can serve as a preliminary analysis tool to determine where most of the improvement efforts should be directed.

3 | Fundamentals of process improvement

Good process breeds good quality

This chapter presents the fundamental aspects of improving quality through process improvement. The human and equipment aspects of improving a process are discussed. To achieve long-term success, a company must increase its willingness to change and improve continuously its competitiveness in all its functions. This is more so because the quality perceptions of users continue to change. Many organizations are striving to implement projects such as continuous process improvement, total quality management, total productivity management, and so on in order to improve the quality of their products and services, yet very few have actually achieved their objectives. The premise of this chapter is that there are several underlying elements which are being ignored. These elements must be understood and addressed adequately to lay the foundation for a lasting process improvement.

3.1 DEFINING A PROCESS

A process is a collection of interrelated activities that are designed to generate specific outputs based on the application of specific inputs. A process can be only one task or a sequence of tasks where people, tools, materials, and environment act together to perform operation(s) which cause one or more characteristics of a product to be altered or generated.

A process can be contained within a functional department or it can be spread over several related functional areas. The outputs of a process may be actual physical and tangible items or intangible service elements. A process may be designed to consist of a collection of subprocesses. Figure 3.1 is a representation of the hierarchy of process components. Each level of the process hierarchy is a function of the preceding level. To improve the overall process, we must start at the very elementary level and build up the improvement process.

Process performance refers to the degree of effectiveness of a process to satisfy customer requirements. Performance may be based on a measurable

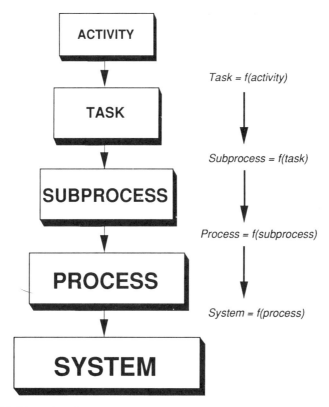

Figure 3.1 Hierarchy of process components.

quantity or it may be based on subjective reactions of customers to the outputs of the process. Performance is determined from a process study which is conducted over an extended period of time under normal operating conditions.

Process capability refers to the long-term performance of a process after the process has been brought under control. This involves a standardized evaluation of the inherent ability of the process to perform under a set of operating conditions. Process capability is also the performance of a process after significant causes of variation have been eliminated. For manufacturing purposes, process capability is usually set to six standard deviations of the variability.

Process capability study refers to a controlled collection of statistics from a process for the purpose of statistically determining the capability of the process to perform well under specified conditions.

Process control refers to using data collected about a process to control the output of the process. This may include the use of control techniques such as SPC (statistical process control) and the establishment of a feedback loop to prevent the manufacture of nonconforming products.

Process quality refers to a statistical measure for the quality of the products generated by a process.

Process tolerance refers to the tolerance allowed on the product from a process. The process tolerance may be considerably tighter than the design tolerance in order to take into consideration such aspects as measurement accuracies and the effects of further processing.

Process under control refers to a process in which the various contributors to variability of the product are monitored and maintained within defined control limits.

Process improvement refers to taking advantage of opportunities to move a process from a current state to another state of higher performance. Measures of process improvement include product quality, process flexibility, work-in-process inventory, lead times, material handling, and throughput.

Process transition is the manner is which process improvement is accomplished. Figure 3.2 shows an example of process transition paths for process improvement. Given that the performance of a process is in an initial *state i*, three possible changes can occur. Further performance may be achieved in moving to *state i+j*, the performance may be stagnant between *state i* and *state i+j*, or the performance may regress from *state i* to *state i+j*. Planning, scheduling, and control strategies must be developed to determine which is the next desired state of a process, when the next state is expected to be reached, and how to move towards that next state. Resource availability, as well as other internal and external factors, will determine the nature of the performance of a process from one state to another. The concept of continuous process improvement discussed in Chapter 2 requires that small increments in performance be pursued continually.

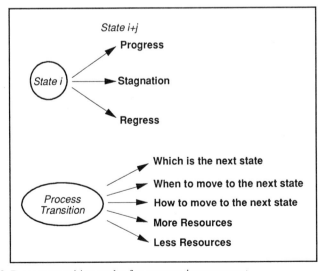

Figure 3.2 Process transition paths for process improvement.

3.2 BARRIERS TO QUALITY AND PROCESS IMPROVEMENT

Regardless of the preparation and efforts committed to quality and process improvement, there may still exist some barriers to improvement. Examples of typical obstacles to implementing quality and process improvement are discussed below.

Lack of employee commitment

There may be an indifferent attitude to organizational goals among employees. The general feeling that prevails among employees is that management exploits workers to pursue unachievable goals. This feeling must be removed and employees must be positively motivated. Workers should be made to feel that they belong to the process and the process belongs to them.

Emphasis on short runs

Some companies are after short-term goals or immediate returns. This is one of the main obstacles to a lasting improvement. If front-end efforts are committed to improvement, approaches such as continuous process improvement will pay off in the long run. A company should be ready for some initial pain in order to realize future gains.

Resistance to change

It is natural for people to resist changes. All organizations experience some form of opposition from the employees whenever a new change is introduced. Juran (1988) refers to this as 'the immune reaction'. This can be reduced by designing the new process closely parallel to the existing process and involving people right from the conceptual stage of the proposed changes. Constant motivation may also reduce this resistance.

Interdepartmental problems

These problems are not uncommon in any organization. These problems arise due to the general tendency of individual departments to conceal their shortcomings, while blaming others for their problems. The other sources of these problems are poor communication, lack of cooperation, personality clashes, and competition for scarce resources.

Inadequate need assessment

Inadequate assessment of the needs of the organization is a major obstacle to implementing CPI. The strategic needs of the organization with respect to market needs should be evaluated prior to making implementation commitment.

Premature termination of the planning process

Any noble effort can fail without proper and complete planning. In the haste to institute quality improvement efforts, a company may not allocate enough time and resources to the planning phase. With proper time commitment to planning, the improvement effort will evolve with no organization problems.

Lack of focus or priority

To be successful, a quality improvement effort must have focus and carry high priority within the organization. Too much concentration on short-term returns can preclude focus and priority for long-term quality improvement.

Management naivety

Uninformed management may put too much emphasis on technology as the only means to improve quality. This view neglects the personnel roles and interactions essential for the success of quality and process improvement. Management should realize that there is a limitation on the capability of technology.

Few precedents

Due to the relatively recent emergence of quality improvement concepts and techniques, there is a limited collection of precedents or models to follow in implementing continuous quality improvement strategies. Fortunately, this situation is changing rapidly. As more and more companies report their success stories, other companies will follow with well-planned procedures. Despite the extensive publications that have covered the successful Japanese examples, many western companies have been slow in following the examples.

Lack of clear responsibility

As we stated at the beginning of Chapter 1, 'Good quality is everybody's responsibility while bad quality is everybody's fault.' If it is not clearly stated that everybody is responsible for quality improvement, nobody will assume the responsibility. The quality control department should serve as the facilitator for quality improvement rather than as a quality enforcement group.

Technology obsolescence

Obsolete technology is another obstacle to quality improvement. It is not uncommon to have technologies that are decades old in companies that are aspiring to improve quality to world-class levels. Efficient technology must be acquired to support quality improvement efforts. Up-to-date technologies must be combined with human resource capabilities to assure success of improvement efforts.

Lack of foresight

To remain competitive, a company must have the foresight and sense of anticipation for what the customer wants and what the competition is doing. Inability to respond quickly to the changing needs of the customer is a major obstacle to quality improvement.

Organizational politics

Organizational politics at the expense of product quality creates an atmosphere where nobody wins. Politics must be put aside so that everyone can contribute to the concerted effort to improve quality.

The above obstacles can be caused by both internal and external circumstances. In order to alleviate these obstacles, several factors must be taken into consideration. These include level of management control, communication interaction, cooperation level, coordination effectiveness, maturity of process technology, consumer tastes and preferences, government regulations, industry incentives, required capital for quality improvement, and cost of maintaining high quality. In addition to these, there are internal and external business trends regarding quality improvement that should not be overlooked. Despite the noted obstacles to quality improvement, companies should not despair. Quality improvement has several advantages. The end reward justifies the agony of the effort. Some examples of the advantages of quality improvement are:

- quality improvement provides opportunities for people from all functional areas – design, process planning, manufacturing, and maintenance – to contribute suggestions and ideas to improve the quality of outgoing products;
- quality improvement improves an organization's market image based on the high quality products it offers;
- quality improvement increases market share through increased customer satisfaction;
- quality improvement provides benefits to all employees of the company.

3.3 IMPROVING QUALITY THROUGH PROCESS IMPROVEMENT

Process improvement must be guided by a comprehensive quality improvement program. A lasting quality improvement can be achieved only by improving the underlying process. The underlying process must be improved bottom-up. Some specific guidelines for achieving quality improvement through process improvement are presented below:

- develop a solid quality policy;
- scrutinize the process to find out its basic components;
- identify processes and subprocesses, and determine how they impact on business and customer needs;
- establish a quality-driven environment that facilitates harmony of human resources, management, and physical equipment;
- set achievable goals;
- set process priorities and resolve conflicts;
- disseminate and enforce priorities uniformly and consistently throughout the organization;
- establish an assessment procedure to evaluate the contribution of each unit of process improvement to quality improvement.

3.3.1 Human aspects of process improvement

People make quality happen
Process improvement requires synthesizing technical, business, quantitative, and qualitative considerations in the production environment. The role of the human is a significant aspect of achieving process improvement. No matter how technically capable a process is, the tangible and intangible contributions of workers will play a major role in its successful implementation.

Operators are required to interact with process hardware. The design and installation of the hardware must consider the human interactions needed for successful operation. Both the behavioral and performance aspects of human interaction with the process should be evaluated. Even in highly automated installations, the human role remains a significant factor.

With the proliferation of sophisticated process hardware, there is a danger of complacency in the design and installation approaches. Such complacency must be overcome by incorporating human interaction considerations in the early stages of planning for process improvement. Issues involving worker safety, labor/management relations, job enrichment, and personnel training are important in process improvement.

3.4 PROCESS IMPROVEMENT FEASIBILITY STUDY

Process improvement must be feasible to be achievable. A formal feasibility study should be conducted to ascertain the practicality of the proposed improvement. The practicality is considered in terms of available technology, cost constraints, production process, labor skills availability, organizational goals, and market structure.

Technical feasibility

Technical feasibility refers to the ability of the process to take advantage of the current state of the technology in pursuing further improvement. The technical capability of the personnel, as well as the capability of the available technology, should be considered.

Managerial feasibility

Managerial feasibility involves the capability of the infrastructure of a process to achieve and sustain process improvement. Management support, employee involvement, and commitment are key elements required to ascertain managerial feasibility.

3.5 PRODUCT REDESIGN AND PROCESS IMPROVEMENT

Quality begins with design, but should not end there

Current and future decades will be driven by quality expectations. This will have a major impact on the design process. Product redesign may be one way of improving a process. Complicated designs require complicated processes which may be difficult to improve. Redesigning a product may offer an opportunity to simplify and improve the process required to make the product. Good designs that are made just for the purpose of tickling the fancy of the designer or to show off the designer's creativity may not meet customers' needs. Old designs that originated in the old days of *laissez faire* can no longer be tolerated.

New processes should take advantage of new technologies to improve process and product quality. There are several measures of product quality. One important measure is the number of quality control points in the product design. Significant benefits can be realized by redesigning a product to minimize the potential areas for quality failures. Some guidelines for redesigning a product for process improvement are:

- scrutinize product characteristics;
- scrutinize the process required to make the product;
- scrutinize all aspects of the product design;
- review customer requirements;
- evaluate how current design is meeting customer requirements;
- determine areas where the product design can be modified and still meet customer requirements;
- determine if the redesign can lead to process improvement;
- if redesign is justified, start implementing continuous process improvement approach.

A documentation should be developed to show how a product should be used and how it can be misused. The potential hazards of a product in case of accidental or deliberate misuse should be outlined to help identify areas for improvement. Product redesign can be categorized as discussed below.

Redesign for quality

This refers to the redesign of a product to take advantage of new and existing technologies to improve the production process. Redesign for quality can positively impact the cost and value of the product. The scope and timing of redesign should agree with the existing organization capability.

Redesign for safety

This refers to the redesign of a product to enhance its operating procedures and characteristics so that the potential for hazard is minimized. Redesign for safety has obvious advantages to the user (customer) in terms of safe operating characteristics. The advantages to the producer are not so obvious. The producer's advantages can be expressed in terms of worker protection against harm when handling the product, and in terms of avoidance of liability law suits.

Redesign for reliability

If a product is reliable, it is less likely that it will be misused. Redesign for reliability addresses the time-based dependability of the product to perform its intended functions. Product failure or improper function due to low quality can lead to users bypassing built-in safety features. A later section in this chapter presents further discussion on product reliability and process improvement.

Redesign for usability

Fitness for use is one of the classical definitions of quality. A product should be evaluated for potential areas to enhance its usability. If the use of a product is impeded, for whatever reason, the perception of high quality may be lost. Sequence and frequency of use should be considered when redesigning a product for usability. Prototype models of the redesign are essential for a proper ergonomics analysis.

Redesign for comfort

A comfortable product provides an incentive for proper use. This is, perhaps, the most difficult redesign issue to be addressed. Comfort is user dependent. Thus, it is difficult to anticipate what the comfort levels of the various users of a product might be. However, redesign for comfort can still be effectively pursued by using test users and documenting all comments and suggestions. It may not be possible, or even practical, to expect to implement all the suggestions gathered during test uses. The documentation, nevertheless, can serve as a guide to future improvements in the product.

When all the above redesign issues are combined, it is possible to achieve an improved product with better quality that offers more achievable opportunities for process improvement.

3.6 QUALITY–VALUE BREAKEVEN ANALYSIS

The relationship between quality and productivity was discussed in Chapter 2. Improved quality leads to improved productivity, improved process leads to improved quality, and improved productivity leads to improved profitability. These hierarchical relationships can be summarized as shown below:

Process Improvement $\Rightarrow$ Quality Improvement

Quality Improvement $\Rightarrow$ Productivity Improvement

Productivity Improvement $\Rightarrow$ Profitability Improvement

Profitability Improvement $\Rightarrow$ Process Improvement

When profitability improves, more resources become available to pursue further process improvement. Thus, the improvement loop repeats itself. Profitability is determined by product cost while product price is based on value. High quality will command high prices. Chen and Tang (1992) presented a poor-quality cost model to illustrate the relationship between quality level and production cost. In this section, we present cost breakeven analysis and we use examples to illustrate the implication on quality and process improvement.

The total cost of an operation may be expressed as the sum of the fixed and variable costs with respect to output quantity. Recall that if quality is high, the net output quantity will increase. The total cost is expressed as:

$$TC(x) = FC + VC(x),$$

where x is the number of good units produced, $TC(x)$ is the total cost of producing x units, FC is the total fixed cost, and $VC(x)$ is the total variable costs associated with producing x units. The total revenue resulting from the sale of x units is defined as:

$$TR(x) = px,$$

where p is the price per unit. Our assumption here is that if quality is high, then all the good units produced can be sold. The profit due to the production and sale of x units of the product is calculated as:

$$P(x) = TR(x) - TC(x).$$

The breakeven point of an operation is defined as the value of a given parameter that will result in neither a profit nor a loss. The parameter of interest may be the number of units produced, the number of hours of operation, the number of units of a resource type allocated, or any other measure of interest. Regardless of which parameter is considered, the implication on process quality is unmistakable. At the breakeven point, we have the following relationship:

$$TR(x) = TC(x) \text{ or } P(x) = 0.$$

In some cases, the relationship between cost and a parameter of interest can be expressed in a mathematical formula. For example, there may be a linear cost relationship between the total cost of production and the number of units produced. The cost expressions facilitate simple analysis to identify potential areas for process improvement. Figure 3.3 shows an example of a breakeven point for a single process. Figure 3.4 shows examples of multiple breakeven points that exist when multiple processes are compared. When two process alternatives are compared, the breakeven point refers to the point of indifference between the two alternatives. In Figure 3.4, $x1^*$ represents the point where both processes A and B are equally desirable, $x2^*$ represents where A and C are equally desirable, and $x3^*$ represents where B and C are equally desirable. The figure shows that if we are operating below a production level of $x2$ units, then process C is the preferred process out of the three. If we are operating at a level more than $x2$ units, then project A is the best choice.

Example

Three process alternatives are being considered for producing a new product. The required analysis involves determining which alternative should be selected, based on how many units of the product are produced per year. Based on past records, there is a known relationship between the number of units, x,

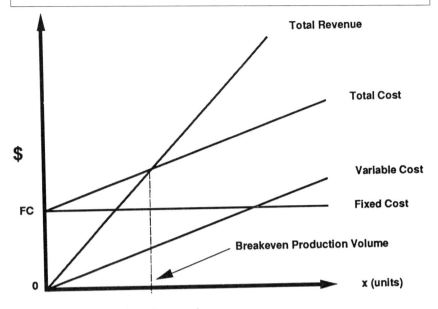

Figure 3.3 Example of breakeven point.

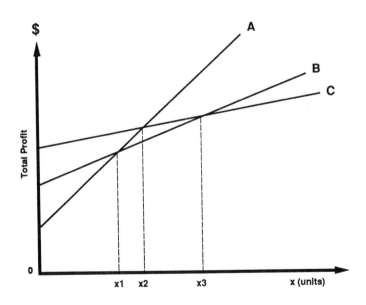

Figure 3.4 Breakeven points for multiple projects comparison.

produced per year and the net annual profit, $P(x)$, from each alternative. The level of production is expected to be between 0 and 250 units per year. The net annual profits (in thousands of dollars) are given below for each alternative:

Project A: $P(x) = 3x - 200$
Project B: $P(x) = x$
Project C: $P(x) = (1/50)x^2 - 300$

Solution: This problem can be solved mathematically by finding the intersection points of the profit functions and evaluating the respective profits over the given range of product units. However, it is much easier and visually helpful to solve it by a graphical approach. Figure 3.5 presents the simultaneous plot (breakeven chart) of the profit functions. The plot shows that process B should be selected if between 0 and 100 units are to be produced. Process A should be selected if between 100 and 178.1 units (178 actual units) are to be produced. Process C should be selected if more than 178 units are to be produced. It should be noted that if less than 66.7 units (66 actual units) are produced, Process A would generate net loss rather than net profit. Similarly, Process C would generate

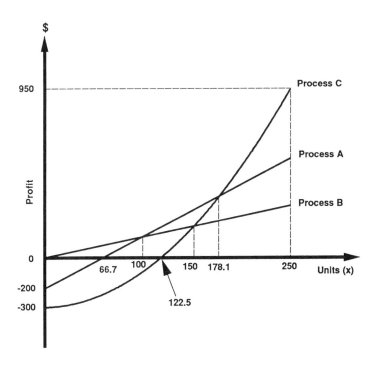

Figure 3.5 Plot of profit functions.

losses if less than 122.5 units (122 actual units) are produced. Once the breakeven production volumes are determined, management must put in place the elements required to improve the process so that the target volumes can be achieved.

Profit ratio due to process improvement

Breakeven charts offer opportunities for several different types of analysis. In addition to determining the breakeven points, other measures of worth or criterion measure may be derived from the charts. A measure, called profit ratio, is discussed here for the purpose of obtaining a further comparative analysis relevant for process improvement.

Profit ratio is defined as the ratio of the profit area to the sum of the profit and loss areas in a breakeven chart. That is,

$$\text{Profit ratio} = \frac{\text{Area of profit region}}{\text{Area of profit region} + \text{Area of loss region}}.$$

For example, suppose the expected revenue and the expected total cost associated with a process are given, respectively, by the following expressions:

$$R(x) = 100 + 10x$$
$$TC(x) = 2.5x + 250$$

where x is the number of units produced and sold from the process. Figure 3.6 shows the breakeven chart for the process. The breakeven point is shown to be 20 units. Net profits are realized from the process if more than 20 units are produced, whereas net losses are realized if less than 20 units are produced. It should be noted that the revenue function in Figure 3.6 represents an unusual case where a revenue of $100 is realized when zero units are produced. The reader is invited to speculate as to why and when such a fixed revenue might occur.

Let us calculate the profit ratio for this process if the number of good units that can be produced is limited to between 0 and 100 units. From Figure 3.6, the surface area of the profit region and the area of the loss region can be calculated by using the standard formula for finding the area of a triangle. That is, Area = $(\frac{1}{2})$(Base)(Height). Using this formula, we have the following:

$$\text{Area of Profit Region} = \frac{1}{2}(\text{base})(\text{height})$$

$$= \frac{1}{2}(1100 - 500)(100 - 20)$$

$$= 24{,}000 \text{ square units}$$

$$\text{Area of Loss Region} = \frac{1}{2}(\text{base})(\text{height})$$

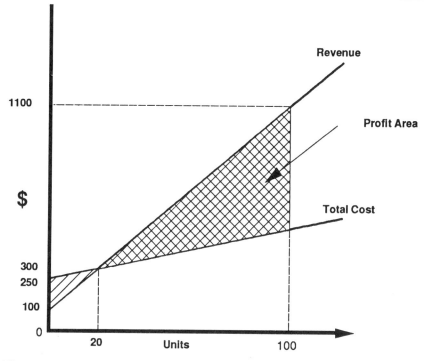

Figure 3.6 Area of profit versus area of loss.

$$= \frac{1}{2}(250 - 100)(20)$$

$$= 1500 \text{ square units.}$$

Therefore, the profit ratio is computed as:

$$\text{Profit Ratio} = \frac{2400}{24000 + 1500}$$

$$= 0.9411$$

$$= 94.11\%.$$

The profit ratio may be used as a criterion for selecting among process improvement alternatives. If this is done, the profit ratios for all the alternatives must be calculated over the same values of the independent variable. The process with the highest profit ratio will then be selected. For example, Figure 3.7 presents the breakeven chart for an alternate process, say Process II. It is seen that both the revenue and cost functions for the process are nonlinear. The revenue and cost are defined as follows:

$$R(x) = 100x - x^2$$
$$TC(x) = 500 + x^2$$

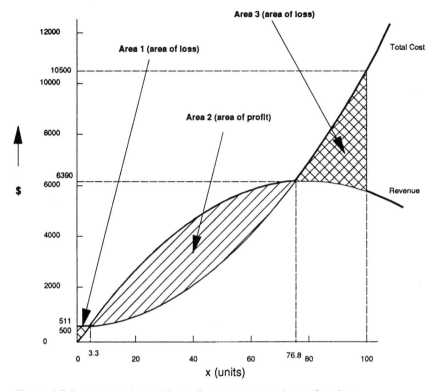

Figure 3.7 Breakeven chart with nonlinear revenue and cost functions.

If the cost and/or revenue functions for a process are not linear, the areas bounded by the functions may not be easily determined. For those cases, it may be necessary to use other methods of finding the bounded areas. An example of such a method is the use of definite integrals. Interested readers should consult calculus books for the procedures for evaluating definite integrals. Figure 3.7 indicates that the process generates a loss if fewer than 3.3 units (3 actual units) or more than 76.8 units (76 actual units) are produced. The respective profit and loss areas on the chart are calculated as shown below:

$$\text{Area 1 (loss)} \quad = \int_0^{3.3} [(500 + x^2) - (160x - x^2)]dx$$

$$= 802.8 \ unit-dollars$$

$$\text{Area 2 (profit)} \quad = \int_{3.3}^{76.8} [(160x - x^2) - (500 + x^2)]dx$$

$$= 132,272.08 \ unit-dollars$$

$$\text{Area 3 (loss)} \quad = \int_{76.8}^{100} [(500 + x^2) - (160x - x^2)]dx$$

$$= 48,135.98 \ unit-dollars.$$

Consequently, the profit ratio for Process II is computed as:

$$\text{Profit Ratio} \quad = \frac{\text{Total Area of Profit Region}}{\text{Total Area of Profit Region} + \text{Total Area of Loss Region}}$$

$$= \frac{132,272.08}{802.76 + 132,272.08 + 48,135.98}$$

$$= 0.7299$$

$$= 72.99\%.$$

The profit ratio approach evaluates the performance of each process over a specified range of operating levels. Most of the existing evaluation methods use single-point analysis with the assumption that the operating condition is fixed at a given production level. The profit ratio measure allows the evaluation of the net yield of a process, given that the production level may shift from one level to another. An alternative, for example, may operate at a loss for most of its early life, while it may generate large incomes to offset the losses in its later stages. The conventional methods cannot capture this type of transition from one performance level to another. The premise of continuous process improvement is that attempts be made gradually to overcome the low performance levels during the process transition periods.

In addition to being used to compare alternate processes, the profit ratio may also be used for evaluating the economic feasibility of a single process. In such a case, a decision rule will need to be developed. An example of a decision rule that may be used for this purpose is:

If profit ratio is greater than 75%, then the process is economically feasible. If profit ratio is less than or equal to 75%, the process is not economically feasible.

3.7 IMPORTANCE OF ERGONOMICS IN PROCESS IMPROVEMENT

Worker performance improves with worker comfort
Ergonomics is the science that relates human capabilities and limitations to job performance. If a worker feels better, he or she will work better. Fitting the task to the worker is an effective approach to improving the work process and, consequently, improving product quality. Alexander and Pulat (1985) defined ergonomics as 'the study of the interface between humans and the objects they use and the environment they function in.' Work designs requiring worker

postures that conflict with the normal biomechanics of the human body lead to muscular fatigue, which can adversely affect product quality.

As Naderi and Baggerman (1992) pointed out, the relationship between quality and ergonomics is very complex. Even if the work itself is well designed and the worker is well trained, environmental factors can still affect product quality. For example, poor lighting and glare can adversely affect an inspector's ability to make accurate judgments about product quality. The emergence of the information age, with the proliferation of desktop computers, has created new problems in ergonomics and product quality. While the use of computers greatly improves productivity, certain elements of the work environment have worsened in cases where the worker–computer interface is not given adequate ergonomics consideration. For example, on an assembly line where product characteristics are displayed on a computer screen, eye strain may become a problem that impedes the worker's ability effectively to review product quality. Process improvement requires that the totality of the work environment be scrutinized to remove potential threats to product quality.

The lack of proper ergonomics studies in the work place has resulted in a dramatic increase in the occurrence of cumulative trauma diseases (CTDs) over the past few years. CTDs are injuries of the soft tissues that result from repetitive motion, awkward, and/or excessive force. These injuries seem to be a symptom of the change in modern industry. The trend in industry has been to move away from physically intensive tasks to a more technical society, where humans conduct tasks that assist the mechanical machinery. This often means doing tasks that require extensive finger manipulation and/or forearm movement such as in the use of desktop computers. These types of activities have been known to contribute to the development of CTDs and, subsequently, affect the quality of work. Three important factors must be considered when performing ergonomics analysis for quality improvement. The components are:

- personal characteristics of the worker;
- work place conditions;
- environmental factors.

Naderi and Baggerman (1992) reviewed the impact of various occupational disorders on quality. A summary based on their review is presented in Table 3.1.

Ergonomics can improve the comfort and well-being of workers. Both the mental and physiological needs of the worker can be enhanced with ergonomics in the work place. In summary, ergonomics have the following advantages:

- improved product quality;
- increased productivity;
- decrease in absenteeism and lost time;
- reduction in medical costs;

Table 3.1 Impact of occupational disorders on quality

Type of Job	Occupational Disorders	Work Characteristics	Impact on Quality
Hand assembly	Tenosynovitis, Carpal Tunnel Syndrome, Tendonitis of wrist and shoulder	Repetitive wrist motion, flexed shoulders, ulnar deviation, arm pronation	Inaccuracies in manual operations (e.g. improper insertion and misplacement)
Pneumatic screw drivers	Tendonitis, Tenosynovitis, Carpal Tunnel Syndrome	Repetitive wrist motion, excessive grip force, exposure to vibration	Loose screws in parts, misaligned screws
Materials handling	Thoracic outlet syndrome, shoulder tendonitis, lower back pain	Lifting and lowering, carrying heavy loads, high frequency lifting & lowering	Dropped and damaged products
Computer use	Tendonitis of shoulder and wrist, Carpal Tunnel Syndrome	Static restricted posture, flexed arms, high speed finger movement	High error rate in data entry

- improved worker morale;
- reduction in work hazards;
- improved community relations.

3.7.1 Using the right tools for the right jobs

An important aspect of quality and process improvement involves using the right tools. Any process is subject to deficiency if the correct tools and methods are not being used. For example, do-it-yourself home owners often do low quality home repair jobs, not necessarily because they are not proficient as 'handy men', but because they typically don't have the right tools. A plan for process improvement calls for an adequate investment in the right tools for the right jobs.

3.8 LEARNING CURVES AND PROCESS IMPROVEMENT

Learning breeds quality, forgetting breeds regret
Learning is a natural phenomenon that improves employee performance. As workers learn an operation, their performance level improves, resource

expenditure per unit of product decreases, and product quality improves. Learning curve, also known as manufacturing progress function, represents the improved efficiency obtained from repetition of an operation. Human performance improvement due to learning has been extensively studied in the literature, starting with the pioneer work of T. P. Wright in 1936. The learning achieved by employees is one avenue through which process improvement can be achieved. Many of the interacting factors that influence product quality are subject to learning effects. The effects of learning result in improved overall performance of the process.

Applications of learning curves include production planning, cost estimation and control, resource allocation, lot sizing, and product pricing. Typical univariate learning curves present a relationship between production cost and cumulative output. Worker performance (productivity) and product quality (loss) can be quantified in terms of appropriate cost indices, which can then be modeled by learning curves. Wright (1936) discovered the '80% learning effect' in airplane production plants. This indicates that a given operation is subject to a 20% productivity improvement whenever cumulative production doubles. Because of the several variables that interact in manufacturing, there has been recent interest in multivariate learning curves. These interacting factors can have significant impacts on product quality. Tapiero (1987) discusses the relationship between production learning and quality control.

A major factor that has not been adequately addressed in learning studies is the fact that workers also forget during the process of learning. Without considering the effect of forgetting, conventional learning curves may be overestimating the potential effect of learning. In this section, we discuss the modeling of a bivariate learning curve model that accounts for the learning and forgetting components in employee performance. The inclusion of a forget model creates a realistic representation of manufacturing operations that are subject to interruption in the learning process. Important questions that should be of interest in this regard include the following.

- What factors influence learning?
- What factors influence forgetting?
- What effects do learning and forgetting have on worker performance and product quality?

3.8.1 Basic log-linear model

The univariate learning curve expresses a dependent variable (e.g. production cost) in terms of some independent variable (e.g. cumulative production). There have been numerous alternate learning curve models. A comprehensive survey of the various models is presented by Badiru (1992b). Figure 3.8 shows comparative plots of some of the existing univariate models on a log-log scale. It has been established that learning and forgetting affect worker performance, which ultimately may affect product quality.

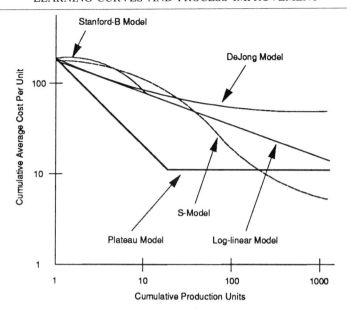

Figure 3.8 Examples of learning curves on a log scale.

The log-linear learning curve model is recognized as the basic model for most performance analysis. The model presents the relationship between cumulative average cost per unit and cumulative production:

$$C_x = C_1 x^b,$$

where C_x = cumulative average cost of producing x units, C_1 = cost of the first unit, x = cumulative production, and b = the learning curve exponent. Figure 3.9 presents a hyperbolic plot of the log-linear model on a linear graph scale.

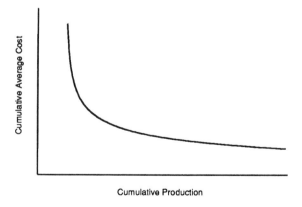

Figure 3.9 Basic log-linear model.

In a log-log plot, shown in Figure 3.10, the model appears as a straight line of the form:

$$\log C_x = \log C_1 + b \log x,$$

where b is the constant slope of the line. The expression for the learning rate, p, is defined as the percent productivity gain based on two production levels, x_1 and x_2, where $x_2 = 2x_1$. It is computed as C_{x2}/C_{x1}, which yields:

$$p = 2^b.$$

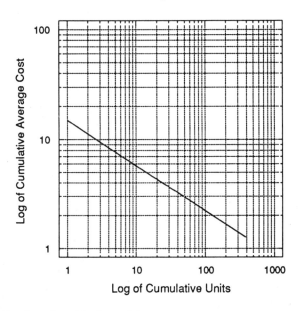

Figure 3.10 Log-log plot of basic model.

3.8.2 Bivariate learning curve models

Extensions of the univariate learning curve are important for realistic analysis of worker performance and process improvement. In real operations, several quantitative and qualitative factors intermingle to compound the performance analysis problem. There are numerous factors that can influence how fast, how far and how well a worker learns within a given time span. A standard form of the multivariate model is defined as:

$$C_x = K \prod_{i=1}^{n} c_i x_i^{b_i},$$

where C_x = cumulative average cost per unit, K = cost of first unit of the product, x = vector of specific values of independent variables, x_i = specific value of the ith factor, n = number of factors in the model, c_i = coefficient for the ith factor, and b_i = learning exponent for the ith factor. A bivariate form of the model is presented below:

$$y = \beta_0 x_1^{\beta_1} x_2^{\beta_2},$$

where y is a measure of cost and x_1 and x_2 are independent variables of interest. A study conducted for the RAND Corporation (Alchian, 1963) using Second World War data used learning curves to estimate direct labor per pound of airframe needed to manufacture the Nth airframe in a cumulative production of N planes. The alternate functions presented below were used by Alchian to describe the relationships between direct labor per pound of airframe (m), cumulative production (N), time (T), and rate of production per month (DN):

1. $\log m = a_2 + b_2 T$
2. $\log m = a_3 + b_3 T + b_4 DN$
3. $\log m = a_4 + b_5(\log T) + b_6(\log DN)$
4. $\log m = a_5 + b_7 T + b_8 (\log DN)$
5. $\log m = a_6 + b_9 T + b_{10} (\log N)$
6. $\log m = a_7 + b_{11}(\log N) + b_{12}(\log DN)$

Goldberger (1968) studied the multiplicative power function, generally referred to as the Cobb-Douglas function, of the form:

$$C = b_0 x_1^{b_1} x_2^{b_2} \ldots x_n^{b_n} \varepsilon,$$

where C = estimated cost, b_0 = model coefficient, x_i = ith independent variable ($i=1,2,\ldots, n$), b_i = exponent of the ith variable, and ε = error term. The error term is defined as $\varepsilon = e^u$, where $u \sim N(0, s^2)$ and independent of $X_1, \ldots, X_n$. For parametric cost analysis, Waller and Dwyer (1981) presented an additive model of the form:

$$C = c_1 x_1^{b_1} + c_2 x_2^{b_2} + \ldots + c_n x_n^{b_n} + \varepsilon,$$

where c_i ($i=1,2,\ldots,n$) is the coefficient of the ith independent variable. The model was reported to have been fitted successfully for missile tooling and equipment cost. A variation of the power model was used by Bemis (1981) to study an actual weapon system production. Cox and Gansler (1981) also discuss the use of a bivariate model for the assessment of the costs and benefits of a single-source versus multiple-source production decision with variations in quantity and production rate in major DOD (Department of Defense) programs. A similar study by Camm, Gulledge, and Womer (1987) also uses the multiplicative power model to express program costs in terms of cumulative quantity and production rate in order to evaluate contractor behavior.

McIntyre (1977) introduced a nonlinear cost–volume–profit model for learning curve analysis. The nonlinearity in the model is effected by incorporating a nonlinear cost function that expresses the effects of employee learning. McIntyre applied sensitivity analysis to the nonlinear model to assess the impact of estimation errors in the learning rate and steady-state production time on estimated profit and break-even quantities. Some of the nonlinear models he investigated are discussed below.

Basic profit function

The profit equation for the initial period of production for a product subject to the usual learning function is expressed as:

$$P = px - c(ax^{b+1}) - f,$$

where P = profit, p = price per unit, x = cumulative production, c = labor cost per unit time, f = fixed cost per period, and b = index of learning.

Multiprocess model

The profit function for the initial period of production with n production processes operating simultaneously is given as:

$$P = px - nca \left(\frac{x}{n}\right)^{b+1} - f,$$

where x is the number of units produced by n labor teams consisting of one or more employees each. Each team is assumed to produce x/n units. This model indicates that when additional production teams are included, more units are produced over a given time period. However, the average time for a given number of units increases because more employees are producing while they are still learning. That is, more employees with low (but improving) productivity are engaged in production at the same time.

Multiskill model

The preceding model is extended to the case where different skill levels of employees produce different learning parameters between production runs. This is modeled as:

$$P = p \sum_{i=1}^{n} x_i - c \sum_{i=1}^{n} a_i x_i^{b_i+1} - f,$$

where a_i and b_i denote the parameters applicable to the average skill level of the ith production run and x_i represents the output of the ith run in a given time period. This model is useful for analyzing concurrent engineering processes.

Womer (1979) presents a multivariate model that incorporates cumulative production, production rate, and program cost. His approach involves a production function that relates output rate to a set of inputs with variable utilization rates:

$$q(t) = AQ^{\delta}(t)x^{1/\gamma}(t),$$

where, A = constant, $q(t)$ = program output rate at time t, $Q(T)$ = cumulative production at time T, δ = learning parameter, l = returns to scale parameter, and $x(t)$ = rate of variable resource utilization at time t. To optimize the discounted program cost, the cost function is defined as:

$$C = \int_0^T x(t)e^{-pt}dt,$$

where p is the discount rate and T is the time horizon for the analysis.

Example of a bivariate learning curve

Suppose a learning curve contains the following two independent variables: cumulative production (x_1) and cumulative training time (x_2). Assume the model to be represented as:

$$C_{x_1x_2} = Kc_1x_1^{b_1}c_2x_2^{b_2},$$

where C_x = cumulative average cost per unit for a given set of factor values, K = intrinsic constant, x_1 = specific value of first factor, x_2 = specific value of second factor, c_i = coefficient for the ith factor, and b_i = learning exponent for the ith factor. The set of illustrative data used for the modeling is shown in Table 3.2. Two data replicates are used for each of the ten combinations of cost and time values. Observations are recorded for the number of units representing double production volumes. The model is transformed to the logarithmic form below:

$$\log C_x = [\log K + \log(c_1c_2)] + b_1\log x_1 + b_2\log x_2$$
$$= \log a + b_1\log x_1 + b_2\log x_2,$$

where 'a' represents the combined constant in the model such that $a = (K)(c_1)(c_2)$. The fitted model is:

$$\log C_x = 5.70 - 0.21(\log x_1) - 0.13(\log x_2),$$
$$C_x = 298.88x_1^{-0.21}x_2^{-0.13},$$

where $\log(a) = 5.70$ (i.e. $a = 298.88$), C_x = cumulative average cost per unit, x_1 = cumulative production units, and x_2 = cumulative training time in hours. Figure 3.11 shows the response surface for the fitted model. Diagnostic statistical analysis indicates that the model is a good fit for the data. The 95% confidence intervals for the parameters in the model are shown in Table 3.3.

The result of analysis of variance for the full regression is presented in Table 3.4. The P-value of 0.0000 in the table indicates that we have a highly significant regression fit. The R-squared value of 0.966962 indicates that most of the variabilities in cumulative average cost are explained by the terms in the model. Table 3.5 shows the breakdown of the model component of the sum of squares. Based on the low P-values shown in the table, it is concluded that both units and training time contribute significantly to the regression model.

Table 3.2 Data for modeling bivariate learning curve

Treatment Number	Observation Number	Cumulative Average Cost ($)	Cumulative Production (Units)	Cumulative Training Time (Hours)
1	1	120	10	11
	2	140	10	8
2	3	95	20	54
	4	125	20	25
3	5	80	40	100
	6	75	40	80
4	7	65	80	220
	8	50	80	150
5	9	55	160	410
	10	40	160	500
6	11	40	320	660
	12	38	320	600
7	13	32	640	810
	14	36	640	750
8	15	25	1280	890
	16	25	1280	800
9	17	20	2560	990
	18	24	2560	900
10	19	19	5120	1155
	20	25	5120	1000

Table 3.3 95% confidence interval for model parameters

Parameter	Estimate	Lower Limit	Upper Limit
$\log (a)$	5.7024	5.4717	5.9331
b_1	−0.2093	−0.2826	−0.1359
b_2	−0.1321	−0.2269	−0.0373

Table 3.4 ANOVA for the full regression of the learning curve model

Source	Sum of Squares	df	Mean Square	F-Ratio	P-value
Model	7.41394	2	3.70697	248.778	0.0000
Error	0.253312	17	0.00149007		
Total	7.66725	19			

R-squared = 0.966962
R-adjusted (adjusted for degrees of freedom) = 0.963075
Standard error of estimate = 0.122069

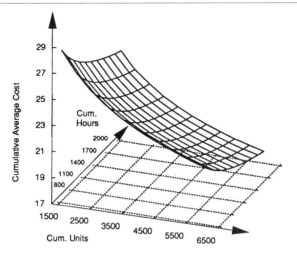

Figure 3.11 Response surface for bivariate learning curve example.

Table 3.5 Further ANOVA for the variables in the model fitted

Source	Sum of Squares	df	Mean Square	F-Ratio	P-value
LOG (units)	7.28516187	1	7.2851619	488.91	0.000
LOG (time)	0.12877864	1	0.1287786	8.64	0.0092
Model	7.41394052	2			

Table 3.6 Correlation matrix for coefficient estimates

	Constant	LOG (units)	LOG (time)
Constant	1.0000	0.3654	−0.6895
LOG (units)	0.3654	1.0000	−0.9189
LOG (time)	−0.6895	−0.9189	1.000

The correlation matrix for the estimates of the coefficients in the model is shown in Table 3.6. It is seen that log of units and log of time are very negatively correlated, and the constant is positively correlated with log of units, while it is negatively correlated with log of time. The strong negative correlation (−0.9189) between units and training time suggests that there is strong multicollinearity. Multicollinearity normally implies that one of the correlated variables can be omitted without jeopardizing the fit of the model. Variables that are statistically independent will have an expected correlation of zero. As expected, Table 3.6 does not indicate any zero correlations. The source of strong correlations may be explained by the fact that it is difficult to separate the effects of training time from the effect of cumulative production. Obviously, the level of training will influence productivity, which may be reflected in the level of cumulative production within a given length of time.

3.9 LEARN–FORGET MODELS

Retention rate and retention capacity of different workers will influence the modeling of forget functions. Whenever interruption occurs in the learning process, it results in some forgetting. The resulting drop in performance rate depends on the initial level of performance and the length of the interruption. Any operation that is subject to interruption in the learning process is suitable for the application of forget functions. Sule (1978) postulated that the forget model can be represented as:

$$Y_f = X_f R_f^{B_f},$$

where Y_f = number of good units that could be produced on Rth day, X_f = equivalent production on first day of the forget curve, R_f = cumulative number of days in forget cycle, and B_f = forgetting rate. The above forget model is of the same form as the standard learning curve, except that the forgetting rate will be negative where the learning rate is positive and vice versa. Potential forms of univariate forget functions are shown in Figure 3.12.

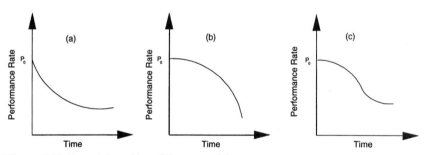

Figure 3.12 Potential profiles of forget models.

Model (a) shows a case where the worker forgets rapidly from an initial performance level. Model (b) shows a case where forgetting occurs more slowly in a concave fashion. Model (c) shows a case where there is some residual retention of performance after a period of progressive forgetting.

The combination of the learning and forget models will present a more realistic picture of what actually occurs in a learning process and it will help determine how much process improvement can be expected. The combination is not as simple as resolving two curves to obtain a resultant curve because only

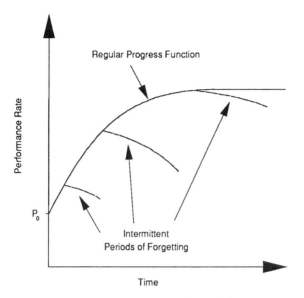

Figure 3.13 Intermittent periods of forgetting during training.

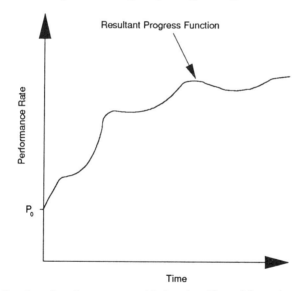

Figure 3.14 Resultant learning curve considering the effect of forgetting.

intermittent periods of forgetting are involved. Figure 3.13 presents a conceptual view of some periods where forgetting takes place. Figure 3.14 presents an hypothesized resultant learn–forget curve.

An example of a bivariate learning function, $l(t,u)$, is presented in Figure 3.15. Note that in this example, the learning effect is represented in terms of

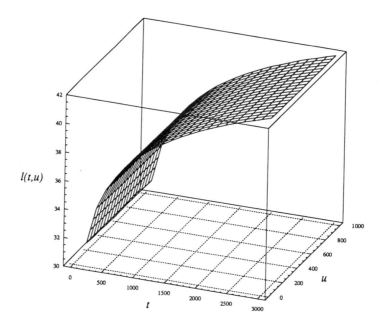

Figure 3.15 Bivariate performance-based learning function.

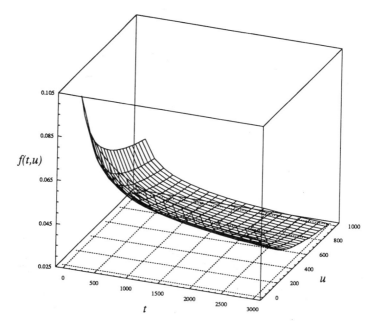

Figure 3.16 Bivariate performance-based forget function.

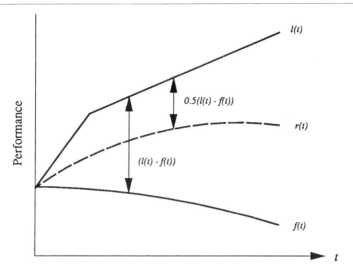

Figure 3.17 Univariate representation of function resolution.

performance rate. Thus, in the figure, performance rate increases with time. The second independent variable in the model is production level in units. A hypothetical bivariate forget function, $f(t,u)$, is shown in Figure 3.16. Due to the effect of forgetting, the performance level tends to decrease with time. Mathematical representations of the functions are presented respectively below:

$$l(t,u) = 20t^{0.09} + u^{-0.05}$$
$$f(t,u) = t^{-0.20}u^{-0.30}$$

The resultant performance function, $r(t,u)$, is computed as shown below:

New performance function = Old performance function − 1/2(Old performance function − Forget function),

which is represented mathematically as:

$$
\begin{aligned}
r(t,u) &= l(t,u) - 0.5[l(t,u) - f(t,u)] \\
&= 20t^{0.09} + u^{-0.05} - 0.5[20t^{0.09} + u^{-0.05} - t^{-0.20}u^{-0.30}] \\
&= 10t^{0.09} + 0.5u^{-0.05} + 0.5t^{-0.2}u^{-0.3}
\end{aligned}
$$

which is simply the point-by-point average of the learning and forgetting functions. That is,

$$r(t,u) = \frac{l(t,u) + f(t,u)}{2}$$

The justification for using the above approach for resolving the two functions can be seen by considering the univariate plots in Figure 3.18. In the figure, the learn function, $l(t)$, is above the forget function, $f(t)$. The forget function will create a downward pull on the learn function. This creates the resultant

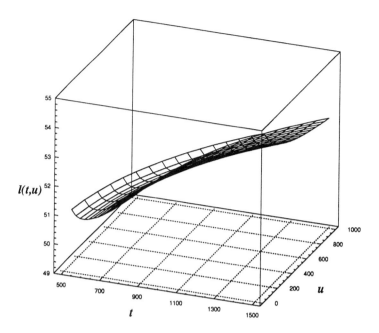

Figure 3.18 Selected portion of learn function.

function, $r(t)$. The resolution of the two functions is applicable only for the time periods over which forgetting occurs.

The plot of the resultant model of the bivariate learning and forgetting functions will exhibit a 'wave-like' form if plotted with intermittent occurrence of forgetting. As an abridged illustration, Figure 3.18 shows a portion of the learn function, $l(t,u)$, over the time interval from 500 to 1500 hours. Note that this time interval, as seen in the plot, represents a region of steep performance improvement. Figure 3.19 shows a portion of the forget function, $f(t,u)$, over the same time interval. Figure 3.20 shows the resultant performance function over the selected time interval.

It is noted that the forget function is defined as an absolute function with very low performance levels over the time period used in the example. These low values result in net performance levels that are about half the performance level without the effect of forgetting. It should be recalled that the resolution approach used in the illustrative example is particularly strict in terms of the hypothesized detrimental effect of the forget function. Alternate resolution approaches may be considered whereby the negative impact of the forget function is reduced. This can be accomplished by using an integer multiple of the learning function when resolving the learn and forget functions. For example, the learning function may be given N times as much weight as the

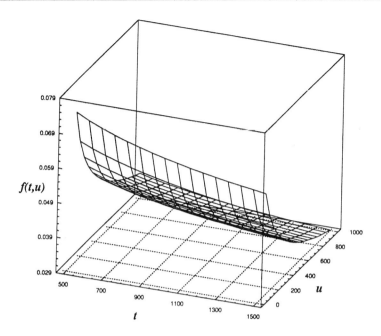

Figure 3.19 Selected portion of forget function.

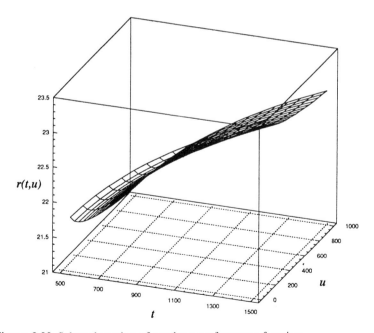

Figure 3.20 Selected portion of resultant performance function.

forget function in obtaining the point-by-point average of the functions. Another approach is to define the forget function as a relative function, based directly on the level of decrement it creates in the overall performance. In this case, the two functions may be added directly to obtain the resultant performance function.

3.9.1 Impact on product quality

The learn–forget model is useful in assessing actual worker performance. The resultant performance model can yield very valuable information relating expected worker performance to expected product quality. The loss in worker performance due to the effect of forgetting can translate into poor workmanship, which will be reflected in product quality. The level of worker performance can be quantified in terms of resource expenditure per unit of product. This quantification may be done on a cost or time basis. Referring back to Figure 3.15, it is seen that performance level increases as time increases. The quantification of performance in this case is done on the basis of incremental cost or time savings achieved over time due to the effect of learning.

3.10 PROCESS TECHNOLOGY TRANSFER

Processes should take advantage of existing developments rather than reinventing the 'wheel'. In production processes, the transfer of existing technology to achieve current objectives should be one of the basic approaches to process improvement. Figure 3.21 shows how products, ideas, concepts, and decisions that have been developed and tested in other processes are transferred to a target process. The receiving process (sink), uses the transferred technology to generate new products, ideas, concepts, and decisions, which follow a reverse technology transfer path to the origin of the technology (source). Thereby, both processes operate on a symbiotic basis, with each one having something to contribute to the transfer process. Consequently, both processes are improved. Figure 3.22 shows a specific cycle of technology adaptation and modification for a given process.

The transfer of process technology can be achieved in various forms. Badiru (1991) presented three technology transfer modes that represent basic strategies for getting one technological product from one point (source) to another point (sink). The three modes are discussed below.

1. *Product transfer*: This refers to the transfer of completed products. In this case, a fully developed product is transferred from one process to another process. Very little product development effort is carried out at the receiving point. However, information about the operations of the product is fed back

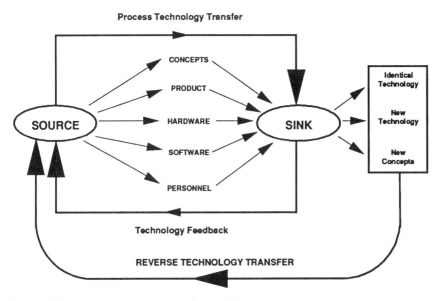

Figure 3.21 Process technology transfer model.

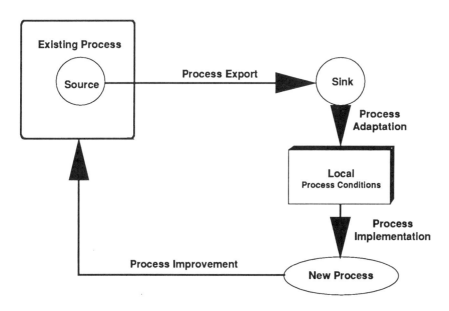

Figure 3.22 Project technology transfer loop.

to the source so that necessary product improvement can be pursued. So, the technology recipient generates an information-based product which serves as a resource for the technology source.

2. *Transfer of guidelines*: This refers to the transfer of technology procedures and guidelines. In this technology transfer mode, procedures (e.g. blueprints) and guidelines are transferred from one process to another. The technology blueprints are implemented locally to generate the desired services and products. The use of local raw materials and manpower is encouraged for the local production. Under this mode, the implementation of the transferred technology procedures can generate new operating procedures that can be fed back to improve the original process. With this symbiotic arrangement, a loop system is created whereby both the transferring and the receiving processes derive useful benefits.

3. *Concept transfer*: This refers to the transfer of technology concepts, theories, and ideas. This strategy involves the transfer of the basic aspects of a process. The transferred elements can then be improved, modified, or customized within local constraints to generate new products. The local modifications and enhancements have the potential to generate an identical technology, a new related technology, or a new set of technology concepts, theories, and ideas. These derived products may then be transferred back to the original technology source.

The important questions to ask when transferring technology from one project to another include the following.

- What exactly is being transferred?
- What is the cost of acquiring the technology?
- How is the subject process similar to transferring process?
- How is the subject process different from transferring process?
- Are the goals of the processes identical?
- What is expected from the transferred technology?
- Is there enough technical skill to make effective use of the transferred technology?
- Is the prevailing management culture receptive to the new technology?
- Is the present infrastructure suitable to support the technology?
- What modifications will be necessary for the technology?
- Where will the new technology be used?
- Who will use the technology?
- What is required to maintain the technology?

3.11 PROCESS CONVERSION STRATEGIES

After an improvement has been achieved, the next step is to ensure an effective conversion to the new process. The implementation of a new improved process can be effected through one of several strategies. Some strategies are more suitable than others for certain types of processes. Below are listed the most commonly used conversion strategies.

Parallel conversion: The existing process and the new process operate concurrently until there is confidence that the new process is satisfactory.

Direct conversion: The old process is removed totally and the new process takes over. This method is recommended only when there is no existing process or when both processes cannot be kept operational due to incompatibility or cost considerations.

Phased conversion: Modules of the new process are gradually introduced one at a time using either direct or parallel conversion.

Pilot conversion: The new process is fully implemented on a pilot basis in a selected department within the organization. Figure 3.23 shows a graphical representation of the process conversion options.

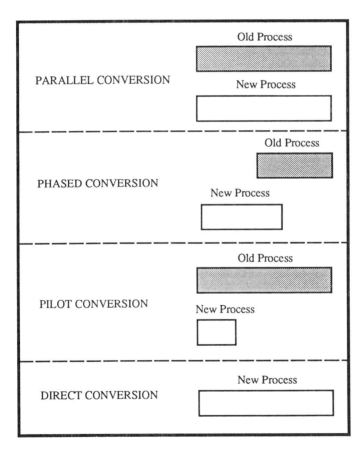

Figure 3.23 Process conversion strategies.

Process integration can facilitate effective sharing of resources to improve utilization and performance levels. Process resource sharing can involve physical equipment, facilities, technical information, ideas, and technical personnel. Process integration is a major effort in process adoption and implementation. Process integration is required for proper product coordination. Integration facilitates the coordination of diverse technical and managerial efforts to improve quality, reduce cost, increase productivity, and increase the utilization of resources. Process integration ensures that all performance goals are satisfied with a minimum of expenditure of time and resources. It may require the adjustment of functions to permit sharing of resources, development of new policies to accommodate product integration, or realignment of managerial responsibilities. Important factors to consider in process integration include:

- unique characteristics of each component in the integrated processes;
- relative priorities of each component in the integrated processes;
- how the components of the processes complement one another;
- physical and data interfaces between the components;
- internal and external factors that may influence the integrated processes;
- how the performance of the integrated system will be measured;
- the human interface required for the process implementation.

3.12 FUZZY SET MODELING FOR PROCESS IMPROVEMENT

Fuzzy sets (Zadeh, 1965) represent one approach to handling probabilistic analysis for quality and process improvement. Fuzzy sets generalize the notions of a set and propositions to accommodate the type of fuzziness or vagueness in decision problems. Recently, fuzzy logic has found a wide variety of applications ranging from industrial process control, quality control, and consumer electronics to medical diagnosis and investment management. In contrast to classical logic, fuzzy logic is aimed at providing a body of concepts and techniques for dealing with modes of reasoning which are approximate rather than exact. Extensions of fuzzy sets now include concepts such as fuzzy arithmetic, possibility distributions, fuzzy statistics, fuzzy random variables, and fuzzy set functions. Fuzzification is a concept which permits the incorporation of fuzzy reasoning into any normal set.

In formal truth logic, it is required that every proposition be either true (1) or false (0). While '0' or '1' treatment fits conventional computer processing perfectly, it can impose serious restrictions in situations dealing with human reasoning. Fuzzy logic is a technique for dealing with sources of imprecision and uncertainty that may not be statistical in nature.

Fuzzy logic uses a multi-valued membership function to denote membership of an object in a class rather than the classical binary true or false values used to denote membership. In fuzzy logic, the source of imprecision is the absence of sharply defined criteria for class membership rather than the presence of random variables. Each class contains a continuum of grades of membership. Thus, a product will not be considered to be either good or bad. Depending on the product's actual quality level, it will have a certain degree of being good or being bad. A question of interest is to determine when a product makes the transition from being a bad product to being a good product.

In many practical real world problems, the transition point is not clearly defined. It is fuzzy! The degree of membership in one category or another will depend on the membership functions that users or producers define to convey the varying levels of quality of the product. A fuzzy set is described by a membership function that maps a set of objects on to the interval of real numbers between 0 and 1. In standard set theory, an object is either a member of a set or not a member of the set. In fuzzy set, the transition from membership to nonmembership is gradual rather than abrupt because there are no distinguishable boundaries. To illustrate the concept of fuzzy sets to process improvement, let us define set A to be the class of 'high' customer ratings for a process. Suppose average rating points based on a sample of customer surveys are on a scale of 1 to 4. Because the definition of high is subjective, we assign a range of rating points and the corresponding possibility values to the set A as shown in Table 3.7.

Table 3.7 Degree of membership in a fuzzy set

Rating Points	Grade of Membership
2.00	0.00
2.25	0.12
2.50	0.25
. . .	. . .
3.50	0.82
3.60	0.90
4.00	1.00

The term high can be modified with linguistic hedges such as 'quite', 'very', and 'somewhat'. Figure 3.24 shows a distribution of rating points based on linguistic hedges. Given a particular specification of rating point level, the distribution can be used to determine an appropriate classification of the rating point level. For example, a rating point of 3.6 may have a classification of 'very high' with fuzzy confidence of 0.7, a classification of 'high' with confidence of 0.9, or a classification of 'quite high' with a fuzzy confidence of 0.99. Thus, a

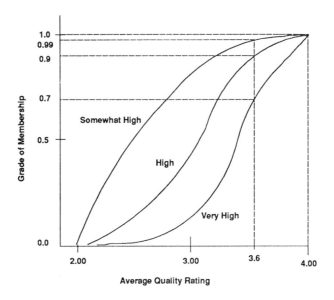

Figure 3.24 Example of fuzzy set distribution with modifiers.

process that gets a very high rating point in a loose market may only get a low rating point in a competitive market.

Definition of fuzzy set

Let A be a set of objects defined over a sample space X. For a finite set defined as:

$$X = x_1, x_2, \ldots, x_n,$$

we can represent A as a fuzzy set with the linear combination below:

$$A = u_1(x_1), u_2(x_2), \ldots, u_n(x_n),$$

where u_i is the grade of membership of x_i in A. In general, for a sample space of objects defined as $X = \{x\}$, the fuzzy set A in X is a set of ordered pairs defined as:

$$A = \{x, u_a(x)\}, \xi \in X.$$

A value of $u_a(x) = 0$ indicates that x is not a member of A, while $u_a(x) = 1$ implies that x is completely contained in A. Values of $u_a(x)$ between 0 and 1 indicate that x is a partial member of A. Characteristic membership functions for fuzzy sets are different from probabilities and should not be confused with probabilities. Probability is a measure of the degree of uncertainty based on the frequency or proportion of occurrence of an event. By contrast, a fuzzy characteristic function relates to the degree of vagueness which measures the ease with which an event can be attained.

3.13 FUZZY QUALITY MODEL

With the definition of fuzzy set, we have a means of expressing a function GOOD(x) to convey the information about the quality level of the manufactured product mentioned earlier. The fuzzy set A can be defined as:

$$A = \{good\}.$$

That is, A is the set containing those items that can be classified as good. Obviously, some items will be stronger members of the set than other items. There will be some items at the low end of good and some items at the high end of good.

For this example, we can define x as a quantitative measure of a particular quality characteristic of the product. An example is the measure of the surface finish or surface roughness of the product. If the measures of surface roughness range from, say, 1 to 50, then we might assign the membership values shown in Table 3.8. A surface roughness of 1 is the most desirable, while a surface roughness of 50 is the least desirable in this particular example. Note that Table 3.8 indicates that the highest degree of membership is 0.95 (less than 1). This is logical since it may be impossible to obtain a perfect surface finish without any roughness at all. A fuzzy set is said to be normal if its highest degree of membership is one.

Table 3.8 Product quality classification using fuzzy set

Surface Roughness (x)	Degree of Membership in the GOOD set $u_a(x)$
1.00	0.95
5.20	0.88
10.50	0.70
. . .	. . .
35.00	0.10
45.00	0.05
50.00	0.00

Figure 3.25 presents what Badiru (1992) refers to as a fuzzy set grid. The grid shows the gradual change in the degree of membership from one level to another. In the grid, the changes in membership grade are so gradual that no discrete boundaries can be seen. The figure represents a bivariate set whereby an item is classified as 'good' based on two quality characteristics: surface roughness and porosity. Items with low values of surface roughness (i.e. high surface finish) and low values of porosity have the strongest degree of membership in the fuzzy set A, which is defined as A = {good}. That is, A is the set of good products. The degree of membership in A slowly decreases as surface roughness and porosity increase.

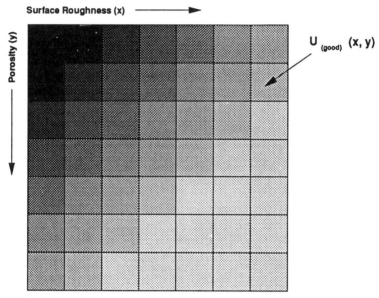

Figure 3.25 Fuzzy set membership grid.

An item located in the upper left-hand corner of the grid has the highest degree of membership in A. That is, it is the best of the good items. An item located in the lower right-hand corner of the grid has the lowest degree of membership in A. That is, it is the worst of the good items. The bivariate fuzzy set grid may be extended to a trivariate (three factors) case. In such a case, the grid would be represented as a box with nonhomogeneous density. The density of the box would change gradually in different directions to indicate varying degrees of membership in the trivariate fuzzy set.

Referring to the example in Table 3.8, the membership values for the set GOOD are based on the observed surface finish of the product. Such membership values may be obtained through empirical studies or subjective experimentations. In some cases, it is possible to define a function that generates the membership values directly. Such a function might be of the form presented below.

$$u_A(x) = \begin{cases} \sqrt{x-1} & \text{if } 1 \leq x \leq 2 \\ 0, & \text{otherwise} \end{cases}$$

Figure 3.26 presents a plot of the function $u_A(x)$. The functional form of the membership function may be based on characteristics relating to the utility of the item with respect to its various quality levels or some other criterion of interest.

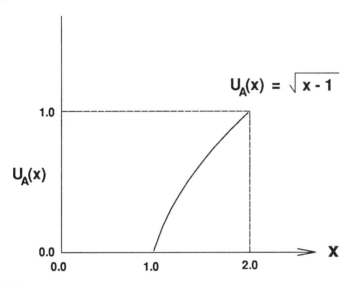

$$U_A(x) = \sqrt{x-1}$$

Figure 3.26 Plot of degree of membership function.

Certain operations that are unique to fuzzy sets are presented below:

Dilation: The dilation of A is defined as:

$$\text{DIL}(A) = \sqrt{u_A(x)}, \ \forall \ \xi \in X$$

Concentration: The concentration of A is defined as:

$$\text{CON}(A) = [u_A(x)]^2, \ \forall \ \xi \in X$$

Normalization: The normalization of A is defined as:

$$\text{NORM}(A) = \frac{u_A(x)}{\max_x \{u_A(x)\}}, \ \forall \ \xi \in X$$

For the function presented in Figure 3.26, DIL(A), CON(A), and NORM(A) are shown in Figure 3.27. Dilation tends to increase the degree of membership of all partial members. Concentration is the opposite of dilation. It tends to

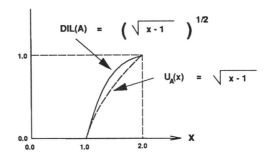

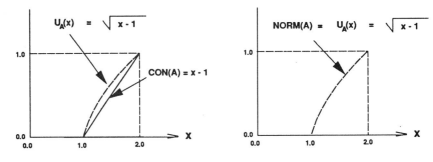

Figure 3.27 Unique operations on fuzzy membership functions.

decrease the degree of membership of all partial members. Normalization performs the function of normalizing the membership function.

Fuzzy membership functions can be used to generate confidence factors about product quality as an alternative to probability and statistical inferences. For example, referring to the product quality example presented earlier, we may have the following rule:

IF surface-roughness is-less-than 10
THEN product-quality is good

Now, suppose we are given the following premise:

Surface-roughness is 10.5.

Our conclusion would be that the product is good but with a certain level of fuzzy membership level (FML). That is,

Product-quality is good (FML = 0.70),
where FML = $U_A(10.5)$ = 0.70 as presented in Table 3.8.

Figure 3.28 presents two unidirectional membership functions. Curve A is defined for the set of good products based on the surface roughness. Note that as surface roughness increases, the degree of membership in the GOOD set

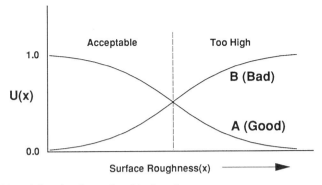

Figure 3.28 Unidirectional membership functions.

decreases. Curve B is defined for the set of bad products. As the surface roughness increases the degree of membership in the BAD set increases. Under fuzzy set reasoning, a product can be classified as being both good and bad. It is the degree of membership in the specific fuzzy set that makes a difference. Note that an item with a surface roughness located at the intersection of curves A and B has equivalent degrees of membership in either of the two sets GOOD and BAD. At this point, we would be indifferent to classifying the item as either good or bad.

Figure 3.29 presents two bidirectional membership functions. A bidirectional function is defined as one that starts at one end, reaches a peak or valley, and then changes direction. Curve B may be suitable for applications dealing with parameters, such as temperature, where both the low end and high end of the function are desirable. As shown in Figure 3.29, temperatures at the low end and at the high end have lower degrees of membership in the set of

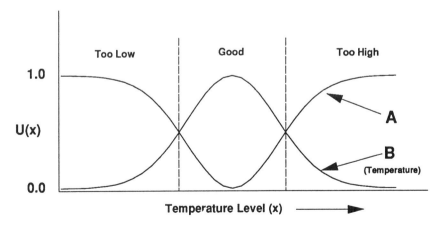

Figure 3.29 Bidirectional membership functions.

ACCEPTABLE-TEMPERATURE, while temperature values in the middle range have higher degrees of membership. This, for example, may be the case when monitoring the ambient temperature of a work station for the comfort of workers. Temperatures that are too low are not desirable and temperatures that are too high are not desirable.

Curve A in Figure 3.29 presents a situation that is opposite to the temperature example. Curve A indicates that both the values at the low and high ends are more desirable than those in the middle range. An example of this situation may be the preparation of glues for post-it note pads. If the glue is weak, then it is desirable for use in the post-it pad. If the glue is very strong, then it is desirable for regular glueing applications. Glue strengths in the middle range are not acceptable because they are either too strong for use in post-it pads or not strong enough for regular uses.

3.13.1 Customer-oriented fuzzy reliability modeling

The application of fuzzy set theory to the problem of multi-state reliability appears to be a fertile area for practical applications for process improvement. Consider the reliability of the braking system for a modern five-passenger vehicle with a curb weight of 1500 kg and a maximum weight of 2000 kg. The vehicle is equipped with all-weather radial tires and the braking system is of the dual diagonal, power-assisted, hydraulic type with front disk brakes, rear drum brakes, and an anti-skid subsystem. Assume that tires and dampers are replaced with original equipment manufacturer equivalents before they have a significant adverse effect on braking ability. People tend to think of an attribute like braking performance in linguistic terms such as 'very poor,' 'poor,' 'good,' etc. rather than 'exact' measures like stopping distance on a dry test track from various speeds. Environmental factors have a major influence on braking performance so the states of the braking system must apply to the range of conditions that customers may expect to encounter which strengthens the case for modeling a multi-state system with fuzzy numbers.

The effects of subsystem degradation or failure depend upon environmental factors. For instance, if the anti-skid system fails, leaving a regular braking system, the effect would be small on a good, dry road surface for a heavily loaded vehicle, but large for a vehicle carrying only the driver on a wet or icy road surface.

3.14 MANAGERIAL ASPECTS OF PROCESS IMPROVEMENT

In today's competitive environment, quality is the key to the success and survival of any organization. Organizations can come closer to achieving ideal goals of 'Zero defect', 'Total Customer Satisfaction', and so on only with continuous improvement. The major ingredients for achieving world class manufacturing (WCM) status are continual improvement in quality, costs, lead time, and customer service. An organization that does not continually change and improve will not keep up with its competitors. The requirements for continual improvement will involve drastic managerial changes. Project management is one approach that can help ensure the success of quality improvement efforts. Project management provides a mechanism for addressing the planning, scheduling, and control aspects of quality improvement projects. The next chapter presents guidelines for using project management techniques for quality improvement.

4 | Project management approach to quality and process improvement

A short cut on quality is always a wrong cut

As companies all over the world strive for quality improvement through TQM, they are increasingly recognizing the importance of project management approaches in accomplishing TQM goals. Project management facilitates on-time within-budget programs. Project management techniques are used widely in many enterprises including construction, banking, manufacturing, marketing, health care services, transportation, R&D, public services, and so on. Total quality management has emerged in recent years as another fertile area for the application of project management techniques. The basic benefits of project management are:

- it increases the awareness of the importance of continuous quality improvement throughout an organization;
- it coordinates and integrates the efforts of all the functional groups in an organization;
- it clearly outlines the responsibility of individuals and groups, and defines the required interfaces;
- it helps clarify objectives and priorities;
- it increases scheduling effectiveness;
- it facilitates better resource allocation;
- it improves task coordination;
- it facilitates intra-group and inter-team communication;
- it provides a mechanism for measuring project progress.

The benefits listed above are consistent with the objectives of quality improvement. Consequently, much attention has been directed at the marriage of TQM and project management (Badiru, 1991).

4.1 IMPORTANCE OF PROJECT MANAGEMENT

Project management is the process of managing, allocating, and timing resources to achieve a given goal in an efficient and expedient manner. Project objectives may be in terms of time, costs, or technical results. A project can be quite simple or very complex. An example of a simple project is painting a small, vacant room. An example of a complex project is launching a space shuttle. A quality improvement project is a complex project because of the number and complexity of the interactions required to make it successful. Juran advocates a project approach to quality improvement. He says:

> The project approach is important. When it comes to quality, there is no such thing as improvement in general. Any improvement in quality is going to come about project-by-project and no other way.

Similar to the hierarchy of a process presented in Chapter 3, project management also has a hierarchy of components, as discussed below.

System: A project system consists of interrelated elements organized for the purpose of achieving a common goal. The elements are expected to work synergistically to generate a unified output that is greater than the sum of the individual outputs of the components.

Program: Program commonly denotes very large and prolonged undertakings. It is a term that is typically applied to project endeavors that span several years. Programs are usually associated with particular systems. For example, a quality improvement effort can be classified as a program because it is expected to be an unending endeavor.

Project: Project is the term generally applied to time-phased efforts of much smaller scope and duration than programs. Programs are sometimes viewed as consisting of a set of projects. Sometimes, both terms are used interchangeably. Many government projects are referred to as programs because of their broad and comprehensive nature.

Task: A task is a functional element of a project. A project is normally composed of contiguous collections of tasks that all contribute to the overall project goal.

Activity: An activity can be defined as a single element of a project. Activities are generally smaller in scope than tasks. In a detailed analysis of a project, an activity may be viewed as the smallest, practically indivisible work element of the project. As an example, we can consider a manufacturing plant as a system. A plant-wide endeavor to improve quality can be viewed as a program. The installation of a flexible manufacturing system is a project within the quality improvement program. The process of identifying and selecting equipment vendors is a task, and the actual process of placing an order with a preferred vendor is an activity. Figure 4.1 presents the functional and hierarchical relationships between the components of a project.

Project management process makes use of collections of principles, concepts,

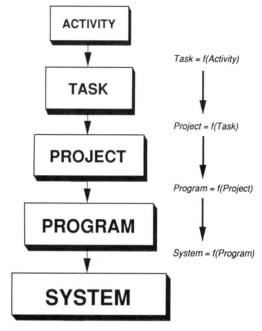

Figure 4.1 Hierarchy of project components.

tools, and techniques to integrate the various components of a project. The goal of project management is to accomplish project objectives on time and within budget. The techniques of project management can help accomplish goals relating to better product quality, improved resource utilization, better customer relations, higher productivity, and fulfillment of due dates. These can generally be expressed in terms of the following project constraints:

- performance specifications;
- schedule requirements;
- cost limitations.

4.2 PROJECT MANAGEMENT STEPS FOR QUALITY IMPROVEMENT

Figure 4.2 presents the major steps in project management for quality improvement. The life cycle of a TQM project consists of several steps going from problem identification, definition, specifications, project formulation, organizing, resource allocation, scheduling, tracking and reporting, and control to project termination. The steps are performed strategically in accordance with the specified project goal.

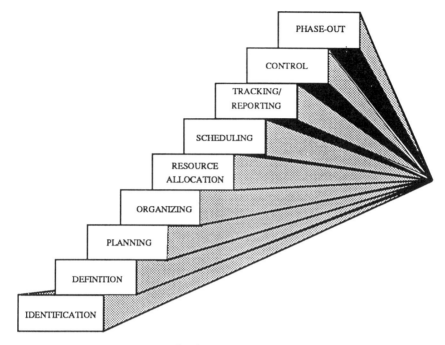

Figure 4.2 Project steps for quality improvement.

Problem identification

This is the stage where a need for quality improvement is identified, defined, and justified. A TQM project may be concerned with the development of new products, implementation of new processes, or improvement of existing facilities.

Project definition

This is the phase at which the purpose of the project is clarified. A mission statement is the major output of this stage. For example, a prevailing low level of productivity may trigger a need for a new CIM technology. The definition should specify how project management may be used to avoid missed deadlines, poor scheduling, inadequate resource allocation, lack of coordination, poor quality, and conflicting priorities.

Project planning

Project planning determines how to initiate and execute the objectives of a TQM project. Planning is discussed in further detail in a subsequent section.

Project organizing

Project organization specifies how to integrate the functions of the personnel involved in a project. Organizing is normally done concurrently with project planning. Directing is an important aspect of project organization. Directing involves guiding and supervising the project personnel. It is a crucial aspect in the management function. Directing requires skilful managers who can interact with subordinates effectively through good communication and motivation techniques. A successful manager improves the performance of his subordinates by directing them, through proper task assignments, towards the project goal. Workers perform better when there are clearly defined expectations. They need to know how their job functions contribute to the overall goals of the project. Workers should be given some flexibility for self-direction in the process of performing their functions. Individual worker needs and limitations should be recognized by the manager when directing project functions. Project directing consists of the following elements.

Approach: Development of a method of approach (communication or otherwise) to subordinates at various levels and in different situations.

Supervising: Monitoring, guiding and reviewing of the day-to-day activities of subordinates with respect to the project goal.

Delegating: Assignment of responsibility or secondary authority to subordinates for the execution of certain functions so as to enhance the utilization of manpower resources.

Motivating: Boosting the morale and interest of subordinates in performing their jobs. This requires understanding the needs, motives, and feelings of subordinates, and an appreciation for the nature of their responses to certain directives.

Resource allocation

Quality improvement goals and objectives are accomplished by applying resources to functional requirements. Resources, in the context of project management, are generally made up of people and equipment, which are typically in short supply. The people needed for a particular task may be committed to other on-going projects. A crucial piece of equipment may be under the control of an uncooperative department.

Project scheduling

Scheduling is often recognized as the major function in project management. The main purpose of scheduling is to allocate resources so that the overall project objectives are achieved within a reasonable time span. In general, scheduling involves the assignment of time periods to specific tasks within the work schedule. Resource availability, time limitations, urgency level, required performance level, precedence requirements, work priorities, technical constraints, and other factors complicate the scheduling process. Thus, the assignment of a time slot to a task does not necessarily ensure that the task will be performed satisfactorily in accordance with the schedule. Consequently, careful control must be developed and maintained throughout the project scheduling process. A separate section is devoted to further discussion of project scheduling.

Project tracking and reporting

This phase involves the process of checking whether or not project results conform to plans and specifications. Tracking and reporting are prerequisites for project control. A properly organized report of the project status will quickly identify the deficiencies in the progress of the project and help pinpoint the necessary corrective actions.

Project control

In this function, necessary actions are taken to correct unacceptable deviations from expected performance. Control is effected by measurement, evaluation, and corrective action. Measurement is the process of measuring the relationship between planned performance and actual performance with respect to project objectives. The variable to be measured, the measurement scale, and measuring approach should be clearly specified during the planning stage.

Project phase-out

This is the last stage of a project. The phase-out of a project is as important as the initiation of the project. The termination of a project should be implemented forthrightly. A project should not be allowed to drag on needlessly after the expected completion time. A terminal activity should be defined for a project during the project planning phase. An example of a terminal activity may be the submission of a final report, the 'power-on' of new equipment, or the signing of a release order. The conclusion of such an activity should be viewed as the completion of the project. However, provisions should be made for follow-up activities or projects that may further improve the results of the project. These follow-up or spin-off projects should be managed as new projects, but with proper input–output relationships between the sequence of projects. If a project is not terminated when appropriate, the motivation for it will wane and subsequent activities may become counter-productive. This is particularly true of TQM projects where 'resistance to change' is already a major obstacle.

4.3 PROJECT IMPLEMENTATION MODEL

It is helpful to have a model that can be adopted for TQM project implementation purposes. Presented below is a comprehensive model for the essential tasks in TQM project planning, scheduling, and control.

1: PLANNING

I.   Specify Project Background
      A.   Define Current Situation and Process
         1.   Document Customer Requirements
         2.   Understand the Process
         3.   Identify Important Variables
         4.   Quantify Variables
      B.   Identify Areas for Improvement
         1.   List and Explain Areas
         2.   Study Potential Strategy for Solution
II.   Define Unique Terminologies Relevant to the Project
         1.   Industry-specific Terminologies
         2.   Company-specific Terminologies
         3.   Project-specific Terminologies
         4.   Customer-specific Terminologies
III.   Define Project Goal and Objectives
      A.   Write Mission Statement
      B.   Solicit Inputs and Ideas from Personnel
IV.   Establish Performance Standards
      A.   Schedule
      B.   Performance
      C.   Cost
V.   Conduct Formal Project Feasibility
      A.   Determine Impact on Cost
      B.   Determine on Organization
      C.   Determine Project Deliverables
      D.   Determine Benefits to the Customer
VI.   Secure Management Support

2: ORGANIZING

I.   Identify Project Management Team
      A.   Specify Project Organization Structure
         1.   Matrix Structure
         2.   Formal and Informal Structures
         3.   Justify Structure
      B.   Specify Departments Involved and Key Personnel
         1.   Purchasing
         2.   Materials Management
         3.   Engineering, Design, Manufacturing, etc.

4. Customers, Vendors
C. Define Project Management Responsibilities
1. Select Project Manager
2. Write Project Charter
3. Establish Project Policies and Procedures

II. Implement Triple C Model
A. Communication
1. Determine Communication Interfaces
2. Develop Communication Matrix
B. Cooperation
1. Outline Cooperation Requirements
C. Coordination
1. Develop Work Breakdown Structure
2. Assign Task Responsibilities
3. Develop Responsibility Chart

3: SCHEDULING AND RESOURCE ALLOCATION

I. Develop Master Schedule
A. Estimate Task Duration
B. Identify Precedence Task Precedence Requirements
1. Technical Precedence
2. Resource-imposed Precedence
3. Procedural Precedence
C. Use Analytical Models
1. CPM
2. PERT
3. Gantt Chart
4. Optimization Models

4: TRACKING, REPORTING, AND CONTROL

I. Establish Guidelines for Tracking, Reporting, and Control
A. Define Data Requirements
1. Data Categories
2. Data Characterization
3. Measurement Scales
B. Develop Data Documentation
1. Data Update Requirements
2. Data Quality Control
3. Establish Data Security Measures

II. Categorize Control Points
A. Schedule Audit
1. Activity Network and Gantt Charts
2. Milestones
3. Delivery Schedule
B. Performance Audit

      1. Employee Performance
      2. Product Quality
      3. Customer Feedback
  C. Cost Audit
      1. Cost Containment Measures
      2. Percent Completion versus Budget Depletion
III. Identify Implementation Process
IV. Phase-out the Project
  A. Performance Review
  B. Strategy for Follow-up Projects
  C. Personnel Retention and Releases
V. Document Project and Submit Final Report

The model above gives a general guideline for TQM project planning, scheduling, and control. The skeleton of the model can be adopted for specific implementation as required for specific projects. Not all projects will be amenable to all the contents of the model and customization will always be necessary when implementing it.

4.3.1 Statement of work

The project implementation model will be driven by the specific statement of work involved in the process improvement effort. The statement of work (SOW) involves a narrative description of the work to be done. This may include the objectives of the project, a brief description of the work, budget, specifications, and schedule.

Project specifications

Project specifications involve identifying man-hour requirements, equipment, and material estimates. This may be made as a part of the SOW. Project specifications must be developed carefully since small variations in the specifications may cause a large impact on the project cost. The specifications should be reviewed periodically and modified as needed. In the context of quality improvement these specifications may include the specifications of raw materials, jigs and fixtures, cutting tools, supplies, product and process drawings, layouts, control charts, and check charts. Quality improvement project specifications should be standardized throughout the organization to avoid confusion. Incorrect specifications will adversely affect quality.

4.4 SELLING THE PROJECT PLAN

The project plan must be sold throughout the organization. Different levels of detail will be needed when presenting the project to various groups in the organization. The higher the level of management, the lower the level of detail. Top management will be more interested in the global aspects of the project. For example, when presenting the project to management, it is necessary to specify how the overall organization will be affected by the project. When presenting the project to the supervisory level staff, the most important aspect of the project will be the operational level of detail. At the worker or operator level, the individual will be more concerned about how his or her job will be affected by the project. The project manager or analyst must be able to accommodate these various levels of detail when presenting the plan to both participants and customers of the project. Regardless of the group being addressed, the project presentation should cover the essential elements below at the appropriate levels of detail.

INTRODUCTION
PROJECT DESCRIPTION
   Goals and Objective
   Expected Outcome
PERFORMANCE MEASURE
CONCLUSION

4.5 QUALITY POLICY

One of the primary items in planning for quality improvement is to develop a quality policy or quality mission statement. A policy states what has to be done. A procedure specifies how the policy should be carried out. The quality policy should be needs-based (customer needs, social needs, business needs, etc.) and it should clearly define the objectives of the organization. Quality policies can be disseminated to employees through posted proclamations. Some of the important factors to be considered while making a quality policy are:

- strengths and weaknesses of the organization;
- existing and desired customer interface;
- level of employee involvement;
- tools available to enforce the policy.

Quality manual

Another important step in the planning stage for quality improvement involves the development of a quality manual. British Standard (BS) 4778 defines a quality manual as a 'document setting out the general quality policies, procedures, and practices of an organization.' A quality manual is an important tool for projecting a company's commitment to quality improvement. The quality manual should serve as the 'Bible' of the organization as far as quality is concerned and should be constantly updated as changes occur in the process.

The contents of a quality manual should cover the following:

- quality policy;
- quality procedures;
- planning procedures;
- responsibility matrix;
- design review and control procedures;
- vendor rating scheme;
- in-process control;
- outgoing product control;
- test and measuring equipment control;
- delivery identification, protection, preservation;
- training procedures;
- system audit.

4.6 PROJECT LEADERSHIP

Good leaders lead by demonstrating good examples. Good managers are not necessarily good leaders. People learn and perform best when good examples are available to follow. A leader should have a spirit of performance which stimulates his or her subordinates to perform at their own best. Rather than dictating what needs to be done, a good leader shows what needs to be done. Showing, in this case, does not necessarily imply actual physical demonstration of what is to be done. Rather, it implies projecting a commitment to the function at hand and a readiness to participate as appropriate. The commitment and participative attitude of a leader will help assure the success of a TQM project.

Good leadership is an essential component of a project management approach to TQM. Project leadership involves dealing with managers and supporting personnel across the functional lines of quality improvement. It is a misconception to think that a leader leads only his or her own subordinates. Leadership responsibilities can cover functions vertically, up and down. A good project leader can lead not only his or her subordinates, but also the entire organization, including the highest superiors. Leadership involves recognizing an opportunity to make an improvement in a project and taking the initiative to implement the improvement. In addition to inherent personal qualities, leadership style can be influenced by training, experience, and dedication. A leader should preach and execute actions needed to achieve TQM objectives.

- Back up words with action.
- Adopt a 'do as I do' attitude.
- Avoid a 'do as I say' attitude.
- Participate in joint problem solving.
- Develop and implement workable ideas.

4.7 PROJECT ORGANIZATION

Project organization structures may be selected on the basis of functional specializations, departmental proximity, standard management boundaries, organizational policies, operational relationships, or product requirements.

Formal and informal organizations

The formal organization is an officially sanctioned structure of an organization. Informal organization develops when people organize in an unofficial way to accomplish an objective that is in line with the overall project goal. The informal organization is often very subtle in that not everyone in the organization is aware of its existence. Even some of those who are aware of its existence may not be welcome to participate in it. Friends and close associates often organize informally to pursue project goals. Both formal and informal organizations are practised in any organization, even those such as military organizations that have strict hierarchical structures.

Functional organizations

Projects that are organized along functional lines are normally found in some departmental area of specialization. That is, the project is located in a specific department. For example, projects that involve manufacturing operations may be under the direction of the vice-president of manufacturing while a project involving new technology may be assigned to the technology development department. Functional organization is the most common type of formal organizations. The advantages of functional organization are:

- flexibility in manpower utilization;
- improved productivity of specially skilled personnel;
- enhanced comradeship of technical staff;
- potential for staff advancement along functional lines;
- improved accountability;
- clear line of control.

The disadvantages of functional organization are:

- conflict between project objectives and regular functions;
- shift in project responsibilities, for example, one quality control project may be assigned to the vice-president of manufacturing while a similar quality control project may go to the vice-president of operations;
- potential for an unreceptive attitude towards the project by the surrogate department;
- multiple layers of management between the project personnel and the beneficiaries of the project;

- lack of concentrated effort (divided attention between project tasks and regular tasks).

Product organization

Another approach to organizing a TQM project is to use the end product or goal of the project as the determining factor for the organization structure. This is often referred to as the project organization. The project is set up as a unique entity within the parent organization. It has its own dedicated technical staff and administration. It is linked to the rest of the organization through progress reports, organizational policies, procedures, and funding. The interface between product organized projects and other elements of the organization may be strict or liberal, depending on the organization.

Project organization is common in large, project-driven organizations. Unlike the other organization structures, project organization decentralizes functions. It creates a group consisting of specialized skills around a given task. The project group is sometimes referred to as a team or a task force. Project organization is also common in public and research organizations where specially organized and designated groups are assigned specific functions. A major advantage of project organization is that it gives the project members a feeling of dedication to and identification with a particular project goal. A possible shortcoming is the requirement that the project group be sufficiently funded to be able to operate independently without sharing resources or personnel with other functional groups or programs. At the conclusion of a project, the project team may be reassigned to other projects. The project organization can facilitate the most diverse and flexible grouping of project participants and permits highly dedicated attention to the project at hand.

The advantages of product organization are:

- full authority is given to the project manager;
- members of the project team are directly responsible to the project manager (one boss);
- condensation of communication lines;
- skill development due to project specialization;
- improved motivation, commitment, and concentration;
- quicker decisions due to centralized authority;
- improved morale of belonging to a given project;
- simplicity of structure;
- unity of project purpose.

The disadvantages of product organization are:

- duplication of efforts on different but similar projects;
- monopoly of organizational resources;
- mutually exclusive allocation of resources (one person to one project);

- narrow view of project personnel (as opposed to global organization view);
- reduced skill diversification;
- concern about new job assignment after the project;
- need for a consistent source of project funding.

Matrix organization

Matrix organization represents a mixture of project organization and functional organization. It permits both vertical and horizontal flows of information. The matrix model is sometimes called a multiple-boss organization. It is a model that is becoming increasingly popular as the need for resource sharing increases. TQM projects, for example, require the integration of specialized skills from different functional areas. Under matrix organization, projects are permitted to share physical resources as well as managerial assets.

A matrix organization is suitable where there is multiple managerial accountability and responsibility for a quality improvement function. There are usually two chains of command, horizontal and vertical, dealing with functional and project lines. Figure 4.3 shows an example of a matrix organization structure.

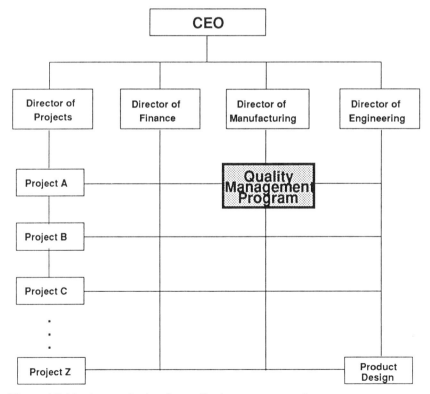

Figure 4.3 Matrix organization for quality improvement project.

The project line in the matrix is usually of a temporary nature, while the functional line is more permanent. The matrix organization is quite dynamic with its actual structure being determined by the prevailing project scenarios. The matrix organization has several advantages and some disadvantages. The advantages are as follows.

- *Consolidation of objectives*: The objectives of the task at hand are jointly shared and pursued by multiple departments.
- *Efficient utilization of resources*: The allocation of company resources is more streamlined. Manpower and equipment can be allocated at the most suitable usage level jointly among departments working towards a common goal.
- *Free flow of information*: Since departments are cooperating rather than competing, there is an unhindered flow of common information both vertically and horizontally in the matrix structure.
- *Interpersonal contacts*: The joint responsibility for projects creates an atmosphere of functional compatibility. Good working relationships that develop under one matrix structure become useful in other projects.
- *High morale*: The success achieved on one project effort motivates workers to cooperate on other projects.
- *Lateral functional interactions*: The multiple responsibility for projects allows workers to be exposed to other functional activities and, thereby, permits smooth transition to other departments, should that become necessary.
- *Post-project interactions*: The matrix structure allows continuity of functions after project conclusion. The functional departments simply redirect their efforts to other responsibilities. Unlike a project organization structure where project shutdown could necessitate layoffs, the matrix structure makes a provision for returning to regular responsibilities.

The disadvantages of the matrix organization are as follows.

- *Multiple bosses*: A major disadvantage of the matrix structure is the fact that workers report to two bosses on a given project. Playing one boss against another is a potential problem in a matrix structure.
- *Power struggle*: A power struggle between the bosses may adversely affect the performance of the project personnel.
- *Complexity of structure*: The number of managers and personnel involved in a given project can easily be confusing. Difficulties can arise with respect to monitoring and controlling personnel activities. Other potential problems are obstruction of information, slow response time, difficulty in resolving conflicts, unclear channels for supervision, and incompatibility of policies and procedures.
- *Overhead cost*: By doubling up the chain of command, the matrix structure leads to higher interdepartmental and intradepartmental overhead costs.

However, as productivity gains are realized, the overhead costs may become negligible.

- *Conflicting priorities*: Since multiple responsibilities are a major characteristic of a matrix organization, it is sometimes difficult to determine which responsibility has higher priority. Each functional manager may view his or her own direct responsibilities as having higher priority than other project responsibilities.

Despite its disadvantages, the matrix organization is widely used in practice. Its numerous advantages tend to outweigh the disadvantages. Besides, the disadvantages can be overcome with proper planning and coordination. This can be achieved through the Triple C model.

Mixed organization

Another possibility for organizing a TQM project is to adopt some combined implementation of functional, product, and matrix models. This permits a combination of the advantages of the various organization structures. The mixed model facilitates flexibility in meeting special problem situations. The structure can adapt to the prevailing needs of the project or the organization. However, a disadvantage is the difficulty in identifying lines of responsibility within a given project. A multilayer matrix organization is another approach suitable for organizing quality improvement projects. This is effective for complex project environments.

4.8 SELECTING A PROJECT MANAGER

A TQM project manager is needed to direct the functional groups within the project organizational structure. The project manager has the overall responsibility for supervising the project planning, scheduling, and control functions. He or she must be very versatile, with a broad range of knowledge covering analytical as well as managerial skills. The project manager must have both the power and authority to effectively pursue quality improvement goals within the limits of the prevailing organizational structure. When selecting a TQM project manager, several desirable characteristics and factors must be considered. These characteristics and factors include:

- commitment to quality;
- analytical and technical background;
- communication skills;
- leadership and managerial skills;
- availability, accessibility, and attentiveness;
- rapport with subordinates, peers, and top management;

- inquisitiveness;
- ability to be a motivator and a facilitator;
- familiarity with company operations;
- familiarity with customer requirements;
- overall personality;
- perseverance;
- technical and administrative credibility.

4.9 WORK BREAKDOWN STRUCTURE

Project decomposition and work simplification are important for enhancing TQM project planning, scheduling, and control. A work breakdown structure (WBS) involves dividing the work into smaller elements called work packages. A work breakdown structure should be used as a hierarchical organization of the work elements contained in a TQM project. Tasks that are contained in the WBS collectively describe the overall project. The WBS serves to describe the link between the end objective and the intermediate tasks. It shows work elements in a conceptual framework for planning, scheduling, and control. The objective of developing a WBS is to study the elemental components of a project in detail. It permits the implementation of the 'divide and conquer' concepts. Overall project planning and control are substantially improved by using WBS. A large project may be broken down into smaller subprojects which may, in turn, be decomposed into task groups. WBS structure has the following advantages:

- it serves as a basis for bottom-up or top-down planning;
- it provides a basis for estimating costs more accurately;
- it helps establish equitable budgeting;
- it helps track time, cost, and performance;
- it facilitates more effective scheduling.

Individual components in a WBS are referred to as WBS elements and the hierarchy of each is designated by a level identifier. Elements at the same level of subdivision are said to be of the same WBS level. Descending levels provide increasingly detailed definition of project tasks. The complexity of a TQM project and the degree of control desired will determine the number of levels in the WBS. The graphical structure of a WBS is similar to an organization chart with different levels associated with different levels of detail about the project. The basic approach to developing a WBS is presented below:

Level 1: Level 1 contains only the final TQM goal.

Level 2: Level 2 contains the major phases or subsections of the project. These phases are usually identified by their adjoining location or by their related purpose.

Level 3: Level 3 contains definable components of the level 2 phases.

Subsequent levels are constructed in more specific details depending on the level of control desired. If a complete WBS is very large, separate WBS diagrams may be drawn for the level 2 components. A specification of work (SOW) or WBS summary should accompany the WBS. A statement of work is a narrative of the work to be done. It should include the objectives of the work, its nature, resource requirements, and tentative schedule. Each WBS element is assigned a code that is used for its identification throughout the project life cycle. Alphanumeric codes may be used to indicate element level as well as task group. The various management phases of a TQM project can be condensed into three major functions of planning, scheduling, and control.

4.10 PROJECT PLANNING

TQM project planning determines the nature of actions and responsibilities needed to achieve quality improvement goals. It entails the development of alternate courses of action and the selection of the best action to achieve the objectives making up the goals. Planning determines what needs to be done, by whom, for whom, and when. Whether it is done for long-range (strategic) purposes or short-range (operational) purposes, planning should address the following components.

1. *Project goal and objectives*: This involves the specification of what must be accomplished at each stage of the project.
2. *Technical and managerial approach*: This involves the determination of the technical and managerial strategies to be employed in pursuing the project goal.
3. *Resource availability*: This requires the allocation of resources for carrying out the actions needed to achieve the project goal.
4. *Project schedule*: This involves a logical and time-based organization of the tasks and milestones contained in the project. The schedule is typically influenced by resource limitations.
5. *Contingency plan and replanning*: This involves the identification of auxiliary actions to be taken in case of unexpected developments in the project.
6. *Project policy*: This involves specifying the general guidelines for carrying out tasks within the project.
7. *Project procedure*: This involves specifying the detailed method for implementing a given policy relative to the tasks needed to achieve the project goal.
8. *Performance standard*: This involves the establishment of a minimum acceptable level of quality for the products of the project.
9. *Tracking, reporting, and auditing*: These involve keeping track of the project plans, evaluating tasks, and scrutinizing the records of the project.

TQM project decisions will involve numerous personnel within the organization with various types and levels of expertise. In addition to the conventional roles of the project manager, specialized roles may be developed within the quality improvement program. Such roles include the following.

1. *Technical specialist*: This person will have responsibility for addressing specific technical requirements of quality improvement. In a large project, there will typically be several technical specialists working together to solve quality problems.
2. *Operations integrator*: This person will be responsible for making sure that all operational components of the project interface correctly to satisfy quality improvement goals. This person should have good technical awareness and excellent interpersonal skills.
3. *Project specialist*: This person has specific expertise related to the specific goals and requirements of the project. Even though a technical specialist may also serve as a project specialist, the two roles should be distinguished. A general electrical engineer may be a technical specialist on the electronics design components of a quality improvement project. However, if the specific setting of the electronics project is in the medical field, then an electrical engineer with expertise in medical operations may be needed to serve as the project specialist.

Project organization is a crucial component of project planning. Organizing a project involves determining the interfaces needed among personnel in order to assure a dedicated pursuit of the project goal. It involves the determination of what activities should be performed in what functional areas and under what supervisory hierarchy. Staffing is a component of organizing. Staffing is the process of defining the required personnel and the assignment of the personnel to appropriate functions with respect to the project goal. The staffing process may include hiring new people, reassignment of existing personnel, training or retraining, and realignment of responsibilities. The Triple C model of communication, cooperation, and coordination, as presented in Chapter 2, is particularly useful for organizing a TQM project.

4.11 PROJECT SCHEDULING

Project scheduling is a major function in project management. A TQM project schedule will show the timing of the efforts and resources committed to the project. A master schedule for the overall effort is often developed for general overview of the project. In addition, detailed work schedules should be developed for specific segments or phases of the project. The detailed schedules serve as operating guides for the personnel.

Project scheduling should be distinguished from sequencing and scheduling in production management, even though the same principles and procedures are applicable to both. Production sequencing involves ordering of operations on each machine (resource) so as to satisfy the sequence of operations required by a job. A sequence of operations on a job may require that the same type of operation be performed on the same job (or product) at different times while the job is in production. This may necessitate repeated routing of the job to the same machine (or resource center) at different times. Production scheduling provides a basis for determining when a job is routed from machine to machine for specific operations. This establishes the starting and finishing times of each operation. Production sequencing and scheduling involve developing relative priorities of operations at each machine in order to meet scheduled due dates of individual jobs. The method of prioritizing jobs is often referred to as the dispatching rule for sending jobs to resource centers. In production management, sequencing and scheduling are performed as complementary functions.

By contrast, project scheduling deals strictly with the timing of tasks that must be performed in a project. This does not require a machine sequencing process. Even when a task requires multiple performance of the same action, each occurrence of the action is viewed as an activity that must be scheduled separately. Thus, project scheduling is a simplified form of the production scheduling problem. Project scheduling can be carried out as the specific means through which the tasks involved in production management are scheduled and accomplished. Project scheduling involves the following functions.

- *Time and resource estimation*: Estimates of the time and resources required to perform activities are made.
- *Basic scheduling*: The basic scheduling computations are performed on a project network by using forward-pass and backward-pass computational procedures. These computations give the earliest and latest start and finish times for each activity. Schedule management often involves performing time–cost trade-off analysis. The scheduling procedure makes use of tools such as CPM (critical path method), PERT (program evaluation and review technique), and Gantt charts. Badiru (1991) presents details of the scheduling tools available for project management.
- *Time–cost trade-offs*: In this function, the time–cost trade-off analysis of activity performance times is conducted to determine the cost of reducing the project duration.
- *Resource allocation*: Constrained resource allocation refers to the process of allocating limited resources to competing activities in a project. Scheduling heuristics or mathematical allocation models are used in allocating the limited resources during the scheduling phase. A data base of resource availability should be developed for each project prior to starting the scheduling process.
- *Resource loading and leveling*: Resource loading develops the profile of the resource units allocated over time. Resource leveling refers to the process of

shifting activities to reduce the period-to-period fluctuations in resource requirements.

- *Schedule control*: When the network plan and schedule have been satisfactorily developed, they are disseminated in final form for operational use. The schedule is tracked and controlled by comparing actual progress to expected progress at selected review times. Schedule tracking facilitates frequent review and revision of the project plan.

4.11.1 Critical path method

The network of activities contained in a project provides the basis for scheduling the project. The critical path method (CPM), and the program evaluation and review technique (PERT) are the two most popular techniques for project network analysis. A project network is the graphical representation of the contents and objectives of the project. The basic project network analysis is typically implemented in three phases: network planning phase; network scheduling phase; and network control phase.

Network planning

Network planning is sometimes referred to as activity planning. This involves the identification of the relevant activities for the project. The required activities and their precedence relationships are determined. Precedence requirements may be determined on the basis of technological, procedural, or imposed constraints. The activities are then represented in the form of a network diagram. The two popular models for network drawing are the activity-on-arrow (AOA) and the activity-on-node (AON) conventions. In the AOA approach, arrows are used to represent activities while nodes represent starting and ending points of activities. In the AON approach, nodes represent activities, while arrows represent precedence relationships. Time, cost, and resource requirement estimates are developed for each activity during the network planning phase. The estimates may be based on historical records, time standards, forecasting, regression functions, or other quantitative models.

Network scheduling

Network scheduling is performed by using forward-pass and backward-pass computational procedures. These computations give the earliest and latest starting and finishing times for each activity. The amount of slack or float associated with each activity is determined. The activity path with the minimum slack in the network is used to determine the critical activities. This path also determines the duration of the project. Resource allocation and time–cost trade-offs are other functions performed during network scheduling.

Network control

Network control involves tracking the progress of a project on the basis of the network schedule and taking corrective actions when needed. An evaluation of actual performance versus expected performance determines deficiencies in the project progress.

Advantages of CPM network analysis

The advantages of project network analysis are presented below.

- Advantages for communication:
  it clarifies project objectives;
  it establishes the specifications for project performance;
  it provides a starting point for more detailed task analysis;
  it presents a documentation of the project plan;
  it serves as a visual communication tool.
- Advantages for control:
  it presents a measure for evaluating project performance;
  it helps determine what corrective actions are needed;
  it gives a clear message of what is expected;
  it encourages team interactions.
- Advantages for team interaction:
  it offers a mechanism for a quick introduction to the project;
  it specifies functional interfaces on the project;
  it facilitates ease of application.

Precedence constraints

Precedence relationships in a CPM network fall into the three major categories listed below:

1. technical precedence;
2. procedural precedence;
3. imposed precedence.

Technical precedence requirements are caused by the technical relationships among activities in a project. For example, in conventional construction, walls must be erected before the roof can be installed. Procedural precedence requirements are determined by policies and procedures. Such policies and procedures are often subjective, with no concrete justification. Imposed precedence requirements can be classified as resource-imposed, state-imposed, or environment-imposed. For example, resource shortages may require that one task be done before another. The current status of a project (e.g. percent completion) may determine that one activity be performed before another. The environment of a project, for example, weather changes, and the effects of concurrent projects, may determine the precedence relationships of the activities in a project.

The primary goal of a CPM analysis of a project is the determination of the 'critical path'. The critical path determines the minimum completion time for a project. The computational analysis involves forward-pass and backward-pass procedures. The forward pass determines the earliest start time and the earliest completion time for each activity in the network. The backward pass determines the latest start time and the latest completion time for each activity. Figure 4.4 shows an example of an activity network using the activity-on-node convention. Conventional network logic is always drawn from left to right. If this convention is followed, there is no need to use arrows to indicate the directional flow in the activity network. The notations used for activity A in the network are explained below:

A: Activity identification
ES: Earliest starting time
EC: Earliest completion time
LS: Latest starting time
LC: Latest completion time
t: Activity duration

During the forward-pass analysis of the network, it is assumed that each activity will begin at its earliest starting time. An activity can begin as soon as the last of its predecessors is finished. The completion of the forward pass determines the earliest completion time of the project. The backward-pass analysis is a reverse of the forward pass. It begins at the latest project completion time and ends at the latest starting time of the first activity in the project network. The rules for implementing the forward-pass and backward-

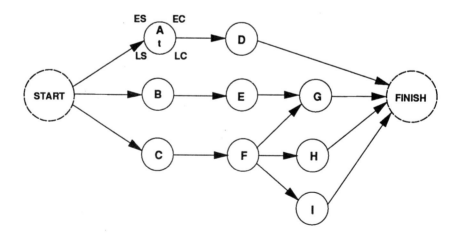

Figure 4.4 Example of activity network (1).

pass analyses in CPM are presented below. These rules are implemented iteratively until the ES, EC, LS, and LC have been calculated for all nodes in the activity network.

Rule 1: Unless otherwise stated, the starting time of a project is set equal to time zero. That is, the first node in the network diagram has an earliest start time of zero. Thus,
ES of first activity = 0.
If a desired starting time is specified, then
ES of first activity = Specified starting time.

Rule 2: The earliest start time (ES) for any activity is equal to the maximum of the earliest completion times (EC) of the immediate predecessors of the activity. That is,
ES = maximum {immediate preceding ECs}.

Rule 3: The earliest completion time (EC) of an activity is the activity's earliest start time plus its estimated time. That is,
EC = ES + {activity time}.

Rule 4: The earliest completion time of a project is equal to the earliest completion time of the very last node in the project network. That is,
EC of project = EC of last activity.

Rule 5: Unless the latest completion time (LC) of a project is explicitly specified, it is set equal to the earliest completion time of the project. This is called the zero project slack convention. That is,
LC of project = EC of project.

Rule 6: If a desired deadline is specified for the project, then
LC of project = specified deadline.
It should be noted that a latest completion time or deadline may sometimes be specified for a project based on contractual agreements.

Rule 7: The latest completion time (LC) for an activity is the smallest of the latest start times of the activity's immediate successors. That is,
LC = minimum {immediate succeeding LSs}.

Rule 8: The latest start time for an activity is the latest completion time minus the activity time. That is,
LS = LC − (activity time).

Illustrative example

Table 4.1 presents the data for a sample project with seven activities. The AON network for the example is given in Figure 4.5. Dummy activities are included in the network to designate single starting and ending points for the network.

Forward pass

The forward pass calculations are shown in Figure 4.6. Zero is entered as the ES for the initial node. Since the initial node for the example is a dummy node,

Table 4.1 Data for sample project for CPM analysis

Activity	Predecessor	Duration (Days)
A	—	2
B	—	6
C	—	4
D	A	3
E	C	5
F	A	4
G	B,D,E	2

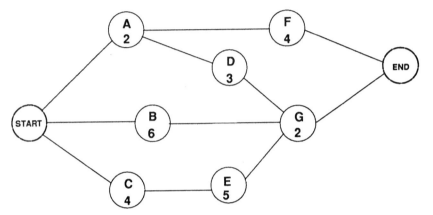

Figure 4.5 Example of activity network (2).

its duration is zero. Thus, EC for the starting node is equal to its ES. The ES values for the immediate successors of the starting node are set equal to the EC of the START node and the resulting EC values are computed. Each node is treated as the 'start' node for its successor or successors. However, if an activity has more than one predecessor, the maximum of the ECs of the preceding activities is used as the activity's starting time. This happens in the case of activity G, whose ES is determined as Max $\{6, 5, 9\} = 9$. The earliest project completion time for the example is 11 days. Note that this is the maximum of the immediate preceding earliest completion times: Max $\{6, 11\} = 11$. Since the dummy ending node has no duration, its earliest completion time is set equal to its earliest start time of 11 days.

Backward pass

The backward pass computations establish the latest start time (LS) and latest completion time (LC) for each node in the network. The results of the backward pass computations are shown in Figure 4.7. Since no deadline is specified, the

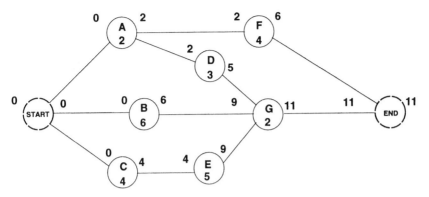

Figure 4.6 Forward pass analysis for CPM example.

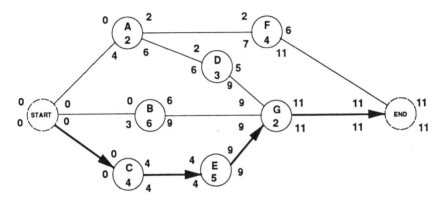

Figure 4.7 Backward pass analysis for CPM example.

latest completion time of the project is set equal to the earliest completion time. By backtracking and using the network analysis rules presented earlier, the latest completion and latest start times are determined for each node. Note that in the case of activity A with two successors, the latest completion time is determined as the minimum of the immediate succeeding latest start times. That is, Min {6, 7} = 6. A similar situation occurs for the dummy starting node. In that case, the latest completion time of the dummy start node is Min {0, 3, 4} = 0. Since this dummy node has no duration, the latest starting time of the project is set equal to the node's latest completion time. Thus, the project starts at time 0 and is expected to be completed by time 11.

Within a project network, there are usually several possible paths, and a number of activities that must be performed sequentially and some activities that may be performed concurrently. If an activity has ES and EC times that are not equal, then the actual start and completion times of that activity may be flexible. The amount of flexibility an activity possesses is called a slack time. The slack time is used to determine the critical activities in the network as discussed below.

Critical activities

The critical path is defined as the path with the least slack in the network diagram. All the activities on the critical path are said to be critical activities. These activities can create bottlenecks in the network if they are delayed. The critical path is also the longest path in the network diagram. In some networks, particularly large ones, it is possible to have multiple critical paths. If there are a large number of paths in the network, it may be very difficult to identify all the critical paths visually. The slack time of an activity is also referred to as its float. There are four basic types of activity slack. They are described below.

- *Total slack (TS)*: Total slack is defined as the amount of time an activity may be delayed from its earliest starting time without delaying the latest completion time of the project. The total slack of an activity is the difference between the latest completion time and the earliest completion time of the activity, or the difference between the latest starting time and the earliest starting time of the activity.
  TS = LC − EC or TS = LS − ES
  Total slack is the measure that is used to determine the critical activities in a project network. The critical activities are identified as those having the minimum total slack in the network diagram. If there is only one critical path in the network, then all the critical activities will be on that one path.
- *Free slack (FS)*: Free slack is the amount of time an activity may be delayed from its earliest starting time without delaying the starting time of any of its immediate successors. Activity free slack is calculated as the difference between the minimum earliest starting time of the activity's successors and the earliest completion time of the activity.
  FS = Min {Succeeding ESs} − EC
- *Interfering slack (IS)*: Interfering slack or interfering float is the amount of time by which an activity interferes with (or obstructs) its successors when its total slack is fully used. This is rarely used in practice. The interfering float is computed as the difference between the total slack and the free slack.
  IS = TS − FS
- *Independent float (IF)*: Independent float or independent slack is the amount of float that an activity will always have, regardless of the completion times of its predecessors or the starting times of its successors. Independent float is computed as: Independent float = Max $\{0, (ES_j - LC_i - t)\}$, where ES_j is the earliest starting time of the preceding activity, LC_i is the latest completion time of the succeeding activity, and t is the duration of the activity whose independent float is being calculated. Independent float takes a pessimistic

view of the situation of an activity. It evaluates the situation whereby the activity is pressured from either side, that is, when its predecessors are delayed as late as possible while its successors are to be started as early as possible. Independent float is useful for conservative planning purposes, but it is not used much in practice. Despite its low level of use, independent float does have practical implications for better project management. Activities can be buffered with independent floats as a way to handle contingencies.

Referring to Figure 4.7, the total slack and the free slack for activity A are calculated, respectively, as:

TS = 6 − 2 = 4 days
FS = Min {2, 2} − 2 = 2 − 2 = 0

Similarly, the total slack and the free slack for activity F are:

TS = 11 − 6 = 5 days
FS = Min {11} − 6 = 11 − 6 = 5 days

Table 4.2 presents a tabulation of the results of the CPM example. The table contains the earliest and latest times for each activity, as well as the total and free slacks. The results indicate that the minimum total slack in the network is zero. Thus, activities C, E, and G are identified as the critical activities. The critical path is highlighted in Figure 4.7 and consists of the following activities: C, E, and G.

The total slack for the overall project itself is equal to the total slack observed on the critical path. The minimum slack in most networks will be zero since the ending LC is set equal to the ending EC. If a deadline is specified for a project, then we would set the project's latest completion time to the specified deadline. In that case, the minimum total slack in the network would be given by: TS_{Min} = (Project Deadline) − EC of the last node.

This minimum total slack will then appear as the total slack for each activity on the critical path. If a specified deadline is lower than the EC at the finish node, then the project will start out with a negative slack. That means that it will be behind schedule before it even starts. It may then become necessary to

Table 4.2 Result of CPM analysis for sample project

Activity	Duration	ES	EC	LS	LC	TS	FS	Critical
A	2	0	2	4	6	4	0	—
B	6	0	6	3	9	3	3	—
C	4	0	4	0	4	0	0	Critical
D	3	2	5	6	9	4	4	—
E	5	4	9	4	9	0	0	Critical
F	4	2	6	7	11	5	5	—
G	2	9	11	9	11	0	0	Critical

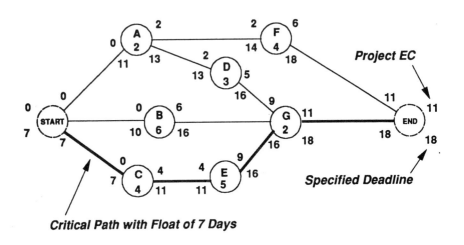

Figure 4.8 CPM network with deadline greater than project EC.

expedite some activities (i.e. crashing) in order to overcome the negative slack. Figure 4.8 shows an example with a specified project deadline. In this case, the deadline of 18 days comes after the earliest completion time of the last node in the network.

Gantt charts

When the results of a CPM analysis are fitted to a calendar time, the project plan becomes a schedule. The Gantt chart is one of the most used tools for presenting a project schedule. A Gantt chart can show planned and actual progress of activities. The time scale is indicated along the horizontal axis, while horizontal bars or lines representing activities are ordered along the vertical axis. As a project progresses, markers are made on the activity bars to indicate actual work accomplished. Gantt charts must be updated periodically to indicate project status.

Figure 4.9 presents the Gantt chart for our illustrative example using the earliest starting (ES) times from Table 4.2. Figure 4.10 presents the Gantt chart for the example based on the latest starting (LS) times. Critical activities are indicated by the shaded bars. Figure 4.9 shows that the starting time of activity F can be delayed from day two until day seven (i.e. TS=5) without delaying the overall project. Likewise, A, D, or both may be delayed by a combined total of four days (TS=4) without delaying the overall project. If all the four days of

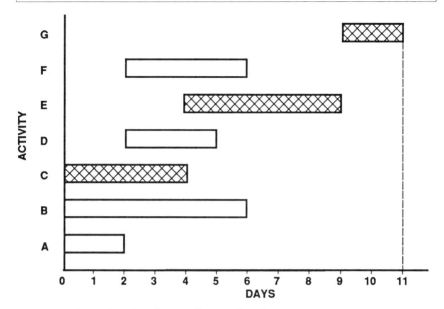

Figure 4.9 Gantt chart based on earliest starting times.

slack are used up by A, then D cannot be delayed. If A is delayed by one day, then D can be delayed by up to three days without causing a delay of G, which determines project completion. The Gantt chart also indicates that activity B may be delayed by up to three days without affecting the project completion time.

In Figure 4.10, the activities are scheduled by their latest completion times. This represents the extreme case where activity slack times are fully used. No activity in this schedule can be delayed without delaying the project. In Figure 4.10, only one activity is scheduled over the first three days. This is compared to the schedule in Figure 4.9 which has three starting activities. The schedule in Figure 4.10 may be useful if there is a situation that permits only a few activities to be scheduled in the early stages of the project. Such situations may involve shortage of project personnel, lack of initial budget, time for project initiation, time for personnel training, allowance for learning period, or general resource constraints. Scheduling of activities based on ES times indicates an optimistic view. Scheduling on the basis of LS times represents a pessimistic approach.

Gantt chart variations

The basic Gantt chart does not show the precedence relationships among activities. However, the relationships can be shown by linking appropriate bars in the chart as shown in Figure 4.11, although the linked bars become cluttered

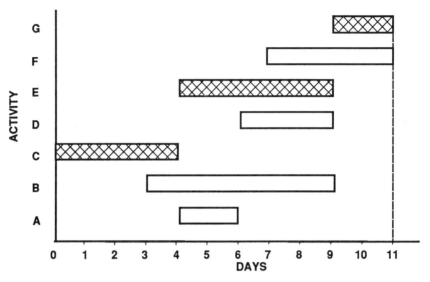

Figure 4.10 Gantt chart based on latest starting times.

and confusing for large networks. Figure 4.12 shows a Gantt chart which presents a comparison of planned and actual schedules. Note that two tasks are in progress at the current time indicated in the figure. One of the on-going tasks is an unplanned task. Figure 4.13 shows a Gantt chart on which important milestones have been indicated. Figure 4.14 shows a Gantt chart in which bars represent a combination of related tasks. Tasks may be combined for scheduling purposes or for conveying functional relationships required on a project. Figure 4.15 presents a Gantt chart of project phases. Each phase is further divided into parts. Figure 4.16 shows a multiple projects Gantt chart. Multiple projects charts are useful for evaluating resource allocation strategies. Resource loading over multiple projects may be needed for capital budgeting and cash flow analysis decisions. Figure 4.17 shows a project slippage chart that is useful for project tracking and control. Other variations of the basic Gantt chart may be developed for specific needs.

4.11.2 Resource consideration

Projects are subject to three major constraints of time limitations, resource constraints, and performance requirements. Since these constraints are difficult to satisfy simultaneously, trade-offs must be made. The smaller the resource base, the longer the project schedule, and the lower the quality of work.

Resource loading refers to the allocation of resources to tasks in a project. A resource loading graph is a graphical representation of resource allocation over

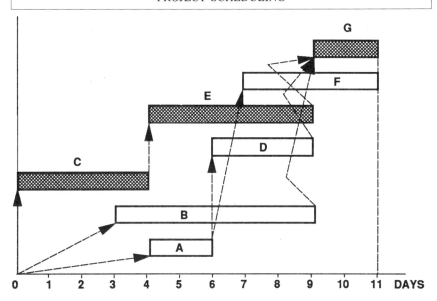

Figure 4.11 Linked bars in Gantt chart.

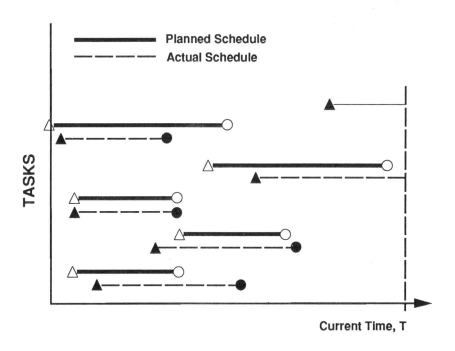

Figure 4.12 Progress monitoring Gantt chart.

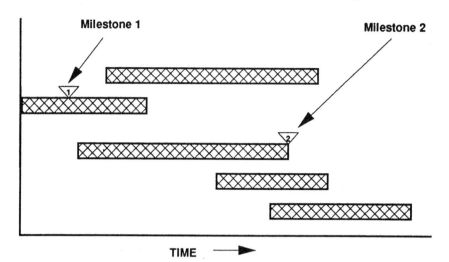

Figure 4.13 Milestone Gantt chart.

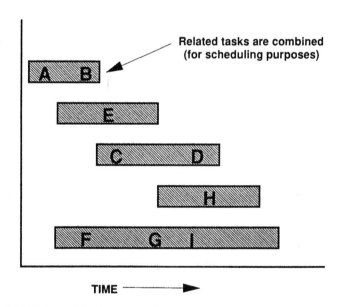

Figure 4.14 Task combination Gantt chart.

time. Figure 4.18 shows an example of a resource loading graph. A resource loading graph may be drawn for the different resource types involved in a project.

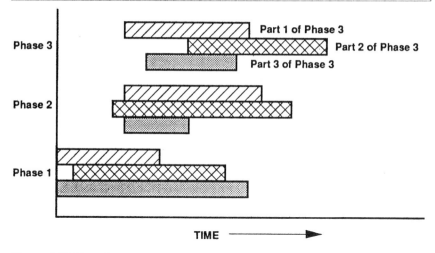

Figure 4.15 Phase-based Gantt chart.

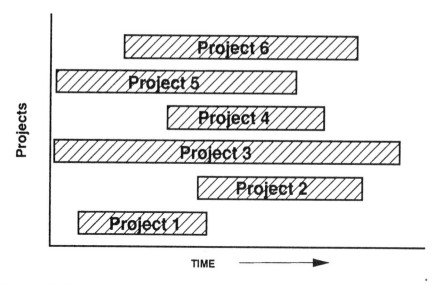

Figure 4.16 Multiple projects Gantt chart.

The graph provides information useful for resource planning and budgeting purposes. A resource loading graph gives an indication of the demand a project will place on an organization's resources. In addition to resource units committed to activities, the graph may also be drawn for other tangible and

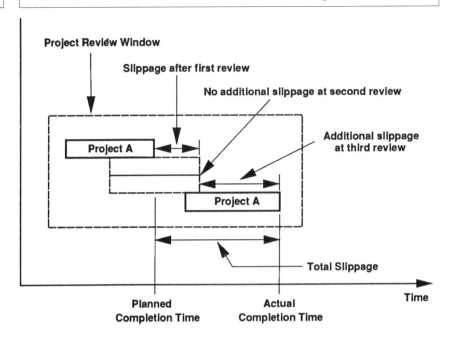

Figure 4.17 Project slippage tracking Gantt chart.

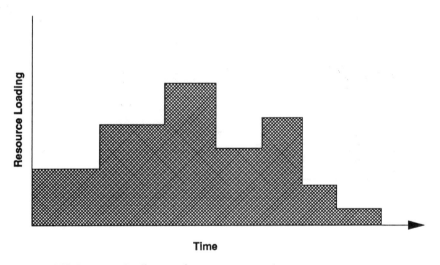

Figure 4.18 Resource loading graph.

intangible resources of an organization. For example, a variation of the graph may be used to present information about the depletion rate of the budget available for a project. If drawn for multiple resources, it can help identify potential areas of resource conflicts. For situations where a single resource unit

Table 4.3 Format for resource availability data base

Resource ID	Brief Description	Special Skills	When Available	Duration of Availability	How Many
Type 1	Technician	Carpentry	8/5/93	Two Months	15
Type 2	Programmer	FORTRAN	12/25/93	Indefinite	2
Type 3	Engineer	Design	Immediate	Five Years	27
•	•	•	•	•	•
•	•	•	•	•	•
•	•	•	•	•	•
Type $n-1$	Operators	Machining	Always	Indefinite	10
Type n	Accountant	Contract Laws	9/2/93	Six Months	1

is assigned to multiple tasks, a variation of the resource loading graph can be developed to show the level of load (responsibilities) assigned to the resource over time. Table 4.3 shows a model of a resource availability data base. The data base is essential when planning resource loading strategies for resource-constrained projects.

Resource leveling refers to the process of reducing the period-to-period fluctuation in a resource loading graph. If resource fluctuations are beyond acceptable limits, actions are taken to move activities or resources around, in order to level out the resource loading graph. For example, it is bad for employee morale and public relations when a company has to hire and lay people off indiscriminately. Proper resource planning will facilitate a reasonably stable level of the work force. Other advantages of resource leveling include simplified resource tracking and control, lower cost of resource management, and improved opportunity for learning. Acceptable resource leveling is typically achieved at the expense of longer project duration or higher project cost. Figure 4.19 shows a somewhat leveled resource loading.

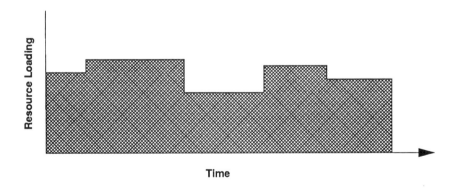

Figure 4.19 Resource leveling graph.

When attempting to level resources, it should be noted that:

1. not all of the resource fluctuations can be eliminated;
2. resource leveling often leads to an increase in project duration.

Resource leveling attempts to minimize fluctuations in resource loading by shifting activities within their available slacks. For small networks, resource leveling can be attempted manually through trial and error procedures. For large networks, resource leveling is best handled by computer software techniques.

4.12 PROJECT CONTROL

Time, cost, and quality form the basis for the operating characteristics of a project. These factors help to determine the basis for project control. Project control is the process of reducing the deviation between actual performance and planned performance. To control a quality improvement project we must be able to measure performance in terms of quality. Measurements are taken on each of the three components of project constraints of time, quality, and cost, as shown in Figure 4.20.

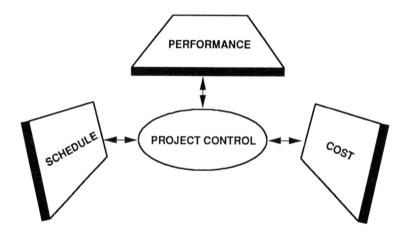

Figure 4.20 Components of project control.

Performance should be expressed in terms of quality, productivity, or any other measure of interest. Cost may be expressed in terms of resource expenditure or budget requirements. Schedule is typically expressed in terms of the timing of activities and the expected project duration. It is impossible to achieve an optimal simultaneous satisfaction of all three project constraints. Consequently, it becomes necessary to compromise one constraint in favor of another. Figure 4.21 presents a model of the trade-offs between quality, time, and resource (cost).

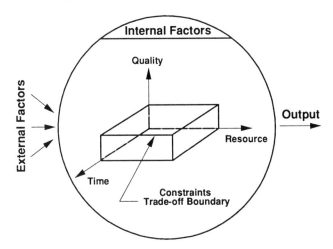

Figure 4.21 Quality–time–resource trade-off.

Better quality can be achieved if more time and resources are available for a TQM project. If lower costs and tighter schedules are desired, then quality may have to be compromised and vice versa. From the point of view of management, the project should be at the highest point along the quality axis. Of course, this represents an extreme case of getting something for nothing. From the point of view of the project personnel, the project should be at the point indicating highest quality, longest time, and most resources. This, of course, may be an unrealistic expectation since time and resources are typically in short supply. Thus, a feasible trade-off strategy must be developed. Even though the trade-off boundary is represented by a box in Figure 4.22, it is obvious that the surface of the box will not be flat. If a multifactor mathematical model is developed for the three factors, the nature of the response surface will vary, depending on the specific interactions of the factors for any given project. A hypothetical response surface is presented in Figure 4.22.

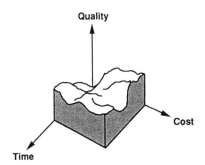

Figure 4.22 Hypothetical quality–time–cost response surface.

If we consider only two of the three constraints at a time, we can better study their respective relationships. Figure 4.23 shows some potential two-factor relationships. In plot (a), performance is modeled as the dependent variable, while cost is the independent variable. Performance increases as cost increases up to a point where performance levels off. If cost is allowed to continue to increase, performance eventually starts to drop. In plot (b), performance is modeled as being dependent on time. The more time that is allowed for a project, the higher the expected performance up to a point where performance levels off. In plot (c), cost depends on time. As project duration increases, cost increases. The increases in cost may be composed of labor cost, raw material cost, and/or cost associated with decreasing productivity. Note that there may be a fixed cost associated with a project even when a time schedule is not in effect.

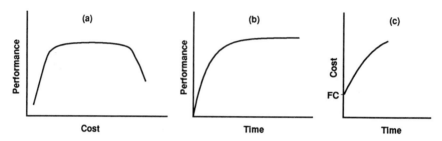

Figure 4.23 Potential trade-off relationships.

Figure 4.24 shows an alternate time–cost trade-off relationship. In this case, the shorter the desired project duration, the higher the cost of the project. If more time is available for the project, then cost can be reduced. However, there is a limit to the possible reduction in cost. After some time, the cost function turns upward due to the increasing cost of keeping manpower and resources tied up on the project for a long period of time. The optimal duration of the project corresponds to the point where the lowest cost is realized.

Some of the causes of schedule, performance, and cost control problems in TQM project are summarized below.

Causes of schedule problems:

- bad time estimates;
- technical problems;
- change of due dates;
- precedence structure;
- unreliable time estimates;
- delay of critical activities.

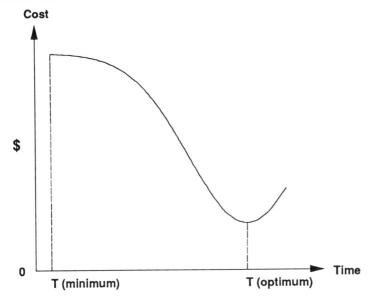

Figure 4.24 Time–cost trade-off example.

Tools for schedule control

The Gantt charts developed in the scheduling phase of a project can serve as the yardstick for measuring project progress. Project status should be monitored frequently. A record should be maintained of the difference between the expected progress of an activity and its actual progress. This information should be conveyed to the appropriate personnel. The more milestones or control points there are in the project, the better the monitoring function. The larger number allows for more frequent and distinct avenues for monitoring the schedule. Thus, problems can be identified and controlled before they accumulate into a bigger problem. Some corrective actions that may be taken for schedule problems include:

- crashing tasks;
- redesigning tasks;
- revising milestones;
- adjusting time estimates;
- changing the scope of work;
- combining related activities;
- introduction of new technology;
- eliminating unnecessary activities.

Causes of performance problems:

- poor quality;
- poor mobility;
- lack of training;
- poor functionality;
- maintenance problems;
- lack of clear objectives.

Tools for performance control

Most project performance problems will not surface until after the project is completed. This makes performance control very difficult. However, every effort should be made to measure all the intermediate factors affecting the project. After-the-fact measurements generally do not facilitate good control. Some of the performance problems may be indicated by time and cost deviations. So, when schedule and cost problems exist, an analysis of how the problems may affect performance should be made. Since project performance requirements usually relate to the performance of the end products, controlling performance problems may necessitate the following:

- modifying policies and procedures;
- introducing improved technology;
- adjusting project specifications;
- improving management control;
- reviewing project priorities;
- changing quality standards;
- allocating more resources;
- improving work ethics.

Causes of cost problems:

- high labor cost;
- inadequate budget;
- poor cost reporting;
- effects of inflation;
- high overhead cost;
- increase in scope of work.

Tools for cost control

Cost control has received extensive coverage in the literature. Numerous accounting and reporting systems have been developed over the years for project cost monitoring and control. Some of the strategies suitable for controlling project cost include:

- reducing labor costs;
- using competitive bidding;
- modification of work process;
- adjusting work breakdown structure;
- improving coordination of project functions;
- improving cost estimation procedures;
- using less expensive raw materials;
- controlling inflationary trends;
- cutting overhead costs.

4.13 PROJECT DECISION MODEL

Badiru (1991) presents a decision model for project management. The model can be implemented for TQM projects. The steps of the model facilitate a proper consideration of the essential elements of decisions in a project environment. These essential elements include problem statement, information, performance measure, decision model, and an implementation of the decision. The steps recommended by Badiru for project decisions are outlined below.

Step 1 Problem statement
A problem involves choosing between competing, and probably conflicting, alternatives. The components of problem solving in project management include:

- describing the problem;
- defining a model to represent the problem;
- solving the model;
- testing the solution;
- implementing and maintaining the solution.

Problem definition is very crucial. In many cases, symptoms of a problem are recognized more readily than its cause and location. Even after the problem is accurately identified and defined, a benefit/cost analysis may be needed to determine if the cost of solving the problem is justified.

Step 2 Data and information requirements
Information is the driving force for the project decision process. Information clarifies the relative states of past, present, and future events. The collection, storage, retrieval, organization, and processing of raw data are important components for generating information. Without data, there can be no information. Without good information, there cannot be a valid decision. The essential requirements for generating information are:

- ensure that an effective data collection procedure is followed;

- determine the type and the appropriate amount of data to collect;
- evaluate the data collected with respect to information potential;
- evaluate the cost of collecting the required data.

For example, suppose a manager is presented with a recorded fact that says, 'sales for the last quarter are 10 000 units.' This constitutes ordinary data. There are many ways of using this data to make a decision depending on the manager's value system. An analyst, however, can ensure the proper use of the data by transforming it into information, such as, 'sales of 10 000 units for the last quarter are low.' This type of information is more useful for the manager for decision-making purposes.

Step 3 Performance measure

A performance measure for the competing alternatives should be specified. The decision maker assigns a perceived worth or value to the available alternatives. Setting a measure of performance is crucial to the process of defining and selecting alternatives.

Step 4 Decision model

A decision model provides the basis for the analysis and synthesis of information, and is the platform over which competing alternatives are compared. To be effective, a decision model must be based on a systematic and logical framework for guiding project decisions. A decision model can be a verbal, graphical, or mathematical representation of the ideas in the decision-making process. A project decision model should have the following characteristics:

- simplified representation of the actual situation;
- explanation and prediction of the actual situation;
- validity and appropriateness;
- applicability to similar problems.

The basic types of decision models for project management are as follows.

Descriptive models: These are directed at describing a decision scenario and identifying the associated problem. For example, a project analyst might use a CPM network model to identify bottleneck tasks in a project.

Prescriptive models: These furnish procedural guidelines for implementing actions. The Triple C approach, for example, is a model that prescribes the procedures for achieving communication, cooperation, and coordination in a project environment.

Predictive models: These models are used to predict future events in a problem environment. They are typically based on historical data about the problem situation. For example, a regression model based on past data may be used to predict future productivity gains associated with expected levels of resource allocation.

Satisficing models: These are models that provide trade-off strategies for achieving a satisfactory solution to a problem within given constraints. Goal programming and other multicriteria techniques provide good satisficing solutions. As an example, these models are helpful for cases when time limitation, resource shortage, and performance requirements constrain the implementation of a project.

Optimizing models: These models are designed to find the best-available solution to a problem, subject to a certain set of constraints. For example, a linear programming model can be used to determine the optimum product mix in a production environment.

In many situations, two or more of the above models may be involved in the solution of a problem. For example, a descriptive model might provide insights into the nature of the problem; an optimization model might provide the optimal set of actions to take in solving the problem; a satisficing model might temper the optimal solution with reality; a prescriptive model might suggest the procedures for implementing the selected solution; and a predictive model might predict the expected outcome of implementing the solution.

Step 5 Making the decision

Using the available data, information, and the decision model, the decision maker will determine the real-world actions that are needed to solve the stated problem. A sensitivity analysis may be useful for determining what changes in parameter values might cause a change in the decision.

Step 6 Implementing the decision

A decision represents the selection of an alternative that satisfies the objective stated in the problem statement. A good decision is useless until it is implemented. An important aspect of a decision is to specify how it is to be implemented. Selling the decision and the project to management requires a well-organized, persuasive presentation. The way a decision is presented can directly influence whether or not it is adopted. The presentation of a decision should include at least the following: an executive summary, technical aspects of the decision, managerial aspects of the decision, resources required to implement the decision, cost of the decision, and time frame for implementing the decision.

4.14 RESOLVING PROJECT CONFLICTS

The Triple C model of project management can help avoid conflicts in a TQM project. However, if conflicts do develop, the model can help in resolving the conflicts. Conflict resolution through Triple C can be achieved by following the rules below:

1. confront the conflict and identify the underlying causes;
2. be cooperative and receptive to negotiation as a mechanism for resolving conflicts;
3. distinguish between proactive, inactive, and reactive behaviors in a conflict situation;
4. use communication to defuse internal strife and competition;
5. recognize that short-term compromise can lead to long-term gains;
6. use coordination to work towards a unified goal.

Process management and control

Quality is on the mind of the customer

Process management is like a balancing act; too much to the left is ineptitude; too much to the right is harmful!
Processes must be managed and controlled properly to facilitate improvement. This chapter discusses the key characteristics of a process that must be understood before improvement can take place.

5.1 PROCESS FORMULATION

Any process contains inputs, transformation activities, and outputs in such a way that the inputs are converted into desired output. The inputs which may come from suppliers may be any or a combination of:

- machines;
- materials;
- measurements;
- methods;
- manpower;
- environment.

   The transformation activities convert the input variables into outputs. These outputs may be end products for customers, some may serve as inputs to some other processes. There is a feedback loop between customers, outputs, transformation activities, inputs and suppliers. In order to improve a process, it is necessary to understand the fundamentals of the above three components. It is also important to know the purpose of the process and be knowledgeable of who the suppliers and customers are. We need to understand the suppliers' process. We should also make sure that they, too, understand our process. It is also important to determine if our customers are receiving what they want. A quality function deployment (QFD) approach can be used for this process.

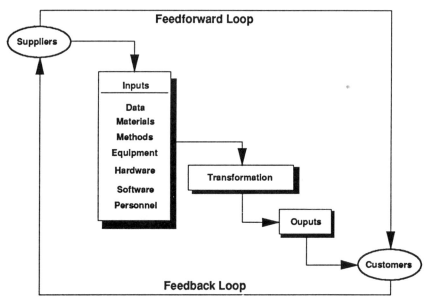

Figure 5.1 Process input, transformation and output.

5.2 KEY QUALITY CHARACTERISTICS

The most important characteristic of a process is the key quality characteristic. The quality of outputs may be described in terms of quality characteristics. A quality characteristic is a description for a process input, transformation activity, or process output. With the description, a measure of quality can be assigned to the particular input, transformation activity, or output. Examples of quality characteristics in a service operation may include information required for service (input), promptness of service (transformation), method of service (transformation), and accuracy of service (output). These quality characteristics help determine the level of customer satisfaction. In a manufacturing operation, examples of quality characteristics may include length, weight, and surface finish.

After the intended features of a product have been defined, the next step is to convert the features to product design and quality characteristics. Quality characteristics should relate to product performance, process performance, customers' needs, and intended product use. Quality function deployment (QFD), fault tree analysis, cause–effect relationships, and design of experiments are some of the methods that can be used to establish quality characteristics. Key quality characteristics are those quality characteristics that determine the performance of a product, process, or service. If a key quality characteristic is not properly established, then performance will be adversely affected.

Operational definitions of key quality characteristics should be developed. An operational definition can help bridge the communication gap between producers, suppliers, and customers in terms of speaking and understanding the same terminologies. An operational definition should include the following:

- important terms associated with the key quality characteristics;
- method for testing the key quality characteristics;
- evaluation criteria such as control limits;
- decision identifier such as Yes or No relating to whether or not the criteria are met;
- actions to be taken based on the outcome of the criteria check.

5.3 PROCESS FLOW DIAGRAM

An effective way of understanding a system and identifying improvement opportunities is to make a flowchart of the system. This flowchart should identify and show processes that add values as well as those that add costs and low quality, and highlight the improvement opportunities. The fundamental theory is that any system consists of two processes (Hacquebord, 1989).

- *Value-added processes*: These are processes that add value to the outputs, and are important for producing the output. A value-added (VA) process is essential for producing the output as expected. The output cannot be achieved without the VA processes at the current level of technology. Without the VA processes, the output will be of less value to the customer.
- *Cost-added processes*: These are processes that do not add value but only add cost, and are not important for producing the output. For process improvement, eliminate or minimize cost-added process steps. A cost-added-only (CAO) process is not essential for producing the output, but may exist for the following reasons:
  (a) occurrence of defects, errors, omissions, or non-conformance;
  (b) redundancy due to the fear of defects;
  (c) waiting period for inspection, clearance, or scheduling;
  (d) correction of errors, rework, or scrap.

5.3.1 Opportunity flowchart

An opportunity flowchart pictorially represents all steps in a process flow diagram. It identifies processes which add values for customers and those which only add costs. The opportunity flowchart can be used to provide a better understanding and communication of a process. It can also highlight improvement opportunities. Figure 5.2 shows the basic symbols used for developing an opportunity flowchart and the layout of the chart.

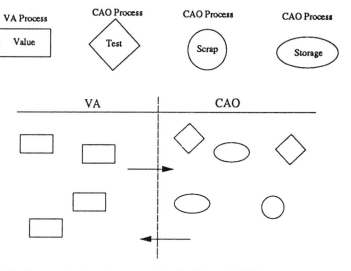

Figure 5.2 Opportunity flowchart symbols for VA and CAO parts.

5.4 MONITORING A PROCESS

The objective of process monitoring is to give the production operators or process engineers the responsibility to investigate and identify problems, and to take corrective action consistently as necessary. One simple and easy-to-use tool for process monitoring is the use of run chart to monitor process behavior and trends over time.

5.4.1 Construction of a run chart

I.   Always plot data in time order
II. Calculate the median

- The first thing is to arrange the data in ascending order
- If the total number of sample is odd, then the median is the middle value.
  Example:
  The ordered values are: 6, 17, 25, 28, 33, 34, 46
  The median is 28.
- If the total number of sample is even, the median is the average of the
  Example:
  The ordered values are: 2, 4, 10, 11, 20, 23, 25, 29
  The median is the average of the two middle values 11 and 20.
  Therefore, the median = 31/2 = 15.5.

III. Draw the median line on the run chart.

Basic rules for run charts

Use the number of runs above and below the median to evaluate a run chart.

- Seven or more points in a row all having the same value.
- Seven or more points continuously increasing or continuously decreasing.
- Eight or more points on the same side of the median.
- Fourteen or more points in a row alternating up and down.
- When counting runs about the median, omit any points on the median.
- When counting runs up or down or alternating, omit entirely any points that repeat the preceding value. The tests for number of runs are presented in Table 5.1. Figure 5.3 shows examples of run charts.

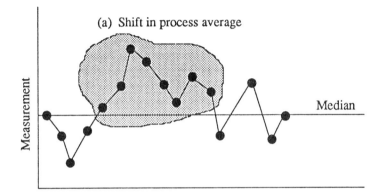

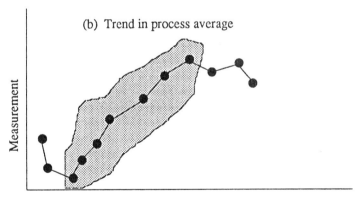

Figure 5.3 Runs chart showing shift and trend in process average.

5.4.2 Process variation

Process varies over time and variation exists in all things. No two processes, two inputs, or two outputs are exactly alike. The different sources of variability

Table 5.1 Tests for number of runs above and below the median

Number of data points	Lower limit for number of runs	Upper limit for number of runs
10	3	8
11	3	9
12	3	10
13	4	10
14	4	11
15	4	12
16	5	12
17	5	13
18	6	13
19	6	14
20	6	15
21	7	15
22	7	16
23	8	17
24	8	17
25	9	17
26	9	18
27	9	19
28	10	19
29	10	20
30	11	20
31	11	21
32	11	22
33	11	22
34	12	23
35	13	23
36	13	24
37	13	25
38	14	25
39	14	26
40	15	26
41	16	26
42	16	27
43	17	27
44	17	28
45	17	29
46	17	30
47	18	30

continued

Table 5.1 *continued*

Number of data points	Lower limit for number of runs	Upper limit for number of runs
48	18	31
49	19	31
50	19	32
60	24	37
70	28	43
80	33	48
90	37	54
100	42	59
110	46	65
120	51	70

which they contain may be large or small, but they are always there. Variation may be hidden by excessive round-off in measurement. Raw data say little about variation. Plots and other data analysis tools are needed to describe and understand variation. All variation is caused, and with proper data collection, the causes contributing the most variation can be identified and attacked for improvement actions. The key to understanding variation is to accept the fact that there are two causes of variation. These are common cause and special cause variations.

Common causes

- These are inherent or natural variations that occur in the inputs and transformation activities. They are part of the process or system.
- They are repeatable, predictable, and possess non-systematic, random-looking appearance.
- They are global (numerous) to the system and originate from many sources, that is, they are not associated with a specific event, operator, etc.
- They provide a process band within which a process is expected to vary.
- The band is determined only by the process and not by the specifications or other means.
- The process will form a distribution due to the stable nature of the process. Figure 5.4 shows examples of stable and unstable processes.

Improvement strategies

- Improvement or reduction of variability requires a change in the inputs and transformation activities that have great influence on process or system outputs.

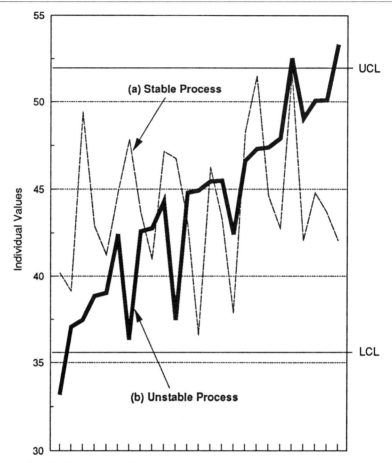

Figure 5.4 Stable and unstable processes.

- Do not attempt to compensate for an individual point. This may lead to tampering or over-controlling of process.
- Management should be personally involved in leading the efforts to change and improve a process or system of common causes. This is because common causes are global in nature, and the solution usually requires management actions in improving or making a fundamental change in the process itself.

Statistical tool

One of the statistical tools useful in studying a process that is in a state of statistical control, and therefore made up of only common cause variations, is the process capability study. In this study, we can either examine the overall capability of the process (C_p and C_{pk}), or examine the individual components or sources of variability which go into the overall capability (nested design). These tools are covered in Chapter 6.

Special causes

- These are variations due to process inputs and transformation activities that contribute sporadically to the process outputs' variability. They are not part of the system, but originate from outside the system.
- They are localized to a specific operator, shift, or piece of equipment, and therefore not part of the process or system.
- Special causes can be reduced, but need to be identified and eliminated because their presence makes it difficult to identify and analyze the common cause variation effectively.
- By eliminating special causes, variation will be reduced, quality will improve, process will be predictable, and unnecessary and costly process tampering will be eliminated.
- Control charts can be used to identify the variability, due to one or more special causes.
- The process or system variability is defined without special causes because they are sporadic contributors, due to specific circumstances coming from outside the process or system.
- The process has no distribution due to the unstable nature of the process. Example of an unstable process was shown earlier in Figure 5.4.

Improvement strategies

- Whenever a control chart signals a special cause, search immediately for what was done differently on that occasion.
- The discovery of special causes of variation is usually the responsibility of someone who is directly connected with the operation. This is because special causes are local in nature, therefore they can be corrected at the point where the effect took place with little or no management involvement.
- Do not make a fundamental change in the process; identify and permanently remove the special cause so as to prevent recurrence.
- For cases where the cause is unknown or cannot be fixed, process adjustment can be made.

The statistical tool useful in studying a process that is out of control is the control chart.

5.5 DIAGNOSING A PROCESS

Data analysis is the basic approach to diagnosing a process. Before diagnosing a process, it is important to collect data that are traceable so as to assist in understanding the current state of the process. Data should be collected over time, and the objectives and goals for collecting the data should be clearly stated in advance. The operational definition of the quality characteristic of interest should also be clearly defined.

5.5.1 Data collection strategy

Proper sampling techniques should be used in collecting data. This is usually problem dependent. There are different types of data. These are:

- variables data;
- attributes data;
- countable data;
- rating data;
- ranking data.

Data measurement scales

The different examples of data measurement scales presented by Badiru (1991a) are applicable to the development of a data collection strategy for quality improvement. The examples are as follows.

1. *Nominal scale* is the lowest level of measurement scales. It classifies items into categories. The categories are mutually exclusive and collectively exhaustive. That is, the categories do not overlap and they cover all possible categories of the characteristics being observed. Operator sex, type of automobile, job classification, and color are some examples of measurements on a nominal scale.
2. *Ordinal scale* is distinguished from a nominal scale by the property of order among the categories. An example is the process of prioritizing tasks for resource allocation. We know that first is above second, but we do not know how far above. Similarly, we know that better is preferred to good, but we do not know by how much. In quality control, the ABC classification of items based on the Pareto distribution is an example of a measurement on an ordinal scale.
3. *Interval scale* is distinguished from an ordinal scale by having equal intervals between the units of measure. The assignment of quality ratings ranging from 0 to 100 to a product is an example of a measurement on an interval scale. Even though an item may have a rating of zero, it does not mean that the item has no worthy quality characteristic at all. Similarly, a score of zero on an examination does not imply that a student knows

absolutely nothing about the material covered by the examination. Temperature is a good example of an item that is measured on an interval scale. Even though there is a zero point on the temperature scale, it is an arbitrary relative measure. No one can touch an item and proclaim that 'it is zero degrees Fahrenheit cold!' Other examples of interval scale are IQ measurements and aptitude ratings.

4. *Ratio scale* has the same properties of an interval scale, but with a true zero point. For example, an estimate of zero time unit for the duration of a task is a ratio scale measurement. Other examples of items measured on a ratio scale are volume, length, height, weight, and inventory level. Many of the items measured in a process and quality improvement program will be on a ratio scale.

In addition to the measurement scale, data can be classified based on their inherent nature. Examples of the relevant classifications are transient data, recurring data, static data, and dynamic data. Transient data is defined as a volatile set of data that is encountered once during an expert system consultation and is not needed again. Transient data need not be stored in a permanent data base record unless it may be needed for future analysis or uses.

Recurring data refers to data that is encountered frequently enough to necessitate storage on a permanent basis. Recurring data may be further categorized into static data and dynamic data. A recurring data that is static will retain its original parameters and values each time it is encountered during an expert system consultation. A recurring data that is dynamic has the potential for taking on different parameters and values each time it is encountered.

For proper data analysis, data should be recorded in such a way that the structure and format are easy to use and understand. This will enable the analyst to identify possible stratifications and populations that exist in the data, if any. The data structure can be described as follows:

- objective(s) of the data collection;
- quality characteristics of the measurement with clear operational definition;
- date of collection;
- identify all operators taking the measurements;
- identify instruments or machines used;
- if samples are coming from more than one process, identify the process;
- identify all other sources of the data collection, including different sites, labs, method, material, etc.

5.5.2 Sample size determination

The success of process analysis depends on the quality and integrity of the data used for the analysis. Since 100% (exhaustive) evaluation is not possible for most processes, a representative sample must be drawn from the process. Determination of a proper sample size is very essential for assuring a high degree of confidence in the results of process analysis. Process experiments are performed with the objective of being $100(1 - \alpha)\%$ confident that the estimate of a parameter is within e (error) units of the actual value of the unknown parameter. For example, we may want to be 95% confident that our estimate is within e units of μ. The question is: How large should our sample size, n, be in order to achieve that level of confidence?

We know that:

$$P\left(\bar{X} - z_{\alpha/2} \ \frac{\sigma}{\sqrt{n}} \le \mu \le \bar{X} + z_{\alpha/2} \ \frac{\sigma}{\sqrt{n}} \right) = 1 - \alpha,$$

which gives us the probability that the true mean is within the specified end points. Therefore, we must choose n such that:

$$e = z_{\alpha/2} \ \frac{\sigma}{\sqrt{n}}$$

That is:

$$n = \frac{\sigma^2 (z_{\alpha/2})^2}{e^2}$$

The above expression requires a knowledge of the process variance, σ^2. For many processes, the true variance may not be known. In such cases, we must use an estimate of the variance based on previous experience or pilot study. The required sample size increases with an increase in the desired confidence level. If we cannot collect a large sample, then we must either decrease our confidence level or increase the acceptable error level.

5.5.3 Process data analysis

Data analysis refers to the various mathematical and graphical operations that can be performed on process data to elicit the inherent information contained in the data. The manner in which process data are analyzed and presented can significantly affect how the inherent information is perceived by the decision maker. Misuse, mishandling, or mismanagement of data can lead to catastrophic process problems. The examples presented in this section illustrate how the basic data analysis techniques can be used to convey important information for process management and control.

It is very important to establish if a process is in control over time before any further analysis can be performed. If a process is out of control, data analysis based on descriptive statistics is of no significance.

In many cases, data are represented as the answer to direct questions such as: When is the process completion time? Who is responsible for process maintenance? What resources are available for the process? What are the quarterly yields of the process for the past two years? Is the process stable or unstable? Is process quality low, average, or high? Who is the person in charge of the process? Answers to these types of questions constitute data of different forms or expressed on different scales such as nominal scale, ordinal scale, interval scale, or ratio scale. The resulting data may be qualitative or quantitative. Different techniques are available for analyzing the different types of data. This section discusses some of the basic techniques for data analysis. The data presented in Table 5.2 is used to illustrate the data analysis techniques.

Table 5.2 Quarterly yields from four processes (in $1000s)

Process	Quarter 1	Quarter 2	Quarter 3	Quarter 4	Row Total
A	3 000	3 200	3 400	2 800	12 400
B	1 200	1 900	2 500	2 400	8 000
C	4 500	3 400	4 600	4 200	16 700
D	2 000	2 500	3 200	2 600	10 300
Column Total	10 700	11 000	13 700	12 000	47 400

Raw data

Raw data consist of ordinary observations recorded about an attribute of a process. Examples of attributes for which data may be collected for process management and control are cost, performance, duration, product quality, and resource availability. Raw data should be organized into a format suitable for visual review and computational analysis. The data in Table 5.2 represent the quarterly yields from each of four multiple processes: Process A, Process B, Process C, and Process D. The yields are expressed in terms of dollar values. For example, the data for quarter number one indicate that Process C produced the highest yield of $4 500 000 while Process B yielded the lowest yield of $1 200 000. Figure 5.5 presents the raw data of process yield as a line graph over time. The same information is presented as a multiple bar chart in Figure 5.6. Note that we have data for only four quarters. This is not sufficient to determine if the processes are in control. We shall, however, assume that the processes are in control and we shall proceed with the illustrative data analysis.

Total yield

Total or sum is a measure that indicates the overall effect of a particular variable. If X_1, X_2, X_3, ..., X_n represent a set of n observations (e.g. yields), then the total is computed as:

$$T = \sum_{i=1}^{n} X_i.$$

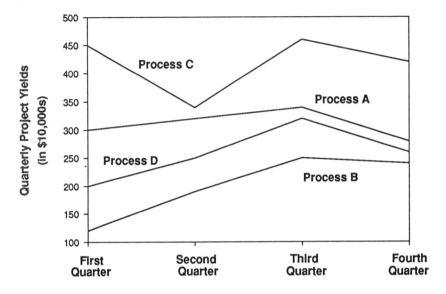

Figure 5.5 Line graph of quarterly process yields.

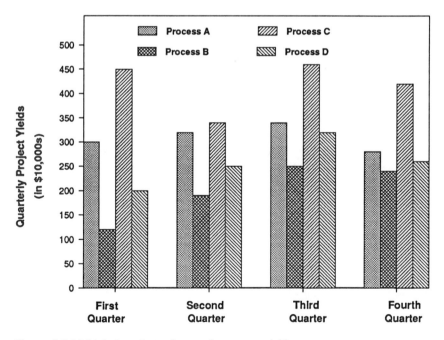

Figure 5.6 Multiple bar chart of quarterly process yields.

For the data in Table 5.2, the total yield for each process is shown in the last column. The totals indicate that Process C produced the largest total yield over the four quarters under consideration, while Process B produced the lowest total yield. The last row of the table shows the total yield for each quarter. The totals reveal that the largest yield occurred in the third quarter. The first quarter brought in the lowest total yield. The grand total yield for the four processes over the four quarters is shown as $47 400 000 in the last cell in the table. Figure 5.7 presents the quarterly total yields as stacked bar charts. Each segment in a stack of bars represents the yield contribution from a particular process. The total yields for the four processes over the four quarters are shown in a pie chart in Figure 5.8. The percentage of the overall yield contributed by each process is also shown in the pie chart.

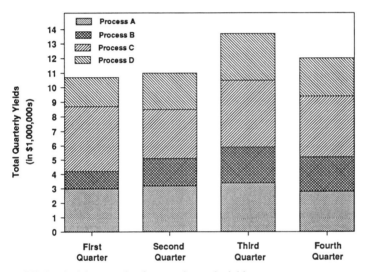

Figure 5.7 Stacked bar graph of quarterly total yields.

Average yield

Average is one of the most used measures in data analysis. Given n observations (e.g. yield), $X_1, X_2, X_3, \ldots, X_n$, the average of the observations is computed as:

$$\bar{X} = \frac{\sum\limits_{i=1}^{n} X_i}{n}$$

$$= \frac{T}{n}.$$

For the data in Table 5.2, the average quarterly yields for the four processes are:

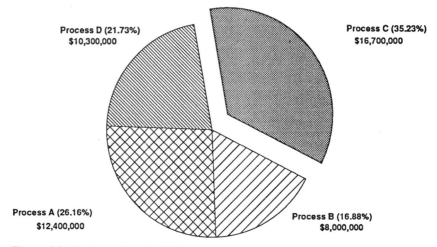

Figure 5.8 Pie chart of total yield per process.

$$\bar{X}_A = \frac{(3000 + 3200 + 3400 + 2800)(\$1\ 000)}{4}$$

$$= \$3\ 100\ 000.$$

$$\bar{X}_B = \frac{(1200 + 1900 + 2500 + 2400)(\$1\ 000)}{4}$$

$$= \$2\ 000\ 000.$$

$$\bar{X}_C = \frac{(4500 + 3400 + 4600 + 4200)(\$1\ 000)}{4}$$

$$= \$4\ 175\ 000.$$

$$\bar{X}_D = \frac{(2000 + 2500 + 3200 + 2600)(\$1\ 000)}{4}$$

$$= \$2\ 575\ 000.$$

Similarly, the expected average yield per process for the four quarters are as presented below:

$$\bar{X}_1 = \frac{(3000 + 1200 + 4500 + 2000)(\$1\ 000)}{4}$$

$$= \$2\ 675\ 000.$$

$$\bar{X}_2 = \frac{(3200 + 1900 + 3400 + 2500)(\$1\ 000)}{4}$$

$$= \$2\ 750\ 000.$$

$$\bar{X}_3 = \frac{(3400 + 2500 + 4600 + 3200)(\$1\ 000)}{4}$$

$$= \$3\ 425\ 000.$$

$$\bar{X}_4 = \frac{(2800 + 2400 + 4200 + 2600)(\$1\,000)}{4}$$

$$= \$3\,000\,000.$$

The above values are shown in a bar chart in Figure 5.9. The average yield from any of the four processes at any given quarter is calculated as the sum of all the observations divided by the number of observations. That is,

$$\bar{X} = \frac{\sum\limits_{i=1}^{N} \sum\limits_{j=1}^{M} X_{ij}}{K},$$

where:

N = number of processes
M = number of quarters
K = total number of observations $(K = NM)$

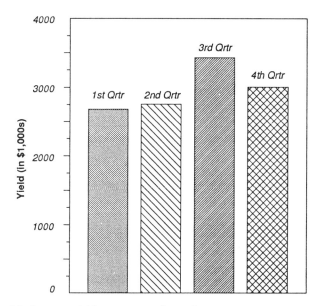

Figure 5.9 Average yield per process for each quarter.

For the data in Table 5.2, overall average per process per quarter is:

$$\bar{X} = \frac{\$47\,400\,000}{16}$$

$$= \$2\,962\,500.$$

As a cross-check, the sum of the quarterly averages should be equal to the sum of the process yield averages, which is equal to the grand total divided by four. That is,

$$(2675 + 2750 + 3425 + 3000)(\$1\ 000) = (3100 + 2000 + 4175 + 2575)(\$1\ 000)$$
$$= \$11\ 800\ 000$$
$$= \$47\ 400\ 000/4.$$

The cross-check procedure above works because we have a balanced table of observations. That is, we have four processes and four quarters. If there were only three processes, for example, the sum of the quarterly averages would not be equal to the sum of the process averages.

Median yield

The median is the value that falls in the middle of a group of observations arranged in order of magnitude. One half of the observations is above the median and the other half is below the median. The method of determining the median depends on whether or not the observations are organized into a frequency distribution. For unorganized data, it is necessary to arrange the data in an increasing or decreasing order before finding the median. Given K observations (e.g. yields), X_1, X_2, X_3, ..., X_K, arranged in increasing or decreasing order, the median is identified as the value in position $(K+1)/2$ in the data arrangement if K is an odd number. If K is an even number, then the average of the two middle values is considered to be the median. If the data in Table 5.2 are arranged in increasing order, we would get the following: 1200, 1900, 2000, 2400, 2500, 2500, 2600, 2800, 3000, 3200, 3200, 3400, 3400, 4200, 4500, 4600.

The median is then calculated as: $(2800 + 3000)/2 = 2900$. Thus, half of the recorded yields are expected to be above \$2 900 000, while half are expected to be below that amount. Figure 5.10 presents a bar chart of the yield data arranged in increasing order. The median is anywhere between the eighth and ninth values in the ordered data above.

Quartiles and percentiles

The median discussed above is a position measure because its value is based on its position in a set of observations. Other measures of position are quartiles and percentiles. There are three quartiles which divide a set of data into four equal categories. The first quartile, denoted Q1, is the value below which one-fourth (one-quarter) of all the observations in the data set fall. The second quartile, denoted Q2, is the value below which two-fourths or one-half of all the observations in the data set fall. The third quartile, denoted Q3, is the value below which three-fourths of the observations fall. The second quartile is identical to the median. It is technically incorrect to talk of the fourth quartile because that will imply that there is a point within the data set below which all the data points fall: a contradiction! A data point cannot lie within the range of the observations and at the same time exceed all the observations, including itself.

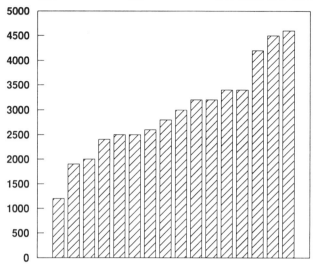

Figure 5.10 Bar chart of ordered data.

The concept of percentiles is similar to the concept of quartiles except that reference is made to percentage points. There are 99 percentiles that divide a set of observations into 100 equal parts. The X percentile is the value below which $X\%$ of the data fall. Thus, the 99th percentile refers to the point below which 99% of the observations fall. The three quartiles discussed previously are regarded as the 25th, 50th, and 75th percentiles. As was explained above, it would be technically incorrect to talk of the 100th percentile. In performance ratings, such as product quality evaluation, the higher the percentile of a product, the better the product. In many cases, recorded data are classified into categories that are not indexed to numerical measures. In such cases, other measures of central tendency or position will be needed. An example of such a measure is the mode.

The mode

The mode is defined as the value that has the highest frequency in a set of observations. When the recorded observations can only be classified into categories, the mode can be particularly helpful in describing the data. Given a set of K observations (e.g. yields), $X_1, X_2, X_3, \ldots, X_K$, the mode is identified as that value that occurs more than any other value in the set. Sometimes, the mode is not unique in a set of observations. For example, in Table 5.2, 2500, 3200, and 3400 all have the same number of occurrences. Thus, each of them is a mode of the set of yield observations. If there is a unique mode in the set of observations, then the data is said to be unimodal. The mode is very useful in expressing the central tendency of a process having qualitative characteristics such as color. The three modes in the raw data can be easily identified in Figure 5.10.

Range of yield

The range is determined by the two extreme values in a set of observations. Given K observations (e.g. yields), X_1, X_2, X_3, ..., X_K, the range of the observations is simply the difference between the lowest and the highest observations. This measure is useful when one wants to know the extent of extreme variations in a factor such as process yield. The range of the yields presented in Table 5.2 is ($4\,600\,000 - $1\,200\,000) = $3\,400\,000$. Because of its dependency on only two values, the range tends to increase as the sample size increases. Furthermore, it does not provide a measurement of the variability of the observations relative to the center of the distribution. This is why the standard deviation is normally used as a more reliable measure of dispersion than the range.

The variability of a distribution is generally expressed in terms of the deviation of each observed value from the sample average. If the deviations are small, the set of data is said to have low variability. The deviations provide information about the degree of dispersion in a set of observations. Unfortunately, a general formula to evaluate the variability of data cannot be based on the deviations. This is because some of the deviations are negative while some are positive and the sum of all the deviations is equal to zero. One possible solution to this problem is to compute the average deviation.

Average deviation

The average deviation is the average of the absolute values of the deviations from the sample average. Given K observations, X_1, X_2, X_3, ..., X_K, the average deviation of the data is computed as:

$$\bar{D} = \frac{\sum_{i=1}^{K} |X_i - \bar{X}|}{K}.$$

Table 5.3 shows how the average deviation is computed for the data presented earlier in Table 5.2. One of the most serious disadvantages of the average of deviation measure is that the procedure ignores the sign associated with each deviation. Despite this disadvantage, its simplicity and ease of computation makes it especially useful to users with limited knowledge of statistical methods. In addition, a knowledge of the average deviation helps in understanding the standard deviation, which is a very important measure of dispersion.

Table 5.3 Computation of average deviation, standard deviation, and variance

Observation Number (i)	Recorded Observation X_i	Deviation from Average $X_i - \bar{X}$	Absolute Value $|X_i - \bar{X}|$	Square of Deviation $(X_i - \bar{X})^2$
1	3 000	37.5	37.5	1 406.25
2	1 200	−1 762.5	1 762.5	3 106 406.30
3	4 500	1 537.5	1 537.5	2 363 906.30
4	2 000	−962.5	962.5	926 406.25
5	3 200	237.5	237.5	56 406.25
6	1 900	−1 062.5	1 062.5	1 128 906.30
7	3 400	437.5	437.5	191 406.25
8	2 500	−462.5	462.5	213 906.25
9	3 400	437.5	437.5	191 406.25
10	2 500	−462.5	462.5	213 906.25
11	4 600	1 637.5	1 637.5	2 681 406.30
12	3 200	237.5	237.5	56 406.25
13	2 800	−162.5	162.5	26 406.25
14	2 400	−562.5	562.5	316 406.25
15	4 200	1 237.5	1 237.5	1 531 406.30
16	2 600	−362.5	362.5	131 406.25
Total	47 400.0	0.0	11 600.0	13 137 500.25
Average	2 962.5	0.0	725.0	821 093.77
Square Root				906.14

Sample variance

Sample variance is the average of the squared deviations computed from a set of observations. If the variance of a set of observations is large, the data are said to have a large variability. For example, a large variability in process performance may indicate a lack of consistency or improper methods in the process. Given K observations, $X_1, X_2, X_3, \ldots, X_K$, the sample variance of the data is computed as:

$$s^2 = \frac{\sum_{i=1}^{K} (X_i - \bar{X})^2}{K - 1}.$$

The variance can also be computed by the following alternate formula:

$$s^2 = \frac{\sum_{i=1}^{K} X_i^2 - \left(\frac{1}{K}\right)\left[\sum_{i=1}^{K} X_i\right]^2}{K - 1}.$$

$$s^2 = \frac{\sum_{i=1}^{K} X_i^2 - K(\bar{X})^2}{K - 1}.$$

Using the first formula, the sample variance of the data in Table 5.3 is calculated as:

$$s^2 = \frac{13\ 137\ 500.25}{16 - 1}$$

$$= 875\ 833.33.$$

Note that the average calculated in the last column of Table 5.3 is obtained by dividing the total for that column by 16 instead of $16 - 1 = 15$. Thus, that average is not the correct value of the sample variance. However, as the number of observations gets very large, the average as computed in Table 5.3 will become a close estimate for the correct sample variance. Statisticians generally make distinction between the two values by referring to the average calculated in Table 5.3 as the population variance when K is very large, and referring to the average calculated by the formulas above as the sample variance particularly when K is small. Thus, for our example, the population variance is given by:

$$\sigma^2 = \frac{\sum_{i=1}^{K} (X_i - \bar{X})^2}{K}$$

$$= \frac{13\ 137\ 500.25}{16}$$

$$= 821\ 093.77,$$

while the sample variance, as shown previously, is given by:

$$s^2 = \frac{\sum_{i=1}^{K} (X_i - \bar{X})^2}{K - 1}$$

$$= \frac{13\ 137\ 500.25}{(16 - 1)}$$

$$= 875\ 833.33.$$

The tabulation of the raw data and the computations shown in Table 5.3 can be quite laborious. For this reason, software tools such as spread-sheet programs are recommended for process data analysis.

Standard deviation

The sample standard deviation of a set of observations is the positive square root of the sample variance. The use of variance as a measure of variability has some drawbacks. For example, the knowledge of the variance is helpful only when two or more sets of observations are compared. Because of the squaring operation, the variance is expressed in square units rather than the original units of the raw data. To get a reliable feel for the variability in the data, it is necessary to restore the original units by performing the square root operation on the variance. This is why standard deviation is a widely recognized measure of variability. Given K observations, $X_1, X_2, X_3, \ldots, X_K$, the sample standard deviation of the data is computed as:

$$s = \sqrt{\frac{\sum_{i=1}^{K} (X_i - \bar{X})^2}{K - 1}}.$$

As in the case of the sample variance, the sample standard deviation can also be computed by the following alternate formulae:

$$s = \sqrt{\frac{\sum_{i=1}^{K} X_i^2 - \left(\frac{1}{K}\right)\left[\sum_{i=1}^{K} X_i\right]^2}{K - 1}}.$$

$$s = \sqrt{\frac{\sum_{i=1}^{K} X_i^2 - K(\bar{X})^2}{K - 1}}.$$

Using the first formula, the sample standard deviation of the data in Table 5.3 is calculated as:

$$s = \sqrt{\frac{13\ 137\ 500.25}{16 - 1}}$$

$$= \sqrt{875\ 833.33}$$

$$= 935.8597.$$

Thus, we can say that the variability in the expected yield per process per quarter is \$935 859.70. As was previously explained for the sample variance, the population sample standard deviation is given by:

$$\sigma = \sqrt{\frac{\sum_{i=1}^{K} (X_i - \bar{X})^2}{K}}$$

$$= \sqrt{\frac{13\ 137\ 500.25}{16}}$$

$$= \sqrt{821\ 093.77}$$

$$= 906.1423,$$

while the sample standard deviation is given by:

$$s = \sqrt{\frac{\sum_{i=1}^{K} (X_i - \bar{X})^2}{K - 1}}$$

$$= \sqrt{\frac{13\ 137\ 500.25}{(16 - 1)}}$$

$$= \sqrt{875\ 833.33}$$

$$= 935.8597.$$

The basic data analysis presented above can play a significant role in conveying quick information about process requirements and performance. Thus, prompt decision making can be effected without resorting to any complex mathematical or statistical procedures. Readers interested in detailed coverage of statistical techniques should consult the many books available on the subject.

Descriptive statistics

Descriptive statistics refers to analyses that are performed in order to describe the nature of a process or operation. The analyses presented previously fall under the category of descriptive statistics because they are concerned with summary calculations and graphical display of observations.

Inferential statistics

Inferential statistics refers to the process of drawing inferences about a process based on a limited observation of the process. The techniques presented below fall under the category of inferential statistics. Inferential statistics is of more interest to many practitioners because it is more dynamic and it provides generalizations about a population by investigating only a portion of the population. The portion of the population investigated is referred to as a sample. As an example, the expected duration of a proposed task can be inferred from several previous observations of the durations of identical tasks. Another set of tools used in statistical analysis involve deductive statistics and inductive statistics.

Deductive statistics

Deductive statistics involves assigning properties to a specific item in a set based on the properties of a general class covering the set. For example, if it is known that 90% of processes in a given organization fail, then deduction can be used to assign a probability of 90% to the event that a specific process in the organization will fail.

Inductive statistics

Inductive statistics involves drawing general conclusions from specific facts. That is, inferences about populations are drawn from samples. For example, if 95% of a sample of 100 people surveyed in a 5000-person organization favor a particular process, then induction can be used to conclude that 95% of the personnel in the organization favor the process.

The different types of statistics play important roles in process management and control. Frequently, inferences must be made about such things as expected duration, performance, resource utilization, and equipment failures.

Sample space and sampling

A sample space of an experiment is the set of all possible distinct outcomes of the experiment. An experiment is some process that generates distinct sets of observations. The simplest and most common example is the experiment of tossing a coin to observe whether heads or tails will show up. An outcome is a distinct observation resulting from a single trial of an experiment. In the experiment of tossing a coin, 'heads' and 'tails' are the two possible outcomes. Thus, the sample space consists of only two items.

There are numerous examples of statistical experiments in a process management environment. An experiment may involve simply checking to see whether it rains or not on a given day. Another experiment may involve counting how many tasks fall behind schedule during a process. Another example of an experiment may involve recording how long it takes to perform a given activity in each of several trials. The outcome of any experiment is frequently referred to as a random event because the outcomes of the experiment occur in a random fashion. We cannot predict with certainty what the outcome of a particular trial of the experiment would be.

Sample

A sample is a subset of a population that is selected for observation and statistical analysis. Inferences are drawn about the population based on the results of the analysis of the sample. The reasons for using sampling rather than complete population enumeration are:

1. it is more economical to work with a sample;
2. there is a time advantage to using a sample;
3. populations are typically too large to work with;
4. a sample is more accessible than the whole population;
5. in some cases, the sample may have to be destroyed during the analysis.

There are three primary types of samples. They differ in the manner in which their elementary units are chosen. The three are the convenience sample, the judgment sample, and the random sample.

Convenience sample

A convenience sample refers to a sample that is selected on the basis of how convenient certain elements of the population are for observation. Convenience may be needed because of time pressures, process accessibility, or other considerations.

Judgment sample

A judgment sample is one that is obtained based on the discretion of someone familiar with the relevant characteristics of the population. This is usually based on the heuristics of an experienced individual. It may also be based on a group consensus.

Random sample

A random sample refers to a sample whereby the elements of the sample are chosen at random. This is the most important type of sample for statistical analysis. In random sampling, all the items in the population have an equal chance of being selected to be included in the sample.

Since a sample is a collection of observations representing only a portion of the population, the way in which the sample is chosen can significantly affect the adequacy and reliability of the sample. Even after the sample is chosen, the manner in which specific observations are obtained may still affect the validity of the results. The possible bias and errors in the sampling process are discussed below.

Sampling and nonsampling errors

A sampling error refers to the difference between a sample mean and the population mean that is due solely to the particular sample elements that are selected for observation. A nonsampling error refers to an error that is due solely to the manner in which the observation is made.

Sampling bias

A sampling bias refers to the tendency to favor the selection of certain sample elements having specific characteristics. For example, a sampling bias may occur if a sample of the personnel is selected from only the engineering department in a survey addressing the implementation of high technology processes.

Stratified sampling

Stratified sampling involves dividing the population into classes, or groups, called strata. The items contained in each stratum are expected to be homogeneous with respect to the characteristics to be studied. A random subsample is taken from each stratum. The subsamples from all the strata are then combined to form the desired overall sample. Stratified sampling is typically used for a heterogeneous population such as data on employee productivity in an organization. Through stratification, groups of employees are set up so that the individuals within each stratum are mostly homogeneous and the strata are different from one another. As another example, a survey of managers on some important issue of worker involvement may be conducted by forming strata on the basis of the types of processes they are involved with. There may be one stratum for technical processes, one for construction processes, and one for manufacturing processes.

A proportionate stratified sampling results if the units in the sample are allocated among the strata in proportion to the relative number of units in each stratum in the population. That is, equal sampling ratio is assigned to all strata in a proportionate stratified sampling.

In disproportionate stratified sampling, the sampling ratio for each stratum is inversely related to the level of homogeneity of the units in the stratum. The more homogeneous the stratum, the smaller its proportion included in the overall sample. The rationale for using disproportionate stratified sampling is that when the units in a stratum are more homogeneous, a smaller subsample is needed to ensure good representation. The smaller subsample helps to reduce sampling cost.

Cluster sampling

Cluster sampling involves the selection of random clusters, or groups, from the population. The desired overall sample is made up of the units in each cluster. Cluster sampling is different from stratified sampling in that differences between clusters are usually small. In addition, the units within each cluster are generally more heterogeneous. Each cluster, also known as primary sampling unit, is expected to be a scaled-down model that gives a good representation of the characteristics of the population.

All the units in each cluster may be included in the overall sample, or a subsample of the units in each cluster may be used. If all the units of the selected clusters are included in the overall sample, the procedure is referred to as a single-stage sampling. If a subsample is taken at random from each selected cluster and all units of each subsample are included in the overall sample, then the sampling procedure is called a two-stage sampling. If the sampling procedure involves more than two stages of subsampling, then the procedure is referred to as a multistage sampling. Cluster sampling is typically less expensive to implement than stratified sampling. For example, the cost of taking a random sample of 2000 managers from different industry types may be reduced by first selecting a sample, or cluster, of 25 industries, and then selecting 80 managers from each of the 25 industries. This represents a two-stage sampling that will be considerably cheaper than trying to survey 2000 individuals in several companies in a single-stage procedure.

Frequency distribution

Once a sample has been drawn and observations of all the items in the sample are recorded, the task of data collection is completed. The next task involves organizing the raw data into a meaningful format. In addition to the various methods discussed earlier, frequency distribution is another tool for organizing data. Frequency distribution involves the arrangement of observations into classes so as to show the frequency of occurrences in each class. An appropriate class interval must be selected for the construction of the frequency distribution. The guidelines for selecting the class interval are as follows.

1. The number of classes should not be so small or so large that the true nature of the underlying distribution cannot be identified. Generally, the number of classes should be between 6 and 20.
2. The interval length of each class should be the same. The interval length should be selected such that every observation falls within some class.
3. The difference between midpoints of adjacent classes should be constant and equal to the length of each interval.

Example

Suppose a set of data were collected about process costs in an organization. Twenty processes are selected for the study. The observations below are recorded in thousands of dollars:

$3 000	$1 100	$4 200	$800	$3 000
$1 800	$2 500	$2 500	$1 700	$3 000
$2 900	$2 100	$2 300	$2 500	$1 500
$3 500	$2 600	$1 300	$2 100	$3 600

Table 5.4 shows the tabulation of the cost data as a frequency distribution. Note how the end points of the class intervals are selected such that no recorded data point falls at an end point of a class. Note also that seven class intervals seem to be the most appropriate size for this particular set of observations. Each class interval has a spread of $500 which is an approximation obtained from the following expression.

$$W = \frac{X_{max} - X_{min}}{N}$$

$$= \frac{4200 - 800}{7}$$

$$= 485.71$$

$$= 500.$$

Table 5.4 Frequency distribution of process cost data (1)

Cost Interval	Midpoint	Frequency	Cumulative Frequency
750–1250	1000	2	2
1250–1750	1500	3	5
1750–2250	2000	3	8
2250–2750	2500	5	13
2750–3250	3000	4	17
3250–3750	3500	2	19
3750–4250	4000	1	20
Total		20	

Table 5.5 shows the relative frequency distribution. The relative frequency of any class is the proportion of the total observations which fall into that class. It is obtained by dividing the frequency of the class by the total number of observations. The relative frequency of all the classes should add up to 1.

Table 5.5 Frequency distribution of process cost data (2)

Cost Interval	Midpoint	Frequency	Cumulative Frequency
750–1250	1000	0.10	0.10
1250–1750	1500	0.15	0.25
1750–2250	2000	0.15	0.40
2250–2750	2500	0.25	0.65
2750–3250	3000	0.20	0.85
3250–3750	3500	0.10	0.95
3750–4250	4000	0.05	1.00
Total		1.00	

From the relative frequency table, it is seen that 25% of the observed process costs fall within the range of $2 250 and $2 750. It is also noted that only 15% (0.10 + 0.05) of the observed process costs fall in the upper two intervals of process costs. Figure 5.11 shows the histogram of the frequency distribution for the process cost data. Figure 5.12 presents a plot of the relative frequency of the process cost data. The plot of the cumulative relative frequency is superimposed on the relative frequency plot. The relative frequency of the observations in each class represents the probability that a process cost will fall within that range of costs. The corresponding cumulative relative frequency gives the

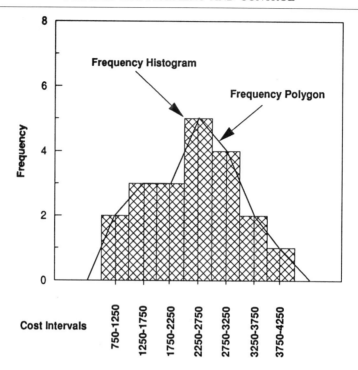

Figure 5.11 Histogram of process cost distribution data.

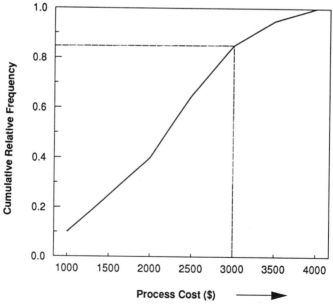

Figure 5.12 Plot of relative frequency and cumulative relative frequency.

probability that process cost will fall below the midpoint of that class interval. For example, 85% of process costs in this example are expected to fall below or equal to $3 000.

Probability concepts

An intuitive understanding of the notions and interpretations of probability is essential to managing most of today's processes. Probability refers to the chances of occurrence of an event out of several possible events in a sample space. This is what people often erroneously refer to as the law of averages. The law of averages is actually a misinterpretation of a mathematical statement called the law of large numbers. In simple terms, the law of large numbers says that if an act is repeated a large number of times, the proportion of those times that a particular event happens tends to be a fixed number. As an example, if a coin is tossed a large number of times, say several million times, the proportion of heads tends to be one-half of the total number of tosses. In that case, the number, one-half, is referred to as the probability that heads will occur on one toss of the coin. As another illustration, if ten items with different colors are placed in a jar and one item is pulled out of the jar at random, the probability of pulling out one specific color is one-tenth. Presented below are some of the general facts about probability.

1. Probabilities are real numbers between 0 and 1 inclusive, that reflect the chances of the occurrence of events.
2. A probability value near 0 indicates that the event in question is not expected to occur. However, it does not mean that the event will not occur. A probability of 0 simply indicates that a particular event is rare.
3. A probability near 1 indicates that the event in question is expected to occur. It does not mean that the event will definitely occur.
4. A probability of one-half indicates that the event in question has an equal likelihood of occurring or not occurring.
5. The sum of the probabilities of all the mutually exclusive events in a sample space is 1. This is one of the most basic facts of probability. And yet, it is the most frequently violated rule in probability analysis.

The assignment of probabilities to physical events does not require a great deal of mathematical training. In the real world, experienced practitioners assign intuitive probabilities to events based on experience and familiarity with previous occurrences of the event. Questions such as, 'What percentage of process attributes affect the quality of output?' can easily be answered by experienced and observant analysts without any mathematical reasoning. Thus, managers can generate probabilities subconsciously. These probability values can be very useful for making inferences about events in a process environment.

Normal probability distribution

A probability density function is a mathematical expression that describes the random behaviors of events in a sample space. Probability density functions are associated with continuous sample spaces where there is an infinite number of possible events. If the number of elements in a sample space is finite or countably finite, then the behavior of the events in the sample space would be described by a discrete probability distribution rather than a continuous probability density function. Countably finite means that there is an unending sequence with as many elements as there are whole numbers. Thus, probability distributions refer to discrete sample spaces while probability density functions refer to continuous sample spaces.

In most practical problems, continuous random variables represent measured data, such as distance, weight, temperature, and height, while discrete random variables represent counted data, such as the number of absent employees on a given day, the number of late jobs in a process, and the amount of dollars available for a particular process. Examples of discrete probability distributions are the binomial distribution, the geometric distribution, and the poisson distribution. Other examples of probability density functions are the exponential probability density function, gamma probability density function, chi-square probability density function, and weibull probability density function.

The normal probability density function is the most important continuous probability density function. It is often referred to as the normal distribution, normal curve, bell-shaped curve, or Gaussian distribution. It has been found that this distribution fits many of the physical events in nature, hence its popularity and wide appeal. The normal distribution is characterized by the following formula:

$$f(x) = \frac{1}{\sqrt{2\pi}\sigma} e^{-\frac{1}{2}\left(\frac{x-\mu}{\sigma}\right)^2}, \quad -\infty < x < \infty$$

where
μ = mean of the distribution
σ = standard deviation of the distribution
e = 2.71828 ... (constant)
π = 3.14159 ... (constant)

The famous bell-shaped appearance of the normal distribution is shown in Figure 5.13. The values of μ and σ are the parameters that determine the specific appearance (fat, thin, long, short, narrow, or wide) of the normal distribution.

Theoretically, the tails of the curve trail on to infinity. When $\mu = 1$ and $\sigma = 1$, the normal distribution is referred to as the standard normal distribution. It is the values of the standard normal distribution that are widely tabulated in books. An appendix at the end of this book presents a tabulation of the standard

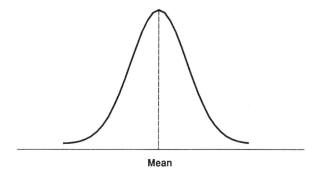

Figure 5.13 The normal curve.

normal distribution. Because of the variety and complexity of working with the general normal distribution, practically all analyses with the normal curve are done based on the standard normal distribution. This is achieved by using the transformation given below:

$$Z = \frac{X - \mu}{\sigma},$$

where Z is the standard normal random variable and X is the general normal random variable with a mean of μ and standard deviation of σ. The variable, Z, is often referred to as the normal deviate. One important aspect of the normal distribution relates to the percent of observations within one, two, or three standard deviations. Approximately 68.27% of observations following a normal distribution lie within plus and minus one standard deviation from the mean. Approximately 95.45% of the observations lie within plus or minus two standard deviations from the mean, and approximately 99.73% of the observations lie within plus or minus three standard deviations from the mean. These are shown graphically in Figure 5.14.

Basic probability calculations

To obtain probabilities for particular values of a random variable, it is necessary to know the probability distribution of the random variable. Because of the infinite possible combinations of means and standard deviation values, there are an infinite number of normal distributions. It is quite impractical to try and calculate probabilities directly from each one of them individually. Fortunately, the standard normal distribution can be applied to each and every possible normal random variable by using the transformation expression presented earlier. The standard normal distribution is of great importance in practice, because it can be used to approximate many of the other discrete and continuous random variables.

Because of the fact that the normal distribution represents a continuous

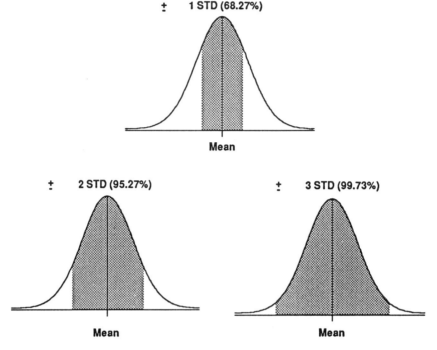

Figure 5.14 Areas under the normal curve.

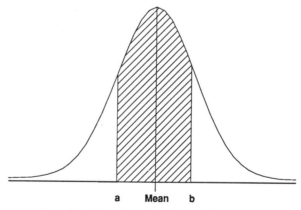

Figure 5.15 Probability of an interval under the normal curve.

random variable, it is impossible to calculate the probability of any particular point on the curve. To determine probabilities, it is necessary to refer to intervals, such as the interval between point *a* and point *b*. In Figure 5.15, the area under the curve from *a* to *b* represents the probability that the random variable will lie between *a* and *b*. That probability is calculated as follows:

Given: Normal random variable X, representing task duration.

Mean of $X = 50$ days

Standard deviation of $X = 10$

Required: The probability that the task duration will lie between 45 and 62 days.

Solution: Let $X1 = 45$ and $X2 = 62$.

Then,

$$z_1 = \frac{45 - 50}{10}$$

$$= -0.5$$

$$z_2 = \frac{62 - 50}{10}$$

$$= 1.2$$

Therefore, we have

$$
\begin{aligned}
P(45 < X < 62) &= P(-0.5 < Z < 1.2) \\
&= P(Z < 1.2) - P(Z < -0.5) \\
&= P(Z < 1.2) - [1 - P(Z < 0.5)] \\
&= 0.8849 - (1 - 0.6915) \\
&= 0.8849 - 0.3085 \\
&= 0.5764.
\end{aligned}
$$

Thus, there is a 57.64% chance that this particular task will require between 45 and 62 days. Note that the area under the curve between 45 and 62 is calculated by first finding the total area to the left of 62 (i.e. 0.8849) and then subtracting the area to the left of 45 (i.e. 0.3085). Note also that $P(Z < -0.5)$ can be computed as $1 - P(Z < 0.5)$ for the case where the normal table does not contain negative values of z. The respective probabilities are read off the normal distribution table given in Appendix C.

To illustrate the use of the table, let us find the probability that Z will be less than 1.23. First, we locate the value of z equal to 1.2 in the left column of the table, and then move across the row to the column under 0.03, where we read the value of 0.8907 inside the body of the table. Thus, $P(Z < 1.23) = 0.8907$. Using a similar process, the following additional examples are presented:

$$
\begin{aligned}
P(X < 55) &= P\left(Z < \frac{55 - 50}{10} \right) \\
&= P(Z < 0.5) \\
&= 0.6915.
\end{aligned}
$$

$$
\begin{aligned}
P(X > 65) &= P\left(Z > \frac{65 - 50}{10} \right) \\
&= P(Z > 1.5)
\end{aligned}
$$

$$= 1 - P(Z < 1.5)$$
$$= 1 - 0.9332$$
$$= 0.0668.$$

Note that since the normal distribution table is constructed as cumulative probabilities from the left, $P(Z > 65)$ is calculated as $1 - P(Z < 65)$. As a general point, it should be noted that:

$P(Z < k) = 1.0$, for any value k that is greater than 3.5
$P(Z < 0) = 0.5$
$P(Z < k) = 0.0$, for any value k that is less than -3.5.

Importance of probability in process management

Variability is a 'reality' in any process. The words 'uncertainty' and 'risk' appear frequently in process management. Uncertainty refers to our inability to predict the future accurately. Risk has two elements: the probability that something will happen and the loss that will result if the thing does happen. A basic function in process management involves making plans for the future; a future that is uncertain. Probability plays a crucial role in helping process analysts formulate and solve problems dealing with uncertainty and risk assessment. Typical examples of elements subject to uncertainty, and thereby necessitating the use of probability, include resource utilization, activity durations, process performance, level of support, weather condition, equipment failures, and process cost. Basic probability calculations are very valuable, not only for planning for the future, but also for evaluating past events in a process.

5.5.4 Seven tools for diagnosing a process

To facilitate data analysis for diagnosing a process, Ishikawa suggests using a collection of seven graphical tools. This collection includes flowcharts, Pareto diagrams, cause-and-effect diagrams, check sheets, scatter plots, run charts, and histograms. The tools are sometimes referred to as Ishikawa's 'seven new tools'. Some of the tools have already been discussed in the preceding sections of this book. They are briefly discussed below to re-emphasize their importance. The tools are very powerful if used properly.

Flow charts

This is used to show the steps that a product or service follows from the beginning to the end of the process. It helps locate the value-added parts of the process steps. It also helps in locating the unnecessary steps in the process, where unnecessary cost and labor exist. These unnecessary steps can be reduced or permanently eliminated.

Pareto diagram

This is used to display the relative importance or size of problems to determine the order of priority for projects. This will help to concentrate efforts on the most serious project. For example, in Figure 5.16, analysts may tend to focus on project I since this is where the greatest dollar loss is being experienced. The seriousness of a project does not necessarily have to be in terms of dollars, it may also be in terms of variability or any parameter of significant importance. In addition, the selection of Project I as the most critical project to focus on should not be made solely on the largest dollar loss alone or any parameter of interest studied. The actual cause of the project should also be considered in determining which project to put most efforts on. For example, if Project I represents the number of accidents per year, and Project II is the number of deaths per year, then Project II should be looked at very closely since focusing on the number of deaths may be more critical than focusing on the number of accidents, even though the frequency of the accident is more than the frequency of the death.

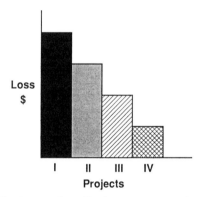

Figure 5.16 Relative dollar losses of quality improvement projects.

Cause and effect (fishbone) diagram

A fishbone diagram is used to develop a relationship between an effect and all the possible causes influencing it. It is also sometimes called a 'tree' or 'river' diagram. Figure 5.17 presents an example of a fishbone diagram. The diagram was originally used for specifying the relationships between a quality characteristic and the ambient factors. The diagram is now used extensively not only for quality related analysis, but also for general applications in business and industry. The steps for developing a fishbone diagram are presented below:

Step 1: Determine the quality characteristic or the response variable to be studied.

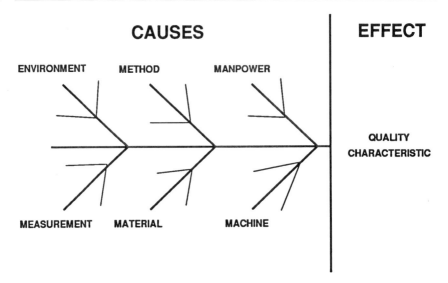

CAUSES   EFFECT

ENVIRONMENT   METHOD   MANPOWER

QUALITY
CHARACTERISTIC

MEASUREMENT   MATERIAL   MACHINE

Figure 5.17 Fishbone diagram.

Step 2: Write the characteristic on the right-hand side of a blank sheet of paper. Start with enough room on the paper because the diagram may expand considerably during the evaluation. Enclose the characteristic in a square. Now, write the primary causes which affect the quality characteristic as big branches (or bones). Enclose the primary causes in squares.

Step 3: Write the secondary causes which affect the big branches as medium-sized branches. Write the tertiary (third-level) causes which affect the medium-sized bones as small bones.

Step 4: Assign relative importance ratings to the factors. Mark the particularly important factors that are believed to have a significant effect on the quality characteristic.

Step 5: Append any necessary written documentation to the diagram.

Step 6: Review the overall diagram for completeness. While it is important to expand the cause-and-effect relationships as much as possible, avoid getting the diagram cluttered. For a fishbone diagram to be presented to upper management, limit the contents to a few important details. At the operational level, more details will need to be provided.

Scatter plots

A scatter plot is used to study the relationships between two variables. It is sometimes called an X–Y plot. The plot gives a visual assessment of the location tendencies of data points. The appearance of a scatter plot can help identify the type of statistical analyses that may be needed for the data. For example, in regression analysis, a scatter plot can help an analyst determine the type of models to be investigated.

Control charts/run charts

A control chart can be used to determine if a process is in control or not. It is also a tool that can be used to monitor the day-to-day performance of a process or used as a tool to assess the past performance of a process. A run chart is a tool which can be used to monitor the trends in a process over time.

Check sheets

A check sheet is a pre-printed table layout that facilitates data collection. Items to be recorded are pre-printed in the table. Observations are recorded by simply checking appropriate cells in the table. A check sheet helps automatically to organize data for subsequent analysis. If properly designed, a check sheet can eliminate the need for counting data points during data analysis.

Histogram

This is used to display the distribution of data by collecting the data points into evenly spaced numerical groupings that show the frequency of values in each group. Histograms are useful for quickly assessing the variation and distribution affecting a process. Important guidelines for drawing histograms are as follows.

Step 1: Determine the minimum and maximum values to be covered by the histogram.

Step 2: Select a number of histogram classes between 6 and 15. Having too few or too many classes will make it impossible to identify the underlying distribution.

Step 3: Set the same interval length for the histogram classes such that every observation in the data set falls within some class. The difference between midpoints of adjacent classes should be constant and equal to the length of each interval. If N represents the number of histogram classes, determine the interval length as:

$$W = \frac{X_{max} - X_{min}}{N},$$

where X_i represents an observation in the data set.

Step 4: Count the number of observations that fall within each histogram class. This can be done by using a check sheet or any other counting technique.

Step 5: Draw a bar for each histogram class such that the height of the bar represents the number of observations in the class. If desired, the heights can be converted to relative proportions in which the height of each bar represents the percentage of the data set that falls within the histogram class.

A frequency polygon may be obtained by drawing a line to connect the midpoints at the top of the histogram bars. The polygon will show the spread and shape of the distribution of the data set. Three possible patterns of distribution may be revealed by the polygon. They are: symmetrical, positively skewed, and negatively skewed. In a symmetrical distribution, the two halves of the graph are identical. In a positively skewed distribution (skewed to the right), there is a long tail stretching to the right side of the distribution. In a negatively skewed distribution (skewed to the left), there is a long tail stretching to the left side of the distribution.

We strongly recommend using computer software tools for developing the diagrams for the seven tools discussed above. Many software tools are now available for drawing a variety of charts and performing extensive data analysis. Examples of the available software packages are spreadsheet programs, and statistical software such as MINITAB and STATGRAPHICS.

5.6 CASE STUDY FOR VENDOR SELECTION

A manufacturing company was interested in purchasing high-quality paper jumbos as raw materials for its products. The company was trying to decide between its four major suppliers. The company analysts, therefore, requested the suppliers to supply data from their processes over time. The analysts instructed each supplier to provide data on 30 stockrolls by taking three crossweb samples every 30 seconds. The average was reported when a stockroll was completed. The characteristic of interest was the basis weight of the paper. The specifications were between 18 and 34. The information obtained from the suppliers is summarized in Table 5.6.

Summary statistics for the supplier data are presented below:

Supplier	N	MEAN	MEDIAN	TRMEAN	STDEV	SEMEAN
A	30	24.390	24.100	24.259	2.258	0.412
B	30	24.722	24.474	24.657	1.933	0.353
C	30	24.690	24.716	24.467	2.898	0.529
D	30	24.483	24.414	24.491	1.635	0.298

Table 5.6 Data on suppliers

Obs.	Supplier A	Supplier B	Supplier C	Supplier D
1	23.0000	23.5425	22.3838	21.9300
2	21.4320	23.6916	26.9865	22.4040
3	26.3524	23.3730	26.1851	22.2875
4	23.6517	23.9634	27.0487	21.2500
5	24.0012	22.7887	27.5525	23.3618
6	26.7580	25.0275	27.9339	22.9909
7	23.6022	25.7711	24.7533	23.3422
8	25.4464	28.1313	24.7150	22.8460
9	21.3195	23.2963	27.5556	23.4495
10	25.6269	21.5161	22.2964	24.0898
11	26.1858	24.7338	23.0874	23.4020
12	22.7996	24.8086	20.5800	23.6095
13	24.2075	25.0708	26.0931	24.2958
14	20.8875	23.9596	21.7602	24.3779
15	24.1979	28.2460	28.7611	23.8950
16	24.2949	24.4640	24.7166	24.4509
17	28.0474	22.7474	25.0488	25.0760
18	23.0223	22.8215	33.8654	24.6969
19	22.9628	26.2595	21.3624	24.7939
20	25.0470	28.0846	22.4919	25.0706
21	22.1606	22.6081	21.4501	24.9345
22	22.8157	23.1440	22.0955	25.1793
23	25.5779	25.5620	23.7537	25.5743
24	26.5116	28.3397	21.6624	26.0820
25	21.9697	24.4840	22.4125	25.9924
26	22.6375	22.5010	22.2181	26.3969
27	25.8168	23.0124	26.3210	27.2147
28	30.7155	25.9185	26.0541	27.1736
29	22.8426	26.3250	25.9320	26.9947
30	27.8194	27.4819	23.6281	27.3404
Average	24.390	24.722	24.690	24.483
Std. Dev.	2.258	1.933	2.898	1.635

	MIN	MAX	Q1	Q3
A	20.887	30.715	22.812	25.909
B	21.516	28.340	23.111	26.004
C	20.580	33.865	22.277	26.487
D	21.250	27.340	23.357	25.679

Figure 5.18 shows the histograms of the observations provided by the suppliers. Figure 5.19 shows a multiple X–Y plot for the suppliers. Figure 5.20 shows a multiple Box-and-Whisker plot for the suppliers.

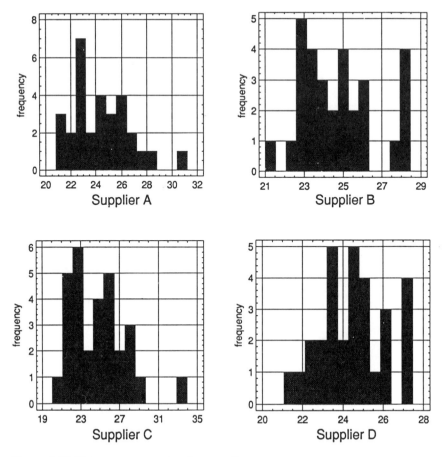

Figure 5.18 Histograms comparing four-supplier processes.

Figures 5.21, 5.22, 5.23, and 5.24 show the individual and moving range charts for the four suppliers respectively. The following observations are made about Supplier D.

TEST 1. One point beyond zone A.
    Test Failed at points: 1 2 3 4 6 8 24 25 26 27 28 29 30.
TEST 2. Nine points in a row in Zone C or beyond (on one side of CL).
    Test Failed at points: 9 10 11 12 13 14 15 16 25 26 27 28 29 30.
TEST 5. Two of 3 points in a row in zone A or beyond (on one side of CL).
    Test Failed at points: 2 3 4 5 6 7 8 9 11 12 24 25 26 27 28 29 30.
TEST 6. Four of 5 points in a row in zone B or beyond (on one side of CL).
    Test Failed at points: 4 5 6 7 8 9 11 12 23 24 25 26 27 28 29 30.$
TEST 8. Eight points in a row beyond zones C (above and below CL).
    Test Failed at points: 8 9 27 28 29 30.

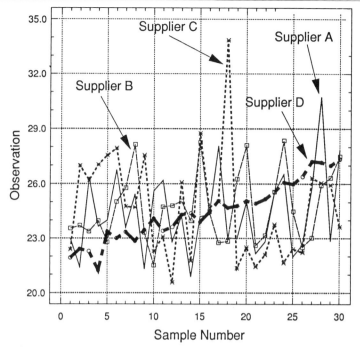

Figure 5.19 Multiple X–Y plot for four suppliers.

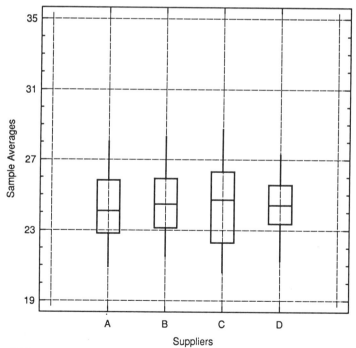

Figure 5.20 Multiple box-and-whisker plot for comparing four suppliers.

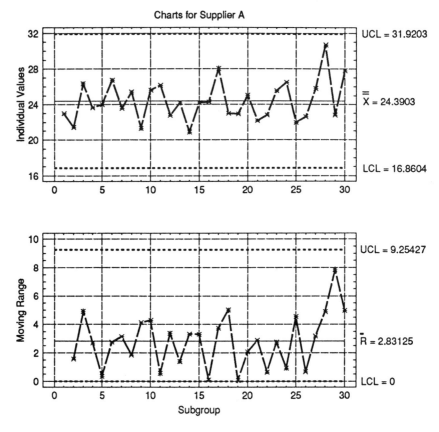

Figure 5.21 Control charts for supplier A.

Descriptive statistics, such as histograms, scatter plots, box plots, averages, and so on did not reveal any major differences between the four suppliers. However, when data from each supplier were plotted over time, it is seen that Suppliers C and D did not have data from a stable process. Therefore, we cannot predict the quality of the paper that Suppliers C and D will supply in the future. Consequently, Suppliers C and D are eliminated from further consideration.

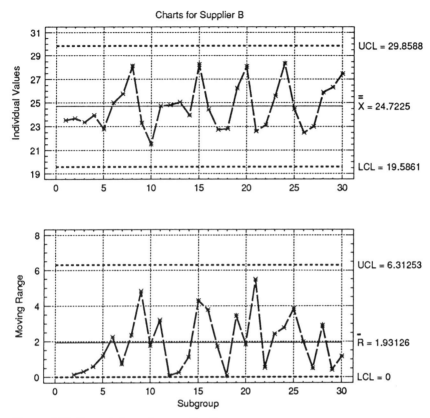

Figure 5.22 Control charts for supplier B.

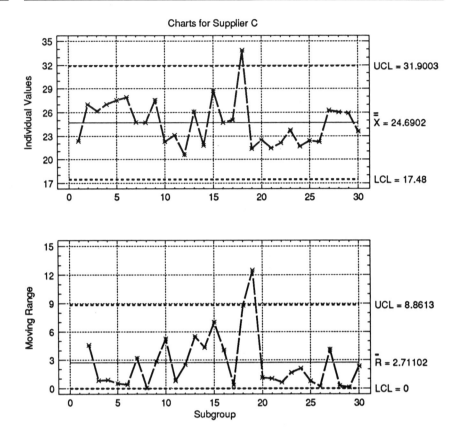

Figure 5.23 Control charts for supplier C.

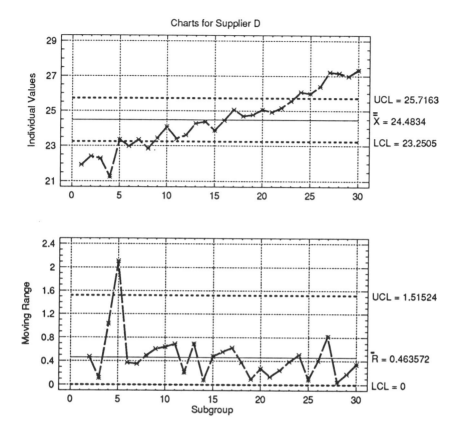

Figure 5.24 Control charts for supplier D.

Statistical tools for quality improvement

Quality needs time and care.
Without care, the long-run tendency of quality is to fall

6.1 STATISTICAL PROCESS CONTROL

Statistical process control (SPC) means controlling a process statistically. SPC originated from the efforts of the early quality control researchers. The techniques of SPC are based on basic statistical concepts normally used for statistical quality control. In a manufacturing environment, it is known that not all products are made exactly alike. There are always some inherent variations in units of the same product. The variation in the characteristics of a product provides the basis for using SPC for quality improvement. With the help of statistical approaches, individual items can be studied and general inferences can be drawn about the process or batches of products from the process. Since 100% inspection is difficult or impractical in many processes, SPC provides a mechanism to generalize concerning process performance. SPC uses random samples generated consecutively over time. The random samples should be representative of the general process. SPC can be accomplished through the following steps:

- control charts ($\bar{X}$-chart, R-chart)
- process capability analysis (nested design, Cp, Cp_k);
- process control (factorial design, response surface).

6.1.1 Control charts

Two of the most commonly used control charts in industry are the X-bar charts and the range charts (R-charts). The type of chart to be used normally depends on the kind of data collected. Data collected can be of two types: variable data and attribute data. The success of quality improvement depends on two major factors:

- the quality of data available;
- the effectiveness of the techniques used for analyzing the data.

6.1.2 Types of data

Variable data

The control charts for variable data are:

control charts for individual (X);
moving range chart (MR-chart);
average chart ($\bar{X}$-chart);
range chart (R-chart);
median chart;
standard deviation chart (σ-chart);
cumulative sum chart (CUSUM);
exponentially weighted moving average (EWMA).

Attribute data

The control charts for attribute data are:

proportion or fraction defective chart (p-chart) (subgroup sample size can vary);
percent defective chart (100p-chart) (subgroup sample size can vary);
number defective chart (np-chart) (subgroup sample size is constant);
number defective (c-chart) (subgroup sample size=1);
defective per inspection unit (u-chart) (subgroup sample size can vary).

The statistical theory useful to generate control limits is the same for all the above charts with the exception of exponential weighted moving average (EWMA) and cumulative sum (CUSUM).

6.1.3 X-bar and range charts

The R-chart is a time plot useful in monitoring short-term process variations, while the X-bar chart monitors the longer term variations where the likelihood of special causes is greater over time. Both charts have control lines called upper and lower control limits, as well as the central lines. The central line and control limits are calculated from the process measurements. They are not specification limits or a percentage of the specifications, or some other arbitrary lines based on experience. Therefore, they represent what the process is capable of doing when only common cause variation exits. If only common cause variation exists, then the data will continue to fall in a random fashion within the control limits. In this case we say the process is in a state of statistical control. However, if a special cause acts on the process, one or more data points will be outside the control limits, so the process is not in a state of statistical control.

6.1.4 Data collection strategies

One strategy for data collection requires that about 20–25 subgroups be collected. Twenty to twenty-five subgroups should adequately show the location and spread of a distribution in a state of statistical control. If it happens that due to sampling costs, or other sampling reasons associated with the process, we are unable to have 20–25 subgroups, we can still use the available samples that we have to generate the trial control limits and update these limits as more samples are made available, because these limits will normally be wider than normal control limits and will therefore be less sensitive to changes in the process. Another approach is to use run charts to monitor the process until such time as 20–25 subgroups are made available. Then control charts can be applied with control limits put on the charts. Other data collection strategies should consider the subgroup sample size, as well as the sampling frequency.

6.1.5 Subgroup sample size

The subgroup samples of size n should be taken as n consecutive readings from the process and not random samples. This is necessary in order to have an accurate estimate of the process common cause variation. Each subgroup should be selected from some small period of time or small region of space or product in order to assure homogeneous conditions within the subgroup. This is necessary because the variation within the subgroup is used in generating the control limits. The subgroup sample size n can be between four or five samples. This is a good size that balances the pros and cons of using large or small sample size for a control chart as provided below.

Advantages of using small subgroup sample size

- Estimates of process standard deviation based on the range are as good and accurate as the estimates obtained from using the standard deviation equation which is a complex hand calculation method.
- The probability of introducing special cause variations within a subgroup is very small.
- Range chart calculation is simple and easier to compute by hand on the shop floor by operators.

Advantages of using large subgroup sample size

- The central limit theorem supports the fact that the process average will be more normally distributed with larger sample size.
- If the process is stable, the larger the subgroup size the better the estimates of process variability.
- A control chart based on larger subgroup sample size will be more sensitive to process changes.

The choice of a proper subgroup is very critical to the usefulness of any control chart.

- If we fail to incorporate all common cause variations within our subgroups, the process variation will be underestimated, leading to very tight control limits. Then the process will appear to go out of control too frequently even when there is no existence of a special cause.
- If we incorporate special causes within our subgroups, then we will fail to detect special causes as frequently as expected.

6.1.6 Frequency of sampling

The problem of determining how frequently one should sample depends on several factors. These factors include, but are not limited to the following.

- *Cost of collecting and testing samples*: The greater the cost of taking and testing samples, the less frequently we should sample.
- *Changes in process conditions*: The larger the frequency of changes to the process, the larger the sampling frequency. For example, if process conditions tend to change every 15 minutes, then sample every 15 minutes. If conditions change every two hours, then sample every two hours.
- *Importance of quality characteristics*: The more important the quality characteristic being charted is to the customer, the more frequently the characteristic will need to be sampled.
- *Process control and capability*: The more history of process control and capability, the less frequently the process needs to be sampled.

6.1.7 Stable process

A process is said to be in a state of statistical control if the distribution of measurement data from the process has the same shape, location, and spread over time. In other words, a process is stable when the effects of all special causes have been removed from a process, so that the remaining variability is only due to common causes. Figure 6.1 shows an example of a stable distribution.

6.1.8 Out-of-control patterns

A process is said to be unstable or NOT in a state of statistical control if it changes from time to time because of a shifting average, or shifting variability, or a combination of shifting averages and variation. Figures 6.2, 6.3, and 6.4 show examples of distributions from unstable processes.

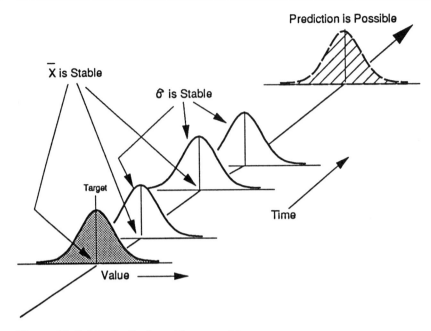

Figure 6.1 Stable distribution with no special causes.

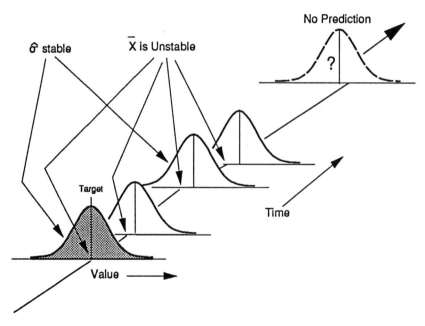

Figure 6.2 Unstable process average.

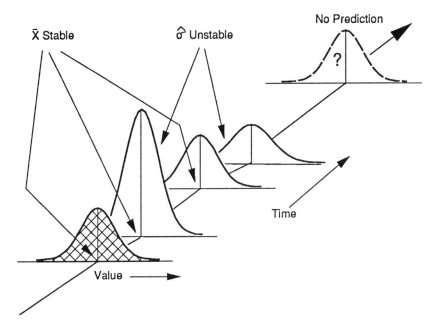

Figure 6.3 Unstable process variation.

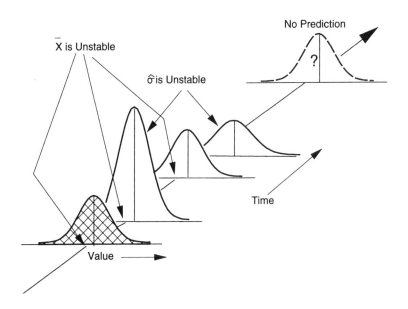

Figure 6.4 Unstable process average and variation.

6.1.9 Calculation of control limits

- Range (R)
  This is the difference between the highest and lowest observations:

$$R = X_{highest} - X_{lowest}$$

- Center lines
  Calculate $\bar{X}$ and $\bar{R}$

$$\bar{X} = \frac{\sum X_i}{m}$$

where,

$$\bar{R} = \frac{\sum R_i}{m}$$

$\bar{X}$ = overall process average
$\bar{R}$ = average range
m = total number of subgroups
n = within subgroup sample size

- Control limits based on R-chart

$$UCL_R = D_4\bar{R}$$
$$LCL_R = D_3\bar{R}$$

- Estimate of process variation

$$\hat{\sigma} = \frac{\bar{R}}{d_2}$$

- Control limits based on $\bar{X}$-chart
  Calculate the upper and lower control limits for the process average:

$$UCL = \bar{X} + A_2\bar{R}$$
$$LCL = \bar{X} - A_2\bar{R}$$

Table 6.1 shows the values of d_2, A_2, D_3, and D_4 for different values of n. These constants are used for developing variable control charts.

Table 6.1 Table of constants for variables control charts

n	d_2	A_2	D_3	D_4
2	1.128	1.880	0	3.267
3	1.693	1.023	0	2.575
4	2.059	0.729	0	2.282
5	2.326	0.577	0	2.115
6	0.534	0.483	0	2.004
7	2.704	0.419	0.076	1.924
8	2.847	0.373	0.136	1.864
9	2.970	0.337	0.184	1.816
10	3.078	0.308	0.223	1.777
11	3.173	0.285	0.256	1.744
12	3.258	0.266	0.284	1.716

6.1.10 Plotting control charts for range and average charts

- Plot the range chart (R-chart) first.
- If R-chart is in control, then plot X-bar chart.
- If R-chart is not in control, identify and eliminate special causes, then delete points that are due to special causes, and recompute the control limits for the range chart. If in control, then plot X-bar chart.
- Check to see if X-bar chart is in control, if not search for special causes and eliminate them permanently.
- Remember to perform the eight trend tests.

6.1.11 Plotting control charts for moving range and individual control charts

- Plot the moving range chart (MR-chart) first.
- If MR-chart is in control, then plot the individual chart (X).
- If MR-chart is not in control, identify and eliminate special causes, then delete special causes points, and recompute the control limits for the moving range chart. If MR-chart is in control, then plot the individual chart.
- Check to see if individual chart is in control, if not search for special causes from out-of-control points.
- Always remember to perform the eight trend tests.

Control chart example

A quality engineer in an automotive trades division of a manufacturing company was trying to study a machining process for producing a smooth surface on a torque converter clutch. The quality characteristic of interest is the surface smoothness of the clutch. The engineer then collected four clutches every hour for 30 hours and recorded the smoothness measurements in micro inches. Acceptable values of smoothness lies between 0 (perfectly smooth) and 45 micro inches. The data collected by the engineer are provided in Table 6.2. Histograms of the individual and average measurements are presented in Figure 6.5.

The two histograms in Figure 6.5 show that the hourly smoothness averages ranges from 27 to 32 micro inches, much narrower than the histogram of hourly individual smoothness which ranges from 24 to 37 micro inches. This is due to the fact that averages have less variability than individual measurements. Therefore, whenever we plot subgroup averages on an X-bar chart, there will always exist some individual measurements that will plot outside the control limits of an X-bar chart. The dotplots of the surface smoothness for individual and average measurements are shown in Figure 6.6.

Table 6.2 Data for control chart example

| Subgroup No. | Smoothness (micro inches) | | | | | |
	I	II	III	IV	Average	Range
1	34	33	24	28	29.75	10
2	33	33	33	29	32.00	4
3	32	31	25	28	29.00	7
4	33	28	27	36	31.00	9
5	26	34	29	29	29.50	8
6	30	31	32	28	30.25	4
7	25	30	27	29	27.75	5
8	32	28	32	29	30.25	4
9	29	29	28	28	28.50	1
10	31	31	27	29	29.50	4
11	27	36	28	29	30.00	9
12	28	27	31	31	29.25	4
13	29	31	32	29	30.25	3
14	30	31	31	34	31.50	4
15	30	33	28	31	30.50	5
16	27	28	30	29	28.50	3
17	28	30	33	26	29.25	7
18	31	32	28	26	29.25	6
19	28	28	37	27	30.00	10
20	30	29	34	26	29.75	8
21	28	32	30	24	28.50	8
22	29	28	28	29	28.50	1
23	27	35	30	30	30.50	8
24	31	27	28	29	28.75	4
25	32	36	26	35	32.25	10
26	27	31	28	29	28.75	4
27	27	29	24	28	27.00	5
28	28	25	26	28	26.75	3
29	25	25	32	27	27.25	7
30	31	25	24	28	27.00	7
Total					881.00	172

The descriptive statistics for individual smoothness are presented below:

N	MEAN	MEDIAN	TRMEAN	STDEV	SEMEAN
120	29.367	29.00	29.287	2.822	0.258
MIN	MAX	Q1	Q3		
24.00	37.00	28.00	31.00		

The descriptive statistics for average smoothness are presented below:

N	MEAN	MEDIAN	TRMEAN	STDEV	SEMEAN
30	29.367	29.375	29.246	1.409	0.257
MIN	MAX	Q1	Q3		
26.75	32.25	28.50	30.25		

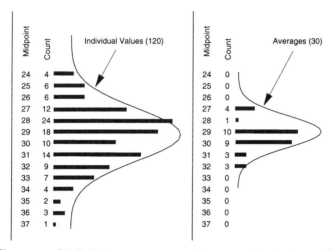

Figure 6.5 Histograms of individual measurements and averages for clutch smoothness.

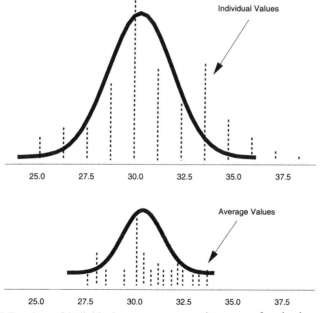

Figure 6.6 Dotplots of individual measurements and averages for clutch smoothness.

Calculations

I.   Natural limit of the process = $\bar{X} \pm 3s$ (based on empirical rule).

   s = estimated standard deviation of all individual samples

   Standard deviation (special and common), $s = 2.822$
   Process average, $\bar{X} = 29.367$
   Natural process limit = $29.367 \pm 3 (2.822) = 29.367 \pm 8.466$
   The natural limit of the process is between 20.90 and 37.83

II. Inherent (common cause) process variability, $\hat{\sigma} = \bar{R}/d_2$

   $\bar{R}$ from the range chart = 5.83
   d_2 (for $n=4$) from Table 6.1 = 2.059
   $\hat{\sigma} = \bar{R}/d_2 = 5.83/2.059 = 2.83$

   Thus, the total process variation, s, is about the same as the inherent process variability. This is because the process is in control. If the process is out of control, the total standard deviation of all the numbers will be larger than $\bar{R}/d_2$.

III. Control limits for the range chart

   Obtain constants D_3, D_4 from Table 6.1 for $n=4$.

   $D_3 = 0$
   $D_4 = 2.282$
   $\bar{R} = 172/30 = 5.73$
   UCL = $D_4 * \bar{R} = 2.282(5.73) = 16.16$
   LCL = $D_3 * \bar{R} = 0(5.73) = 0.0$

   The above limits are slightly different from the Minitab's R-bar or $\bar{X}$ limits. This is because Minitab uses $S_{(pooled)}(d_2)$ as an estimate of $\bar{R}$, and calculates the control limits from this estimate. Minitab will be changing this in version 8.0.

IV. Control limits for the averages

   Obtain constants A_2 from Table 6.1 for $n=4$.

   $A_2 = 0.729$
   UCL = $\bar{X} + A_2(\bar{R}) = 29.367 + 0.729(5.73) = 33.54$
   LCL = $\bar{X} - A_2(\bar{R}) = 29.367 - 0.729(5.73) = 25.19$

V.   Natural limit of the process = $\bar{X} \pm 3(\bar{R})/d_2 = 29.367 \pm 3(2.83) = 29.367 \pm 8.49$

   The natural limit of the process is between 20.88 and 37.86 which is slightly different from $\pm 3s$ calculated earlier based on the empirical rule. This is due to the fact that $\bar{R}/d_2$ is used rather than the standard deviation of all the values. Again, if the process is out of control, the standard deviation of all the values will be greater than $\bar{R}/d_2$. The correct procedure is always to use $\bar{R}/d_2$ from a process that is in statistical control.

VI. Comparison with specification

Since the specifications for the clutch surface smoothness is between 0 (perfectly smooth) and 45 micro inches, and the natural limit of the process is between 20.88 and 37.86, then the process is capable of producing within the spec limits. For a full coverage of process capability, readers should refer to the section on process capability. Figure 6.7 presents the R and X-bar charts for clutch smoothness.

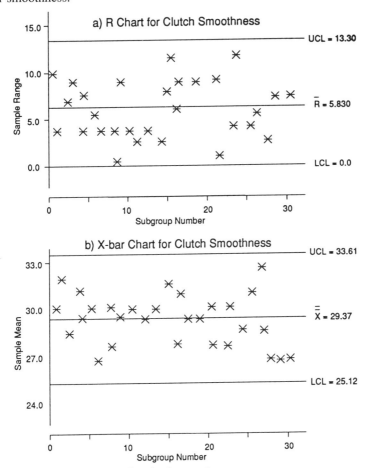

Figure 6.7 R and X-bar charts for clutch smoothness.

The quality engineer examined the above charts and concluded that the process is in a state of statistical control.

Process improvement opportunities

The quality engineer realizes that if the smoothness of the clutch can be held below 15 micro inches, then the clutch performance can be significantly improved. In this situation, the engineer can select key control factors to study in a two-level factorial or fractional factorial design. See section 7.1.

6.2 TREND ANALYSIS

After a process is recognized to be out of control, zone control charting or technique is a logical approach to searching for the sources of the problems. The following eight tests can be performed using MINITAB software. For this approach, the chart is divided into three zones. Zone A is between $\pm 3\sigma$, zone B is between $\pm 2\sigma$ and zone C is between $\pm 1\sigma$. For more information, see Nelson (1984).

Test 1

Pattern: One or more points falling outside the control limits on either side of the average. This is shown in Figure 6.8.

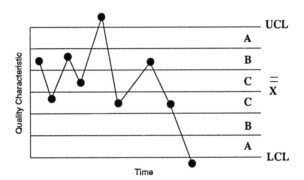

Figure 6.8 Test 1 for trend analysis.

Problem source: A sporadic change in the process due to special causes such as:

- equipment breakdown;
- new operator;
- drastic change in raw material quality;
- change in method, machine, or process setting.

Check: Go back and look at what might have been done differently before the out of control point signals.

Test 2

Pattern: A run of nine points on one side of the average (Figure 6.9).

Problem source: This may be due to a small change in the level of process average. This change may be permanent at the new level.

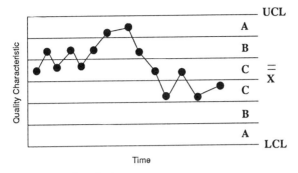

Figure 6.9 Test 2 for trend analysis.

Check: Go back to the beginning of the run and determine what was done differently at that time or prior to that time.

Test 3

Pattern: A trend of six points in a row either increasing or decreasing as shown in Figure 6.10.

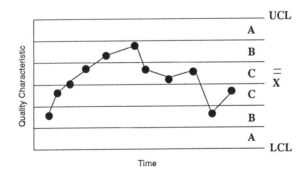

Figure 6.10 Test 3 for trend analysis.

Problem source: This may be due to the following:

- gradual tool wear;
- change in characteristic such as gradual deterioration in the mixing or concentration of a chemical;
- deterioration of plating or etching solution in electronics or chemical industries.

Check: Go back to the beginning of the run and search for the source of the run.

The above three tests are useful in providing good control of a process. However, in addition to the above three tests, some advanced tests (Tests 4:8) for detecting out-of-control patterns can also be used. These tests are based on the zone control chart.

Test 4

Pattern: Fourteen points in a row alternating up and down within or outside the control limits (Figure 6.11).

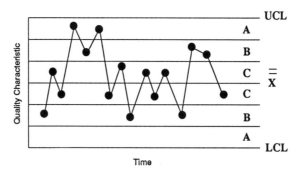

Figure 6.11 Test 4 for trend analysis.

Problem source: This can be due to sampling variation from two different sources such as sampling systematically from high and low temperatures, or lots with two different averages. This pattern can also occur if adjustment is being made all the time (over control).

Check: Look for cycles in the process, such as humidity or temperature cycles, or operator over control of process.

Test 5

Pattern: Two out of three points in a row on one side of the average in zone A or beyond. An example of this is presented in Figure 6.12.

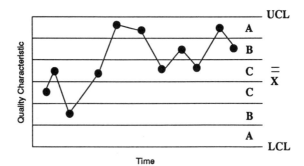

Figure 6.12 Test 5 for trend analysis.

Problem source: This can be due to a large, dramatic shift in the process level. This test sometimes provides early warning, particularly if the special cause is not as sporadic as in the case of Test 1.

Check: Go back one or more points in time and determine what might have caused the large shift in the level of the process.

Test 6

Pattern: Four out of five points in a row on one side of the average in zone B or beyond (Figure 6.13).

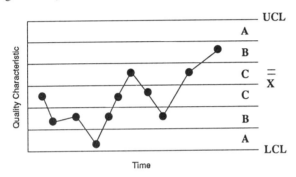

Figure 6.13 Test 6 for trend analysis.

Problem source: This may be due to a moderate shift in the process.
Check: Go back three or four points in time.

Test 7

Pattern: Fifteen points in a row on either side of the average in zone C as shown in Figure 6.14.

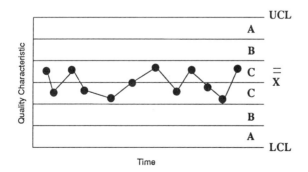

Figure 6.14 Test 7 for trend analysis.

Problem source: This is due to the following.

- Unnatural small fluctuations or absence of points near the control limits.
- At first glance may appear to be a good situation, but this is not a good control.
- Incorrect selection of subgroups. May be sampling from various subpopulations and combining them into a single subgroup for charting.
- Incorrect calculation of control limits.

Check: Look very close to the beginning of the pattern.

Test 8

Pattern: Eight points in a row on both sides of the center line with none in zone C. An example is shown in Figure 6.15.

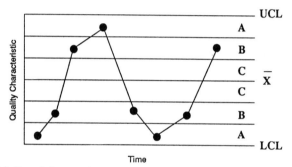

Figure 6.15 Test 8 for trend analysis.

Problem source: No sufficient resolution on the measurement system (see section on measurement system).

Check: Look at the range chart and see if it is in control.

6.3 PROCESS CAPABILITY

The capability of a process is the spread which contains almost all values of the process distribution. It is very important to note that capability is defined in terms of a distribution. Therefore, capability can only be defined for a process that is stable (has distribution) with common cause variation (inherent variability). It cannot be defined for an out-of-control process (it has no distribution) with variation special to specific causes (total variability). Figure 6.16 shows a process capability distribution.

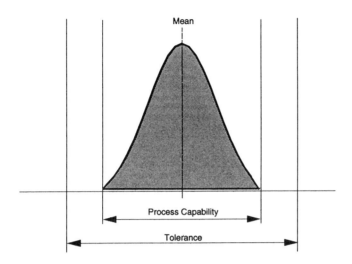

Figure 6.16 Process capability distribution.

6.3.1 Capable process (C_p)

A process is capable ($C_p \geq 1$) if its natural tolerance lies within the engineering tolerance or specifications. The measure of process capability of a stable process is $6\hat{\sigma}$, where $\hat{\sigma}$ is the inherent process variability estimated from the process. A minimum value of $C_p = 1.33$ is generally used for an on-going process. This ensures a very low reject rate of 0.007% and therefore is an effective strategy for prevention of nonconforming items. C_p is defined mathematically as

$$C_p = \frac{USL - LSL}{6\hat{\sigma}}$$

$$= \frac{\text{allowable process spread}}{\text{actual process spread}}$$

where:
USL = upper specification limit
LSL = lower specification limit

C_p measures the effect of the inherent variability only. The analyst should use R-bar/d_2 to estimate $\hat{\sigma}$ from an R-chart that is in a state of statistical control, where R-bar is the average of the subgroup ranges, and d_2 can be obtained for different subgroup sizes n from Table 6.1.

We don't have to verify control before performing a capability study. We can perform the study, then verify control after the study with the use of control charts. If the process is in control during the study, then our estimates of capabilities are correct and valid. However, if the process was not in control, we would have gained useful information, as well as proper insights as to the corrective actions to pursue.

6.3.2 Capability index (C_{pk})

Process centering can be assessed when a two-sided specification is available. If the capability index (C_{pk}) is equal to or greater than 1.33, then the process may be adequately centered. C_{pk} can also be employed when there is only one-sided specification. For a two-sided specification, it can be mathematically defined as:

$$C_{pk} = Minimum \quad \left\{ \frac{USL - \bar{X}}{3\hat{\sigma}} \, , \, \frac{\bar{X} - LSL}{3\hat{\sigma}} \right\}$$

where:
$\bar{X}$ = Overall process average

However, for a one-sided specification, the actual C_{pk} obtained is reported. This can be used to determine the percentage of observations out of specification. The overall long-term objective is to make C_p and C_{pk} as large as possible by continuously improving or reducing process variability, $\hat{\sigma}$ every time so that a greater percentage of the product is near the target value for the key quality characteristic of interest. The ideal is to center the process with zero variability.

If a process is centered but not capable, one or several courses of action may be necessary. One of the actions may be that of integrating designed experiment to gain additional knowledge on the process and in designing control strategies. If excessive variability is demonstrated, one may conduct a nested design with the objective of estimating the various sources of variability. These sources of variability can then be evaluated to determine what strategies to take in order to reduce or permanently eliminate them. Another action may be that of changing the specifications or continuing production and then sorting the items. Three characteristics of a process can be observed with respect to capability:

1. the process may be centered and capable;
2. the process may be capable but not centered;
3. the process may be centered but not capable.

Figures 6.17, 6.18, and 6.19 present the alternate characteristics.

Process capability example

I. Determine if the process is capable for the clutch smoothness data in Table 6.2. The engineer has determined that the process is in a state of statistical control. The specification limits are 0 (perfectly smooth) and 45 micro inches. The inherent process variability as determined from the control chart is:

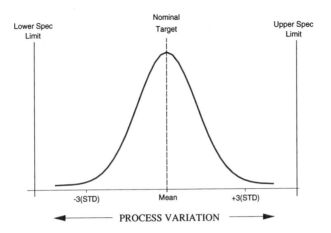

Figure 6.17 A process that is centered and capable.

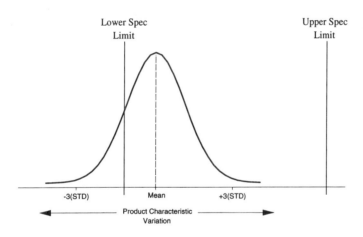

Figure 6.18 A process that is capable but not centered.

$$\hat{\sigma} = \bar{R}/d_2 = 5.83/2.059 = 2.83.$$

The capability of this process to produce within the specifications can be determined as:

$$C_p = \frac{USL - LSL}{6\hat{\sigma}} = \frac{45 - 0}{6(2.83)} = 2.650.$$

The capability of the process, $C_p = 2.65 > 1.0$ indicating that the process is capable of producing clutches that will meet the specifications of between 0 and 45. The process average is 29.367.

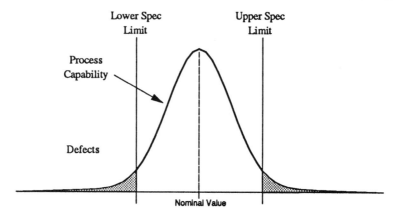

Figure 6.19 A process that is centered but not capable.

II. Determine if the process can be adequately centered. C_{pk} = minimum $[C_1$ and $C_u]$ can be used to determine if a process can be centered.

$$C_u = \frac{USL - \bar{X}}{3\hat{\sigma}} = \frac{45 - 29.367}{3(2.83)} = 1.84.$$

$$C_1 = \frac{\bar{X} - LSL}{3\hat{\sigma}} = \frac{29.367 - 0}{3(2.83)} = 3.46.$$

Therefore, the capability index, C_{pk}, for this process is 1.84. Since C_{pk} = 1.84 is greater than 1.33, then the process can be adequately centered.

6.3.3 Applications of process capability indices

- *Communication*: C_p and C_{pk} have been used in industry to establish a dimensionless common language useful for assessing the performance of production processes. Engineering, quality, manufacturing, etc., can communicate and understand processes with high capabilities.
- *Continuous improvement*: The indices can be used to monitor continuous improvement by observing the changes in the distribution of process capabilities. For example, if there were 20% of processes with capabilities between 1 and 1.67 in a month, and some of these improved to between 1.33 and 2.0 the next month, then this is an indication that improvement has occurred.
- *Audits*: There are so many various kinds of audits in use today to assess the performance of quality systems. A comparison of in-process capabilities with capabilities determined from audits can help establish problem areas.
- *Prioritization of improvement*: A complete printout of all processes with unacceptable C_p or C_{pk} values can be extremely powerful in establishing the priority for process improvements.

- *Prevention of nonconforming product*: For process qualification, it is reasonable to establish a benchmark capability of $C_{pk}=1.33$ which will make nonconforming products unlikely in most cases.

Potential abuse of C_p and C_{pk}

- *Problems and drawbacks*:
  C_{pk} can increase without process improvement though repeated testing reduces test variability;
  the wider the specifications, the larger the C_p or C_{pk}, but the action does not improve the process.
- People tend to focus on number rather than on process.
- *Process control*: People tend to determine process capability before statistical control has been established. Most people are not aware that capability determination is based on process common cause variation and what can be expected from a process in the future. The presence of special causes of variation makes prediction impossible and capability index unclear.
- *Nonnormality*: Some processes result in nonnormal distribution for some characteristics. Since capability indices are very sensitive to departures from normality, data transformation may be used to achieve approximate normality.
- *Computation*: Most computer packages do not use $\bar{R}/d_2$ to calculate σ.

6.3.4 Nested experimental design

A nested design is a tool that can be used to quantify sources of variability or components of variance. If special causes are present in a process, they can be eliminated by taking several cause of actions, depending on the causes. Such actions may include but are not limited to changing raw materials, operators, or making proper adjustments to equipment. However, sometimes it is often necessary to decide on what should be done if the process is in a state of statistical control with unacceptably high common cause variability. In this situation, most quality consultants often suggest making a fundamental change in the process with little or no direction on how this change should be carried out. It is important first to clearly identify the major sources of the common cause variability through a nested designed of experiment. This is because nested design identifies where in the process the bulk of the quality improvement efforts need to be focused.

Figure 6.20 shows a balanced, four-level nested design. In this study there are two levels of operators (Source B) nested within each of the five levels of instruments (Source A). Five levels of samples (Source C) are nested within each level of operator (Source B), and two levels of the tests (Source D) are nested within each level of the samples. A balanced design of this kind is easy to set up and analyze.

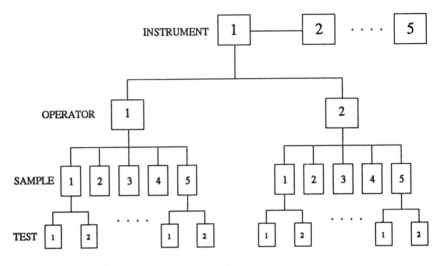

Figure 6.20 Four-level balanced nested design.

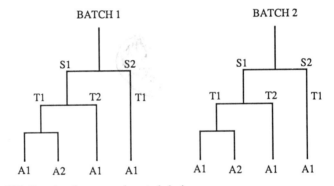

Figure 6.21 Four-level staggered nested design.

A potential drawback of a balanced design is that it gives more degrees of freedom at the lowest level than at the highest level in the hierarchy. In order to balance the degrees of freedom across the design one would have to create a staggered design such as the one shown in Figure 6.21.

Some important points about nested designs are presented below:

- the cost of testing should be minimized as much as possible;
- to minimize time, effort, and cost of the experiment, consider staggered design;
- use a minimum of 25 to 30 data points or a minimum of 25 degrees of freedom at the bottom of the design;

- to balance out the degrees of freedom at each level, then consider staggered design;
- if your software will only analyze balanced designs, then use a balanced design;
- the more data you gather, the better the reliability of the results.

6.3.5 Measurement systems

In evaluating a measurement system, the following six properties should be considered. For a full coverage of measurement systems, see Wheeler and Lyday (1984).

I. The ability of the measurement system to discriminate adequately between several measurements (resolution).
II. The stability of the measurement system over time.
III. The sensitivity of the measurement system over different operators, instruments, or equipment, or machines used (reproducibility).
IV. The ability of the measurement system to detect the product variation (sample effect).
V. The measurement system should be repeatable. This is the ability of the measurement system to detect the variability between the replicate readings on the same sample taken by the same operator (repeatability).
VI. The measurement system should be unbiased.

I. Measurement discrimination

- To determine if there is inadequate measurement discrimination, use control charts. The range chart and X-bar chart can be used for this purpose.
- Let us consider two manufacturing discs with diameters 79.6 mm and 80.3 mm. If the measurements are made to the nearest mm, then the two discs will both yield measurements of 80 mm.
- If these two discs are samples from the same subgroup, then the subgroup range will be zero, when in fact the two discs differ by 0.7 mm.
- If this situation dominates, it will result in an average range that will be small, which will in turn result in artificially tight control limits.
- *Case history*: Table 6.3 presents a case history of replicated data collected on disc diameter measurements for a hypothetical production run. We will use the data to illustrate the distribution of disc diameters and differences between sources of variation.

Figure 6.22 shows a scatterplot of the values in the last two columns of Table 6.3. Figure 6.23 shows the histogram of the data.

Table 6.3 Nested design for disc diameters in centimeters

Instrument (Source A)	Operator (Source B)	Sample (Source C)	Test (Source D) Replicate 1	Replicate 2
1	1	1	14.83	14.62
		2	14.88	15.12
		3	14.76	14.38
		4	13.59	13.66
		5	14.08	14.25
	2	6	13.34	13.01
		7	12.56	13.27
		8	13.33	13.54
		9	13.45	13.78
		10	13.96	13.55
2	3	11	13.21	13.50
		12	13.00	13.25
		13	13.48	13.32
		14	14.09	13.94
		15	13.96	13.77
	4	16	13.20	13.00
		17	13.67	13.45
		18	13.39	13.65
		19	13.28	13.67
		20	13.55	13.48
3	5	21	14.90	15.53
		22	15.41	15.21
		23	15.65	15.98
		24	16.06	15.46
		25	16.02	16.34
	6	26	16.13	15.54
		27	15.27	15.80
		28	15.96	16.34
		29	15.42	16.63
		30	16.14	15.84
4	7	31	16.00	15.76
		32	17.05	16.76
		33	16.22	16.45
		34	17.21	16.68
		35	17.43	17.49
	8	36	16.68	16.32

continued

Table 6.3 *continued*

Instrument (Source A)	Operator (Source B)	Sample (Source C)	Test (Source D)	
			Replicate 1	Replicate 2
		37	15.87	15.54
		38	15.42	15.65
		39	15.23	16.01
		40	15.65	14.87
5	9	41	13.94	13.55
		42	13.49	13.32
		43	14.00	13.65
		44	13.54	13.06
		45	14.11	14.65
	10	46	14.28	14.89
		47	13.35	13.90
		48	14.70	14.10
		49	14.44	14.35
		50	14.96	13.99

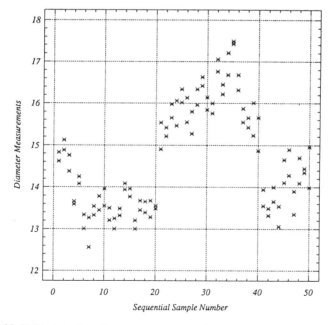

Figure 6.22 X–Y plot of replicated measurement data.

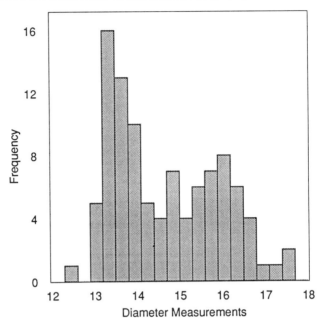

Figure 6.23 Histogram of replicated measurement data.

The descriptive statistics for the measurement data are presented below:

N	MEAN	MEDIAN	TRMEAN	STDEV	SEMEAN
100	14.690	14.410	14.649	1.247	0.125
MIN	MAX	Q1	Q3		
12.560	17.490	13.550	15.790		

The box plots (X–Y scatterplots) for the data categories of instrument, operator, test, and sample are presented in Figure 6.24. The multiple X–Y–Z scatterplot for the categories are presented in Figure 6.25.

Figure 6.26 shows a multivariable plot of measured diameters with respect to instrument categories and sample number. From the plot, we can conclude the following:

- the largest variation is from instruments I and IV;
- instruments III and IV generate larger diameters consistently than instrument I, II, and V;
- the within variation is smallest for instrument II;
- no significant operator effect;
- no significant difference in the sample-to-sample variability.
- The R chart for disc diameter measurements is presented in Figure 6.27, for which:

$$\sigma_{test} = \frac{\bar{R}}{d_2} = 0.3299/1.128 = 0.2925.$$

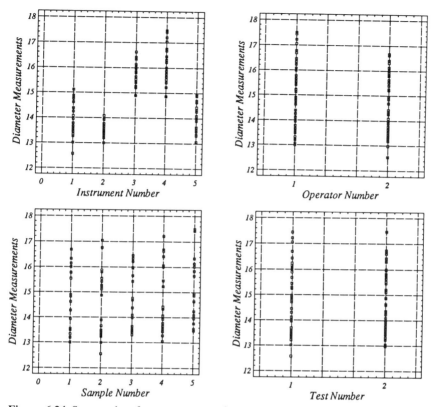

Figure 6.24 Scatter plots for measurement data.

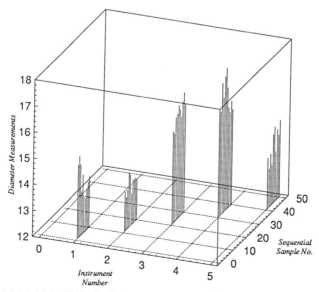

Figure 6.25 Multiple X–Y–Z plot for measurement data.

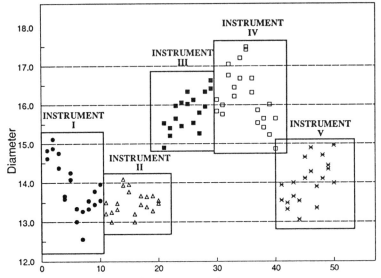

Figure 6.26 Multivariable plot of measurement data.

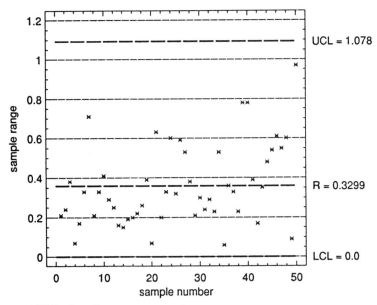

Figure 6.27 R chart for measurement data.

The R chart for sample average from Test I and Test II is presented in Figure 6.28. The figure tells us whether or not sample to sample variability is consistent. The R chart for operator average is presented in Figure 6.29. The following points should be noted:

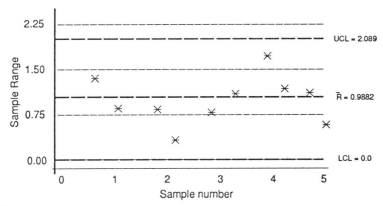

Figure 6.28 R chart for sample average.

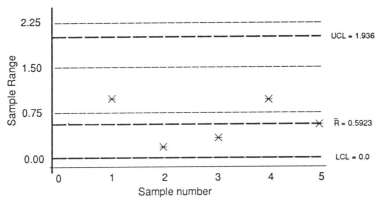

Figure 6.29 R chart for operator average.

- with only five data points, it would be very difficult to find out whether there are special causes among the operators;
- variance component analysis is valid only if there are no special causes in the data.

The variance component result is provided in Table 6.4.

The total standard deviation is given by $\sqrt{1.84597} = 1.3586$. Based on the contents of Table 6.4, we can make the following observations.

- The greatest source of variability is coming from the instrument (76% of total variability).
- Improvement efforts should be focused on the instrument.
- Since the R-chart is in control, check to see if the chart is bottom heavy by calculating the percentage of points below R-bar on the range chart. Sixty-seven % below R-bar will qualify the chart as bottom heavy.
- Estimate of measurement variability is $\bar{R}/d_2 = 0.3299/1.128 = 0.2925$.

Table 6.4 Analysis of variance for diameter measurements

Source	DF	SS	MS	F	P
Instrument	4	122.8969	30.7242	12.31	0.008
Operator (Instrum)	5	12.4808	2.4962	7.00	0.000
Sample (Instrum Operator)	40	14.2604	0.3565	4.21	0.000
Error	50	4.2349	0.0847		
Total	99	153.8731			

Source	Variance Component	Std Deviation	% Variation
Instrument	1.41140	1.1880	76.45%
Operator	0.21396	0.46256	11.59%
Sample	0.13591	0.36866	7.36%
Error	0.08470	0.29103	4.60%
Total	1.84597		100%

6.3.6 SPC for short runs

Most production operations produce different types of products. The frequency of production is usually different for some products. This production frequency may be daily, weekly, or monthly for some products, and may even be quarterly or yearly for some other products. If a separate chart is used to control a process, and a product change occurs, then the control chart also changes. This, therefore, does not allow the process to be continuously monitored when these changes occur. Therefore, it is sometimes very difficult to apply the Shewhart control chart technique for situations where products are changing regularly. However, short-run control chart can be used to control chart a process with different products on the same chart. This will enable products that are not produced frequently to be charted on the same chart with products of regular frequency. Hence, the short-run chart does not change when the product changes, therefore, allowing continuous process monitoring and control.

The procedure for short-run chart is simple and can be accomplished by first standardizing the original data obtained from an actual production process. Even though this standardization allows products with different targets and specifications to be plotted on the same chart, it is also sometimes difficult to implement on the production floor. In addition, another drawback of this method is the inability to chart the actual production values on the control chart. Instead, standardized values are charted, and this can sometimes cause confusion on the production floor because operators are not used to seeing this type of information on the chart.

I. Short-run procedure for X-bar control chart

- Calculate $\bar{X}$ and $\bar{R}$ for all products
- Calculate and plot short-run data points using the following:

$$\text{Short-run data} = \frac{\bar{X} - \bar{\bar{X}}}{\bar{R}}$$

and

$$UCL = +A_2$$
$$LCL = -A_2$$

where:

$\bar{X}$ = Subgroup average of product being charted
$\bar{\bar{X}}$ = Overall subgroup average of product being charted
$\bar{R}$ = Average range of product being charted
A_2 = Control chart constant for different subgroup sizes

II. Short-run procedure for individual chart.

- Calculate $\bar{\bar{X}}$ and $\overline{MR}$ for all products
- Calculate and plot short run data points using the following:

$$\text{Short-run data} = \frac{X - \bar{X}}{\overline{MR}}$$

and
UCL = +2.66
LCL = −2.66
where:
X = Current values of product being charted
$\bar{\bar{X}}$ = Overall average of product being charted
$\overline{MR}$ = Average moving range of product being charted

If the process is going to be adjusted to maintain control, the target can be used rather than $\bar{X}$ or $\bar{\bar{X}}$. If the process is not centered, then adjust it so that $\bar{\bar{X}}$ or $\bar{X}$ will be the target.

Example for short-run control chart for individual

Suppose we have the data in Table 6.5 for short-run data on pull strength. The moving range (MR) table is presented in Table 6.6. The average moving range ($\overline{MR}$) table is presented in Table 6.7.

Sample calculations:

I. For the first data point, the product type is WAX.
    Pull strength (X) = 101.0 (WAX)

Table 6.5 Short-run data on pull strength

Time Order	Product Type	Pull Strength	Short-Run Data
1	WAX	101	−0.273
2	WAX	103	0.333
3	WAX	98	−1.182
4	ROC	102	−0.224
5	ROC	114	1.567
6	ROC	117	2.015
7	ROC	116	1.866
8	ROC	116	1.866
9	ROC	115	1.716
10	ROC	114	1.567
11	CDM	178	1.474
12	CDM	167	0.526
13	CDM	171	0.871
14	CDM	183	1.905
15	WAX	96	−1.787
16	WAX	100	−0.576
17	WAX	106	1.242
18	WAX	101	−0.273
19	CDM	142	−1.629
20	CDM	143	−1.543
21	CDM	148	−1.112
22	CDM	155	−0.509
23	ROC	78	−3.806
24	ROC	87	−2.463
25	ROC	91	−1.866
26	ROC	94	−1.418
27	ROC	98	−0.821
28	WAX	106	1.242
29	WAX	105	0.939
30	WAX	103	0.333

WAX Average $(\bar{X})$ = 101.9
WAX Average $\overline{MR}$ = 3.3

$$\text{Short-run data} = \frac{X - \bar{X}}{\overline{MR}} = \frac{101.0 - 101.9}{3.30} = -0.273.$$

II. For data point No. 6, the product type is ROC.
   Pull strength (X) = 117.0 (ROC)
   ROC Average $(\bar{X})$ = 103.5
   ROC Average $\overline{MR}$ = 6.7

$$\text{Short-run data} = \frac{X - \bar{\bar{X}}}{\overline{MR}} = \frac{117.0 - 103.5}{6.7} = 2.015.$$

Figure 6.30 shows the control chart for the pull strength.

Table 6.6 Moving range table for short-run data

ROW	WAX	ROC	CDM	MR WAX	MR ROC	MR CDM
1	101	102	178	2	12	11
2	103	114	167	5	3	4
3	98	117	171	2	1	12
4	96	116	183	2	0	41
5	100	116	142	6	1	1
6	106	115	143	5	1	5
7	101	114	148	5	36	7
8	106	78	155	1	9	
9	105	87		2	4	
10	103	91			3	
11		94			4	
12		98				

Table 6.7 Moving average table for short-run data

Product	Average	MR Average
WAX	101.9	3.3
ROC	103.5	6.7
CDM	160.9	11.6

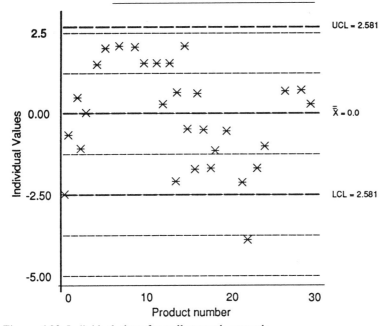

Figure 6.30 Individual chart for pull strength example.

6.4 DESIGN OF EXPERIMENTS

Design of experiments refers to the determination of how observations are to be taken in a study. The design involves questions such as the following.

- How many observations should be used?
- Where should the observations be collected?
- In what order should the observations be collected?
- What variables should be controlled?
- What is the randomization procedure?

The output of an experiment will be a mathematical model describing the process under study. This usually will express a response variable as a function of a set of independent variables. A statement of the research hypothesis should indicate what the experimenter expects to find in the data. For example, the hypothesis of a study might be stated as follows.

Statement: The four processes produce comparable quality levels. Operational decisions are expected to be derived from the results of an experiment.

The following steps are recommended for carrying out a designed experiment.

I.　Objectives of the experiment
　　There should be a clear understanding of the following.

　　What is to be studied?
　　What questions do we want the experiment to answer?
　　What do we want to achieve from the experiment?

　　All these questions should be answered and translated into a set of objectives for the experiment prior to the planning stage of the experiment.

II.　Choice of factors and levels to investigate

- Carefully select the factors or independent variables to be investigated in the experiment.
- Consider quantitative versus qualitative factors.
- Determine whether factor levels should be fixed or random.
- Select two or more levels of the factors or independent variables to be investigated.

III.　Selection of response or dependent variables
　　The following items are very important at this stage:

　　how the response(s) will be measured;
　　the stability and accuracy of the measurement system;
　　the response(s) ability to provide information about the problem under study.

IV. Choice of experimental design

- The experiment must be designed to answer all the objective questions.
- The design must be statistically efficient and economically feasible.
- The design must be balanced.
- In deciding which design to set up, attention should be carefully paid to how data are to be collected and analyzed.
- The results should be simple to interpret.
- The design should adequately cover the experimental region of interest.
- The design should enable the investigator to:

    estimate experimental errors;
    identify significant factors;
    estimate model parameters;
    estimate the effect of each factor independently;
    test model for adequacy.

V. Design verification

- Check to see if the selected design answers all the questions in the objective statement.
- If it does not, redesign the experiment.

VI. Running the experiment

- Data collection strategies

    Determine how data is to be collected and analyzed.

- Particular emphasis should be placed on:

    randomization (full, partial, or none);
    replications;
    repetitions;
    maintaining uniform experimental environment.

VII. Data analysis

- Use statistical methods for the analysis.
- Use available software tools for the analysis.
- Various graphical tools should also be employed, such as the seven new tools.

VIII. Conclusions and recommendations

- Conclusions and recommendations should be drawn based on the results from the experiment.
- Use charts and graphs to present results.

6.4.1 Experiment to compare means

This type of experiment is normally run to detect if differences exist between two or more alternatives, such as differences between two or more machines, temperature levels, testers, suppliers, etc.

Case study

Objective: A small chemical company is interested in comparing two different adhesives, BA-50 and KA-55, for adhesion.

The experimental design: One batch of adhesive can coat two jumbo rolls. Each roll of jumbo is about 1000 ft long. Ten batches of each adhesive type are made. Table 6.8 shows a design in which ten batches of BA-50 were made first, followed by ten batches of KA-55.

Table 6.8 Non-randomized design

Time Order	Adhesive	Time Order	Adhesive
1	BA-50	11	KA-55
2	BA-50	12	KA-55
3	BA-50	13	KA-55
4	BA-50	14	KA-55
5	BA-50	15	KA-55
6	BA-50	16	KA-55
7	BA-50	17	KA-55
8	BA-50	18	KA-55
9	BA-50	19	KA-55
10	BA-50	20	KA-55

There is a possibility that this non-randomized approach can be subjected to non-random sources of variation which may affect the adhesion values. In order to protect the experiment from being biased, the company decided to randomize the order of the batches of the two adhesives.

6.4.2 Randomization

There are three basic ways to set the levels of independent variables in an experimental study.

1. *Rigidly restricted or controlled levels*: In this case, extrapolation is not recommended. An example is an experiment involving only the products from one selected vendor.
2. *Manipulated levels*: In this case, the levels of variables are set as desired. An example is an experiment involving the study of certain batch runs from several vendors.
3. *Randomized levels*: In this case, levels of each variable are selected at

random. An example is an experiment involving the second, fifth, sixth, and tenth batches from each vendor in a study.

Randomization can be achieved through a process that gives all possible sequences equal probability of being selected. In practice, we can randomize by generating random numbers from a computer, or by pulling numbers out of an urn or bowl.

For the experiment in our adhesive example, the company's process engineers use MINITAB random command to generate the order of the experimental run in the format shown below:

Original Order	Run Order	Adhesive
•	1	•
•	2	•
•	3	•
•	•	•
•	•	•
•	•	•

Since the chemical company was unable to randomize individual jumbo in this experiment, then the company elected to randomize batches. The experimental unit therefore is the batch with a sample size of ten batches for each adhesive type.

For careful characterization of each batch, the process engineers decided to sample from each jumbo, resulting in two observations per batch. They then averaged the two observations and analyzed the average adhesion per batch. This resulted in ten replications of the experiment with two repeated measures per batch. Since our experimental unit is a batch, taking multiple samples from the same batch is a repetition, and one must obtain another batch.

- *Replication*: This is when an experimental treatment is repeated on a new experimental unit. Hence, since our experimental unit is a batch, we must obtain another batch to have a replication. This usually increases the precision of the experiment.
- *Repetition or repeated measures*: This is when an experimental treatment is repeated on the same experimental unit. Since our experimental unit is a batch, taking multiple samples from the same batch is a repeated measure.

Statistical analysis

The data in Table 6.9 are analyzed using MINITAB software. The t-test is the statistics used to determine the statistical significance between the two adhesives. Table 6.10 shows the descriptive statistics for the data.

Table 6.9 Data for adhesive example

TOW	BA-50	KA-55
1	68.84	70.46
2	69.22	70.04
3	65.12	66.08
4	71.76	65.36
5	71.28	73.36
6	68.88	73.52
7	67.60	70.80
8	67.97	68.08
9	66.56	63.28
10	65.36	68.02

Table 6.10 Descriptive statistics for adhesive data

	N	MEAN	MEDIAN	TRMEAN	STDEV	SEMEAN
BA-50	10	68.259	68.405	68.214	2.228	0.7051.07
KA-55	10	68.90	69.06	69.03	3.37	

	MIN	MAX	Q1	Q3
BA-50	65.120	71.760	66.260	69.735
KA-55	63.28	73.52	65.90	71.44

Calculation

For the analysis, t-test will be used. The equation for a two-sample t-test is given as:

$$t_{calc} = \frac{(\bar{y}_1 - \bar{y}_2) - (\mu_1 - \mu_2)}{S_p \sqrt{\dfrac{1}{n_1} + \dfrac{1}{n_2}}}$$

The confidence interval is given by:

$$(\bar{y}_1 - \bar{y}_2) \pm t_{v,\frac{\alpha}{2}} S_p \sqrt{\frac{1}{n_1} + \frac{1}{n_2}}$$

where $v = v_1 + v_2$ represents the degrees of freedom associated with the pooled variance.

Suppose we want to compare the two adhesives in our example. The *t-*

distribution is used with degrees of freedom $v = v_1 + v_2$, because we have pooled two variances together. The pooled variance estimate has more degrees of freedom than any one of the two component variances. By pooling variances together, we gain degrees of freedom which moves the *t-distribution* closer to a normal distribution. For our example, we have the following:

$$BA\text{-}50: \bar{y}_1 = 68.259 \ \ s_1 = 2.228$$
$$KA\text{-}55: \bar{y}_2 = 68.90 \ \ s_2 = 3.37$$

$$S_p = \sqrt{\frac{9(2.228)^2 + 9(3.37)^2}{9+9}}$$

$$= 2.857,$$

with 18 degrees of freedom.

$$t_{calc} = \frac{(68.259 - 68.90)}{2.857 \sqrt{\frac{1}{10} + \frac{1}{10}}}$$

$$= -0.502.$$

where $t_{critical} = t_{18,0.025} = 2.10$.

Interpretation

Figure 6.31 presents a graphical representation of the t statistic. With a calculated value of −0.502, we can easily conclude that the two adhesives are statistically the same. Even though there is 0.64 increase in adhesion KA-55 over BA-50, whether or not this difference is of practical significance will be an issue engineers will have to decide.

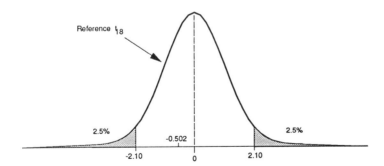

Figure 6.31 Plot for t-test statistic.

6.4.3 Confidence intervals

Confidence interval estimation is another approach to evaluating a process parameter. A confidence interval is the range of values within which we can expect the actual parameter value to fall with a certain level of confidence. For our example, the 95% confidence interval (CI) is computed as:

$$68.259 - 68.90 \pm 2.10(2.857) \sqrt{\frac{1}{10} + \frac{1}{10}}$$

Thus:

$$-5.324 \leq (\mu_1 - \mu_2) \leq 2.042$$

Since zero is contained within the 95% CI, we can conclude that there is no difference between the two adhesive types. Table 6.11 presents a summary of formulae for finding CI intervals for parameters.

Table 6.11 Formulae for confidence intervals

Parameter	Assumptions	$100(1 - \alpha)\%$ CI
μ	n large & σ^2 known or normality & σ^2 known	$\bar{x} \pm z_{\alpha/2} \dfrac{\sigma}{\sqrt{n}}$
μ	n large, σ^2 unknown	$\bar{x} \pm z_{\alpha/2} \dfrac{s}{\sqrt{n}}$
μ	n small, normality, σ^2 unknown	$\bar{x} \pm t_{\alpha/2,n-1} \dfrac{s}{\sqrt{n}}$
p	binomial experiment, n large	$\hat{p} \pm z_{\alpha/2} \sqrt{\dfrac{\hat{p}\hat{q}}{n}}$
σ^2	normality	$\left(\dfrac{(n-1)s_2}{\xi^2_{\alpha/2,n-1}}, \dfrac{(n-1)s^2}{\xi^2_{-\alpha/2,n-1}} \right)$
$\mu_1 - \mu_2$	n_1, n_2 large, independence, σ_1^2, σ_2^2 known or normality, independence, σ_1^2, σ_2^2 known	$(\bar{x}_1 - \bar{x}_2) \pm z_{\alpha/2} \sqrt{\dfrac{\sigma_1}{n_1} + \dfrac{\sigma_2}{n_2}}$
$\mu_1 - \mu_2$	n_1, n_2 large, independence, σ_1^2, σ_2^2 unknown	$(\bar{x}_1 - \bar{x}_2) \pm z_{\alpha/2} \sqrt{\dfrac{s_1}{n_1} + \dfrac{s_2}{n_2}}$
$\mu_1 - \mu_2$	normality, n_1, n_2 small, independence, σ_1^2, σ_2^2 unknown but equal	$(\bar{x}_1 - \bar{x}_2) \pm t_{\alpha/2,n_1+n_2-2}S_p \sqrt{\dfrac{1}{n_1} + \dfrac{1}{n_2}}$ $S_p = \dfrac{(n_1 - 1)s_1^2 + (n_2 - 1)s_2^2}{n_1 + n_2 - 2}$

continued

Table 6.11 *continued*

Parameter	Assumptions	$100(1-\alpha)\%$ CI
$\mu_1 - \mu_2$	normality, n_1, n_2 small, independence, σ_1^2, σ_2^2 unknown and unequal	$(\bar{x}_1 - \bar{x}_2) \pm t_{\alpha/2, v} \sqrt{\dfrac{s_1^2}{n_1} + \dfrac{s_2^2}{n_2}}$ $v = \dfrac{\left(\dfrac{s_1^2}{n_1} + \dfrac{s_2^2}{n_2}\right)^2}{\dfrac{(s_1^2/n_1)^2}{n_1-1} + \dfrac{(s_2^2/n_2)^2}{n_2-1}}$
$\mu_D = \mu_1 - \mu_2$	normality, n pairs, n small, dependence	$\bar{d} \pm t_{\alpha/2, n-1} \dfrac{s_D}{\sqrt{n}}$
$p_1 - p_2$	binomial experiments, n_1, n_2 large, independence	$(\hat{p}_1 - \hat{p}_2) \pm z_{\alpha/2} \sqrt{\dfrac{\hat{p}_1 \hat{q}_1}{n_1} + \dfrac{\hat{p}_2 \hat{q}_2}{n_2}}$
$\dfrac{\sigma_1^2}{\sigma_2^2}$	normality, independence	$\left(\dfrac{s_1^2/s_2^2}{F_{\alpha/2, n_1-1, n_2-1}}, \dfrac{s_1^2/s_2^2}{F_{1-\alpha/2, n_1-1, n_2-1}} \right)$

6.4.4 Hypothesis testing for quality improvement

Statistical inference is usually divided into two categories: hypothesis testing and estimation. Hypothesis testing involves rejecting or accepting statements about process parameters. Estimation involves estimating the values of process parameters. The discussions on data analysis in the preceding chapter deal with estimating parameters such as mean, variance, and proportion.

There are two types of hypotheses: the null hypothesis and the alternate hypothesis. The null hypothesis is denoted as H_0 while the alternate hypothesis is denoted as H_1. The null hypothesis is formed primarily to determine if it can be rejected. It represents a probable statement that is viewed as being correct until it is statistically rejected or accepted. The null hypothesis often involves a statement that a process parameter is equal to a specified value. The idea of 'no action needed' or 'no difference exists' is often conveyed by the null hypothesis. Hence, the name null hypothesis, where null implies 'no action' or 'no difference' or 'do nothing'. The implication is that if the null hypothesis is rejected, then further action will be required either to identify the cause of the difference or to identify the mechanism for improving the process being studied.

As an example, the statement innocent until proven guilty is a judicial null hypothesis that can be stated as follows:

H_0: the suspect is innocent;
H_1: the suspect is guilty.

Rejecting or accepting the null hypothesis in the above example does not confirm or repudiate the suspect's innocence beyond doubt. Rejection or acceptance is based on available evidence which may not be enough to get at the truth. Similarly, in a statistical evaluation of a process, rejecting or accepting the null hypothesis does not mean that we have arrived at the final conclusion about the process. The tentative conclusion may be limited by the caliber of the data (evidence) available.

One-tailed versus two-tailed hypothesis testing

A test of hypothesis may be one-tailed or two-tailed, based on the direction of the statement contained in the alternate hypothesis. An example of a two-tailed test is:

H_0: process average = 200
H_1: process average $\neq$ 200

In the above example, H_0 will be rejected if the process average is above or below 200. The one-tailed tests for the example are explained below:

H_0: process average = 200
H_1: process average > 200

In this case, H_0 will be rejected only if the process average is above 200.

H_0: process average = 200
H_1: process average < 200

In this case, H_0 will be rejected only if the process average is below 200.

Hypothesis testing can be done to evaluate a single process based on a sample from the process. This is referred to as a one-sample study. If the study is done to compare two processes based on samples drawn from the processes, then the study is referred to as a two-sample study. Table 6.12 presents hypothesis tests for one-sample studies, while Table 6.13 presents hypothesis tests for two-sample studies. Readers should refer to Kokoska and Nevison (1989), Jobson (1991), Beyer (1991), or other statistics texts for further details on statistical tables and formulae.

6.4.5 Type I and Type II errors in quality improvement

Type I error refers to the rejection of the null hypothesis when it is true. Type I error is normally expressed in terms of a significance level denoted as α. That is:

Table 6.12 One-sample hypothesis test

H_0	Assumptions	H_1	Test Statistic	Rejection Region
$\mu=\mu_0$	n large & σ^2 known or normality & σ^2 known	$\mu>\mu_0$ $\mu<\mu_0$ $\upsilon\neq\mu_0$	$Z=\dfrac{\bar{X}-\mu_0}{\sigma/\sqrt{n}}$	$Z\geq z_\alpha$ $Z\leq -z_\alpha$ $\lvert Z\rvert\geq z_{\alpha/2}$
$\mu=\mu_0$	n large, σ^2 unknown	$\mu>\mu_0$ $\mu<\mu_0$ $\mu\neq\mu_0$	$Z=\dfrac{\bar{X}-\mu_0}{s/\sqrt{n}}$	$Z\geq z_\alpha$ $Z\leq -z_\alpha$ $\lvert Z\rvert\geq z_{\alpha/2}$
$\mu=\mu_0$	normality, n small, σ^2 unknown	$\mu>\mu_0$ $\mu<\mu_0$ $\mu\neq\mu_0$	$T=\dfrac{\bar{X}-\mu_0}{s/\sqrt{n}}$	$T\geq t_{\alpha,n-1}$ $T\leq -t_{\alpha,n-1}$ $\lvert T\rvert\geq t\delta2\alpha_{/2,n-1}$
$p=p_0$	binomial experiment, n large	$p>p_0$ $p<p_0$ $p\neq p_0$	$Z=\dfrac{\hat{p}-p_0}{\sqrt{p_0(1-p_0)/n}}$	$Z\geq z_\alpha$ $Z\leq -z_\alpha$ $\lvert Z\rvert\geq z_{\alpha/2}$
$\sigma^2=\sigma_0^2$	normality	$\sigma^2>\sigma_0^2$ $\sigma^2<\sigma_0^2$ $\sigma^2\neq\sigma_0^2$	$\xi^2=\dfrac{(n-1)S^2}{\sigma_0^2}$	$\xi^2\geq \xi_{\alpha,n-1}^2$ $\xi^2\leq \xi_{1-\alpha,n-1}^2$ $\xi^2\leq \xi_{1-\alpha/2,n-1}^2$ or $\xi^2\leq \xi_{\alpha/2,n-1}^2$

$$\alpha = P(\text{Type I Error})$$
$$= P(\text{rejecting } H_0 \mid H_0 \text{ is true})$$

The significance level for the test of hypothesis is often denoted as:

$$\text{Significance level} = 1 - \alpha.$$

As an example, $\alpha = 0.0001$ implies taking one chance in 1000 of rejecting the null hypothesis when it is true.

Type II error refers to the acceptance of the null hypothesis when it is false. This is denoted as:

$$\beta = P(\text{Type II Error})$$
$$= P(\text{accepting } H_0 \mid H_0 \text{ is false})$$

In terms of process improvement studies, there will be an opportunity cost associated with accepting the null hypothesis when it is false. The probability of rejecting the null hypothesis when it is false is referred to as the power of the hypothesis test and it is denoted as:

$$\text{Power} = 1 - \beta$$
$$= P(\text{rejecting } H_0 \mid H_o \text{ is false})$$

Table 6.13 Two-sample hypothesis tests

H_0	Assumptions	H_1	Test Statistic	Rejection Region
$\mu_1-\mu_2=D_0$	n_1, n_2 large, independence, σ_1^2, σ_2^2 known or normality, independence, σ_1^2, σ_2^2 unknown	$\mu_1-\mu_2>D_0$ $\mu_1-\mu_2<D_0$ $\mu_1-\mu_2\neq D_0$	$Z = \dfrac{(\bar{X}_1 - X_2) - D_0}{\sqrt{\sigma_1^2/n_1 + \sigma_2^2/n_2}}$	$Z \geq z_\alpha$ $Z \leq -z_\alpha$ $|Z| \geq z_{\alpha/2}$
$\mu_1-\mu_2=D_0$	n_1, n_2 large, independence, σ_1^2, σ_2^2 unknown	$\mu_1-\mu_2>D_0$ $\mu_1-\mu_2<D_0$ $\mu_1-\mu_2\neq D_0$	$Z = \dfrac{(\bar{X}_1 - X_2) - D_0}{\sqrt{s_1^2/n_1 + s_2^2/n_2}}$	$Z \geq z_\alpha$ $Z \leq -z_\alpha$ $|Z| \geq z_{\alpha/2}$
$\mu_1-\mu_2=D_0$	n_1, n_2 small, normality, independence, σ_1^2, σ_2^2 unknown but equal	$\mu_1-\mu_2>D_0$ $\mu_1-\mu_2<D_0$ $\mu_1-\mu_2\neq D_0$	$\dfrac{(\bar{x}_1 - \bar{x}_2) - D_0}{S_p \sqrt{\dfrac{1}{n_1} + \dfrac{1}{n_2}}}$ $S_p = \dfrac{(n_1-1)s_1^2 + (n_2-1)s_2^2}{n_1+n_2-2}$	$T \geq t_{\alpha,n_1+n_2-2}$ $T \leq -t_{\alpha,n_1+n_2-2}$ $|T| \geq t_{\alpha/2,n_1+n_2-2}$
$\mu_1-\mu_2=D_0$	n_1, n_2 small, normality, independence, σ_1^2, σ_2^2 unknown and unequal	$\mu_1-\mu_2>D_0$ $\mu_1-\mu_2<D_0$ $\mu_1-\mu_2\neq D_0$	$\dfrac{(\bar{x}_1 - \bar{x}_2) - D_0}{\sqrt{s_1^2/n_1 + s_2^2/n_2}}$ $v = \dfrac{\left(\dfrac{s_1^2}{n_1} + \dfrac{s_2^2}{n_2}\right)^2}{\dfrac{(s_1^2/n_1)^2}{n_1-1} + \dfrac{(s_2^2/n_2)^2}{n_2-1}}$	$T \geq t_{\alpha/2,v}$ $T \leq -t_{\alpha/2,v}$ $|T| \geq t_{\alpha/2,v}$
$\mu_D=D_0$	n small, n pairs, normality, dependence	$\mu_D>D_0$ $\mu_D<D_0$ $\mu_D\neq D_0$	$\dfrac{\bar{D} - D_0}{S_D/\sqrt{n}}$	$T \geq t_{\alpha,n-1}$ $T \leq -t_{\alpha,n-1}$ $|T| \geq t_{\alpha/2,n-1}$
$\sigma_1^2=\sigma_2^2$	normality, independence	$\sigma_1^2>\sigma_2^2$ $\sigma_1^2<\sigma_2^2$ $\sigma_1^2\neq\sigma_2^2$	$F = S_1^2/S_2^2$	$F \geq F_{\alpha,n_1-1,n_2-1}$ $F \leq F_{1-\alpha,n_1-1,n_2-1}$ $F \leq F_{1-\alpha/2,n_1-1,n_2-1}$

This may be viewed as the discriminating capability of the test. Power of the test may be increased by doing the following.

1. Increasing the sample size.
2. Increasing α which means that the significance level, $1 - \alpha$, will be decreased. Thus, the test will be more effective in detecting differences. The higher the desired significance level, the more difficult it will be for the test to be powerful (or effective).

The p-value of a statistical test is the smallest α level for which H_0 can be rejected. The objective is to minimize the p-value. That is, to minimize the probability of Type I error.

Producer's risk versus the consumer's risk

Type II error is often referred to as the consumer's risk, while Type I error is referred to as the producer's risk. Supposing we have a batch or products from a process and we want to ascertain the quality level of the batch through a test of hypothesis. Rejecting the batch when it is good implies a risk to the producer since a rejected batch never makes it to the market. On the other hand, accepting the batch when it is bad implies a risk to the consumer since there is the potential that a consumer will end up with a bad product. This illustration is summarized in Table 6.14.

Table 6.14 Producer's risk versus consumer's risk

	Good Batch	*Bad Batch*
Accept Batch	Correct decision $1 - \alpha$	Type II Error (Consumer's Risk) β
Reject Batch	Type I Error (Producer's Risk) α	Correct decision $(1 - \beta)$

7	# Additional statistical techniques

Little bits of improvement translate to vast process improvement

This chapter presents additional statistical tools for quality and process improvement. These additional tools can be used for special cases that do not fit the tools presented earlier. Topics covered in this chapter include factorial designs, response surface methodology, central composite designs, and time series analysis. The chapter is designed for practitioners who need more specialized tools to handle special cases.

7.1 FACTORIAL DESIGNS

A factorial experiment is an experiment designed to study the effects of two or more factors, each of which is applied at two or more levels. In a balanced classical factorial experiment, all combinations of all the levels of the factors are tested. In this chapter, we consider only two-level factorial designs. In a 2^k factorial design, 2 represents the number of levels and k represents the number of factors.

A factorial experiment can be used to study how a response variable is influenced by certain factors. It can also be used to assess the effect of changing one factor independent of other factors. The premise of factorial experiments is that an observed response may be due to a multitude of factors. Since a dependent variable interacts with its environment, it is important to assess the simultaneous effects of more than one factor on the dependent variable. The example below shows a case where one response variable is influenced by two independent factors. Each factor is to be studied at three different levels.

Response variable: Epoxy strength
Factor 1: Temperature (75°, 80°, 85°)
Factor 2: Chemical concentration (high, medium, low)

Advantages of factorial experiment

A factorial experiment has several advantages, including those presented below.

- Efficiency
  More robust compared to traditional, single-factor experiments.
  In one-factor study, it may be difficult to identify which one factor should be studied.
  More flexibility.
- Information content
  More information can be derived from factorial experiments compared to single factor experiments.
- Validity of results
  Inclusion of multiple factors increases the validity of results.
  Results can identify direction for further experiments.

Factor

This is an independent variable or condition that is likely to affect the response or quality characteristic of interest. A factor may be a continuous variable such as oven temperature, RPM, pump pressure, web speed, etc., or may be a discrete (qualitative) variable such as catalyst type (A or B), valve (on or off), material type (A or B), cooling step (wet or dry), etc. Temperature, pressure, RPM, etc., are factors that can be controlled and measured. Therefore, they can be regarded as controllable and measurable factors. However, factors such as percent moisture going into an oven, and ambient humidity are measurable but uncontrollable. These factors are known as covariates. Other factors which are uncontrollable and immeasurable are useful in defining experimental error.

Levels

These are the settings of various factors in a factorial experiment, such as high and low values of temperature, pressure, etc. For example, if the range of temperature to be studied is between 120°F and 180°F, then the low level can be set at 120°F and high level set at 180°F.

Response

This is the measurement obtained when an experiment is run at each level of the factors under study. Responses may be continuous (quantitative) variables such as adhesion, percent yield, smoothness, etc., or discrete (qualitative) variables such as good or bad tastes, corrosion or no corrosion, etc.

The basic layout of a factorial design is presented in Table 7.1 for a two-factor experiment. Factor A has a levels. Factor B has b levels. There are n replicates for each cell. Each cell in the layout is referred to as a treatment which represents a specific combination of factor levels. There are a total of $N = abn$ observations in the layout. Factorial designs are referred to as 2^f, 3^f, and

Table 7.1 Layout of data collection for a two-factor factorial design

Factor B Levels	Factor A Levels (sum, average, etc.)				Row Summary
	$i=1$	$i=2$	....	$i=a$	
$j=1$	y_{111} y_{112} . . y_{11n}				α_1 α_2 . . .
$j=2$			y_{ijk}		.
$j=3$ . . $j=b$					. . . α_b
Column Summary	β_1	β_2	....	β_a	....

so on. In a 2^f design, there are f factors, each having two levels. In a 3^f design, there are f factors, each having three levels.

There are three possible models for a factorial experiment depending on how the factor levels are chosen.

- *Fixed model*: In this model, all the levels of the factors in the experiment are fixed.
- *Random model*: In this model, the levels of the factors in the experiment are chosen at random.
- *Mixed model*: In this model, the levels of some of the factors in the experiment are fixed while the levels of some of the factors are random.

The statistical model for the factorial experiment in Table 7.1 is presented below:

$$Y_{ijk} = \mu + A_i + B_j + (AB)_{ij} + \varepsilon_{k(ij)}$$

where
$i = 1, 2, \ldots, a$
$j = 1, 2, \ldots, b$
$k = 1, 2, \ldots, n$
A_i = effect of the ith level of factor A
B_j = effect of the jth level of factor B
$(AB)_{ij}$ = effect of the interaction between A_i and B_j

Y_{ijk} = observation for the kth replicate of the A_i and B_j combination

$\varepsilon_{k(ij)}$ = random error associated with each unique combination of A_i and B_j.

μ = population mean.

The error terms are assumed to be independent and identically distributed normal variates with mean of zero and variance σ_ε^2.

7.2 EXPERIMENTAL RUN

A run is when each control factor is set or fixed at a specific level and the experiment is run at those levels for the factors under study. For example, if an experimenter selects a pressure of 20 psi, a temperature of 150°F and a valve that is open, then this combination will represent a run.

One-variable-at-a-time experimentation

A one-variable-at-a-time experiment can be demonstrated by considering, say, three factors A, B, and C. Let us say initially that each factor is set at its low level. This means that A is at low, B is at low, and C is at low. When this level is run, the response y is 45. Now to determine the effect of factor A, the level of A is changed from low to high, and factors B and C still remained at low. Under this condition, the response value y is, say, 20.

The change in the response value from 45, when all the three factors were set at their low levels, to 20 when only factor A was changed from low to its high level, can only be due to the effect of factor A and/or experimental error. Similarly, the investigator can determine the effect of factor B by setting A at low, B at high, and C still remaining at low, and obtains a response value at this new level, say 39. The investigator can now compare this 39 to 45 obtained for the control (run #1) to determine the effect of factor B. The setup can be described as shown below. This is what is known as one-variable-at-a-time experimentation.

	Factors				Response
Run	A	B	C		Y
1	−1	−1	−1	(control)	45
2	1	−1	−1		20
3	−1	1	−1		39
4	−1	−1	1		52

When experimenting with more than one factor, the one-variable-at-a-time experimental approach is inefficient and can provide misleading results. This type of experimentation presents several serious problems. Some of these problems are:

- the effect of each factor is known at only one chosen level of each of the other factors.
- the effect of each factor is separated in time from the effect of other factors. Unknown extraneous factors which vary with time may therefore influence or bias the real effect of any factor under study.

Let us now consider a larger picture of a one-variable-at-a-time experiment. The objective of this experiment is to minimize MAG, an undesirable tar-like by-product. The investigator considered two variables, temperature and concentration, and studied the effects of these two variables on the response MAG. By setting all factors constant, including the temperature, and allowing the concentration to vary between 10 and 90%, the result (Figure 7.1) shows that MAG is minimum at about 28% concentration.

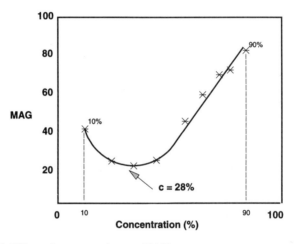

Figure 7.1 Effect of concentration on MAG.

Then the investigator held the concentration constant at 28% and held all other variables constant as well, but varied temperature between 20 and 120°F. The result (Figure 7.2) shows that MAG is minimized at a temperature of 78°F. From this result one can conclude that the minimum MAG we can obtain is 20 at a temperature of 78°F and concentration of 28%.

Figure 7.3 shows a contour plot of temperature and concentration with MAG values plotted within the experimental region. As can be seen, a minimum MAG value of 5 can be achieved at a region of 80% of concentration and 20°F temperature. This example, therefore, demonstrates how a one-variable-at-a-time approach can fail to estimate the effects between two or more factors because the effect of temperature depends on the levels of concentration in this example. This effect between factors is known as interaction, and the one-variable-at-a-time experimental approach lacks the capability of detecting it.

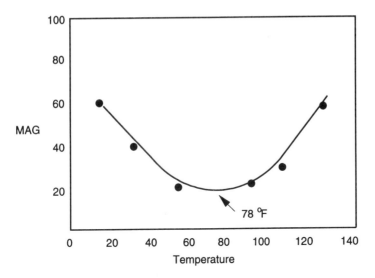

Figure 7.2 Effect of temperature on MAG.

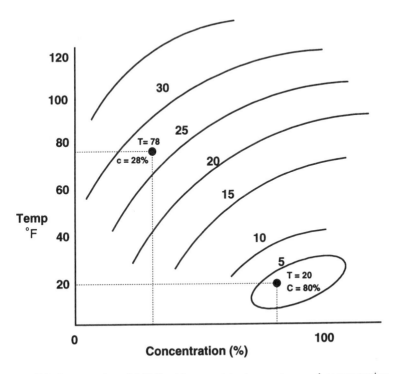

Figure 7.3 Contour plot of MAG with respect to temperature and concentration.

Factorial experiment is superior to one-variable-at-a-time experiment for the following reasons:

- it allows the study of the effects of several factors in the same set of experiment;
- it provides the ability to test for the effect of each factor at all levels of the other factors and determine if this effect changes as the other factors change;
- it is capable of providing not only estimates of the effects separately (main effects), but also the joint effects of two or more factors (interaction effects);
- it provides a more complete picture of what is happening over the entire experimental region than the one variable at a time.

A good factorial experiment should incorporate basic experimental concepts such as randomization, replication, and orthogonality, as well as the iterative nature of experimentation such as conjecture, design, and analysis.

Randomization

Randomization in a design means running the order of experiment in a random (nonsystematic) fashion. This eliminates or balances out the effects of undesirable systematic variation.

Replication

Replication is the running of the same set of conditions more than once. It is very important that, for a true replication to occur, and be distinguished from duplication, one should run the actual set of the condition to be replicated first, record the response, then change at least one or more of the levels, run the experiment at the new levels, and record the response, then come back and run the actual set of the replication again. By running replicate conditions back to back, one would be unable to account for variations that occur due to changes in raw material, operators, etc. In the analysis of the experimental results, it is also important to have an estimate of experimental error (random error) so as to have a meaningful yardstick for determining if estimated effects are real or due to common causes of variability only. Replication runs can be used to provide the estimate of the experimental error.

Orthogonality

Orthogonality in a design implies that the estimates of the main effects and interactions are uncorrelated with each other. Designs having this property ensure that if a systematic change occurs corresponding to any one of the effects, the change will be associated to that effect alone.

7.3 EXPERIMENTING WITH TWO FACTORS: 2^2

Conjecture

A process engineer wants to investigate the effects of two elements, nickel and gold, on the ductility of a new product. The ranges for these variables are as follows:

	Nickel (%)	Gold (%)
Low (−)	10	5
High (+)	20	10

The hypotheses that we will be testing are:

H_0 = Effects are equal to zero (no effects exist)
H_A = Effects are not equal to zero

Design

The design matrix in standard order together with response values for a 2^2 design are presented below:

Design Point	Coded Units			Uncoded Units		
	Nickel	Gold	Strength	Nickel	Gold	Strength
1	−1	−1	52	10	5	52
2	1	−1	58	20	5	58
3	−1	1	75	10	10	75
4	1	1	64	20	10	64

The design point should not be confused with run order. The design point should always be randomized to obtain the run order. The geometry of the design is presented below:

Analysis

Estimation of effects: To calculate an effect, we use the equation

$\bar{Y}$ = response average   Effect Estimate = $\bar{Y}_{High} - \bar{Y}_{Low}$

I.   To estimate the effect of nickel:

$$\text{Effect of nickel} = \frac{58 + 64}{2} - \frac{52 + 75}{2}$$
$$= \bar{Y}_H - \bar{Y}_L$$
$$= 61.0 - 63.5$$
$$= -2.5$$

II.   To estimate the effect of gold:

$$\text{Effect of Gold} = \frac{75 + 64}{2} - \frac{52 + 58}{2}$$
$$= 69.5 - 55$$
$$= 14.5$$

Interpretation

When the amount of nickel is changed from 10% nickel to 20% nickel, the effect on average is a reduction of 2.5 units on the breaking strength, while changing the amount of gold from 5% to 10% increases the breaking strength on average by 14.5 units.

Interaction

The interaction effect is the extent to which the effect of a factor depends on the level of another factor.

III. To estimate the interaction effect between nickel and gold obtain the interaction column by multiplying the nickel column with gold column as follows.

Run	Nickel	Gold	Nickel*gold	Strength
1	−1	−1	1	52
2	1	−1	−1	58
3	−1	1	−1	75
4	1	1	1	64

$$\text{Effect of nickel*gold interaction} = \frac{64 + 52}{2} - \frac{58 + 75}{2}$$
$$= 58.0 - 66.5$$
$$= -8.5$$

Interpretation

By simultaneously changing the amount of nickel and gold, the net effect on average is a reduction of 8.5 units on the breaking strength.

Replication

In order to determine if the above effects are real effects or statistically significant, we must have a good estimate of the experimental error. The investigator, therefore, fully replicated the above design, obtaining a total of eight runs as shown below.

Run	Nickel	Gold	Nickel*gold	Replicate Strength	
1	−1	−1	1	52	49
2	1	−1	−1	58	54
3	−1	1	−1	75	71
4	1	1	−1	64	66

With the new additional data, one can obtain a refined estimate of effect for each factor under study as:

	Strength		
A(+) Nickel	56.00		65.00
A(−)	50.50		73.00
	B(−)	Gold	B(+)

$$\text{Effect of nickel} = \frac{64 + 66 + 58 + 54}{4} - \frac{75 + 71 + 52 + 49}{4}$$

$$= 60.5 - 61.75$$

$$= -2.5$$

$$\text{Effect of gold} = \frac{64 + 66 + 75 + 71}{4} - \frac{58 + 54 + 52 + 49}{4}$$

$$= 69.0 - 53.25$$

$$= 15.75$$

$$\text{Effect of nickel*gold interaction} = \frac{64 + 66 + 52 + 49}{4} - \frac{75 + 71 + 58 + 54}{4}$$

$$= 57.75 - 64.5$$

$$= -6.75$$

The interaction plot for the example is presented in Figure 7.4.

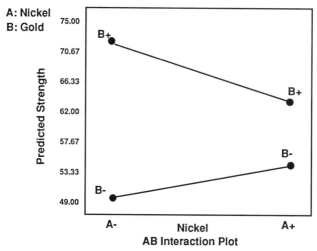

Figure 7.4 Interaction plot for example.

The model

The final model in terms of uncoded factors is:

$$Strength = 9.0 + 1.9*Nickel + 7.2*Gold - 0.27*Nickel*Gold$$

The final model in terms of coded factors is:

$$Strength = 61.125 - 0.625*Nickel + 7.875*Gold - 3.375*Nickel*Gold$$

Estimate of the experimental error

The above estimates of the main effects and the interaction are subjected to errors. Therefore, by running replicates of the experiment we will be able to estimate the experimental error, and this will provide us with the opportunity to interpret the effect of estimates in light of the error.

If we assume that the errors made in taking the observations are independent of one another, then we can estimate the experimental error by calculating the variances of the replicate observations within each design point. The table below shows the results obtained.

	Strength	Variance (s^2)	v=d.f
1.	52 49	4.5	1
2.	58 54	8.0	1
3.	75 71	8.0	1
4.	64 66	2.0	1

If we assume that the variance is homogeneous throughout the experimental region, then we can pool the above variances. The pooled variance can be calculated as:

$$s_{pooled}^2 = \frac{v_1 s_1^2 + v_2 s_2^2 + \ldots v_k s_k^2}{v_1 + v_2 + \ldots + v_k}$$

Therefore,

$$s_{pooled}^2 = \frac{(1)4.5 + (1)8 + (1)8 + (1)2}{1 + 1 + 1 + 1}$$

$$= \frac{22.5}{4}$$

$$= 5.625$$

Therefore, the pooled variance is equal to 5.625 with $v = 4$ degrees of freedom. This pooled variance will be used to construct the confidence intervals about the estimates of effects.

Confidence intervals for the effects

The 95% confidence intervals associated with an effect can be represented as:

$$Effect \pm t_{v,0.25} \sqrt{2s^2/n}$$

where n = total number of observations in each average: $n = 4$, $v = 5$

From t-table, $t_{v,0.025} = t_{5,0.025} = 2.776$

$$s^2 = s_{pooled}^2 = 5.625$$

The 95% confidence intervals for the error are:

$$\pm 2.776 \sqrt{2*(5.625)/4} = \pm 4.655$$

I.   The confidence intervals for the effect of nickel:
     The 95% confidence intervals for the true main effect of nickel is:
     Effect $\pm$ 4.655 = -1.25 ± 4.655 or (-5.905 to 3.405)
II. The confidence intervals for the effect of gold:
     The 95% confidence intervals for the true main effect of gold is:
     Effect $\pm$ 4.655 = 15.75 ± 4.655 or (11.095 to 20.405)
III. The confidence intervals for the interaction effect:
     The 95% confidence intervals for the interaction effect of nickel and gold is:
     Effect $\pm$ 4.655 = -6.75 ± 4.655 or (-11.405 to -2.095)

Conclusion

From the above analysis, we can conclude that the main effect of gold is statistically significant at $\alpha=0.05$. In addition, the interaction between nickel and gold is statistically significant at $\alpha=0.05$. This is because their confidence intervals do not contain zero. However, the main effect of nickel is not statistically significant at $\alpha=0.05$ because its confidence intervals contain zero.

Interpretation

Increasing the amount of gold from 5% to 10% increases the breaking strength by 15.75 units. The practical significance of these 15.75 units needs to be considered further. If this is of practical significance, another experiment on % gold in a different range with some center points may be considered. This new experiment should explore the new range of the percent gold at different levels of the percent nickel since a significant interaction exists between nickel and gold.

7.4 2^3 FACTORIAL DESIGN

Conjecture

We wish to study the effects of webspeed, voltage and webgap on surface roughness of a plating material. It is required that the experiment be capable of estimating all main effects as well as all interactions. Our main objective is to minimize roughness.

Design

A two-level 2^3 full factorial design with some centerpoint replicates will allow us to investigate the three main effects, three two-factor interactions, and one three-factor interaction. The centerpoints will serve two purposes:

- it enables us to test for curvature effect;
- to obtain experimental errors if replicated.

Due to the limited resources, a full 2^3 design with four center points will be considered. These four center points will give us 3 degrees of freedom for our estimate of experimental error. For all practical purposes, 3 degrees of freedom should be considered minimum for error degrees of freedom. The conditions for the factors are:

	Low	Center	High
	(−)	(0)	(+)
Webspeed	20	30	40
Voltage	30	25	30
Webgap	20	20	30

The design matrix in standard order is presented below, together with the roughness response values:

	Speed (S)	Voltage (V)	Gap (G)	S*V	S*G	V*G	S*V*G	Roughness
1.	−1	−1	−1	1	1	1	−1	30
2.	1	−1	−1	−1	−1	1	1	19
3.	−1	1	−1	−1	1	−1	1	37
4.	1	1	−1	1	−1	−1	−1	19
5.	−1	−1	1	1	−1	−1	1	21
6.	1	−1	1	−1	1	−1	−1	18
7.	−1	1	1	−1	−1	1	−1	34
8.	1	1	1	1	1	1	1	20
9.	0	0	0	0	0	0	0	24
10.	0	0	0	0	0	0	0	22
11.	0	0	0	0	0	0	0	23
12.	0	0	0	0	0	0	0	21

The above design is randomized and run. This design is represented geometrically as a cube shown in Figure 7.5.

Analysis

The results obtained for the example are provided below:

Variable	Coefficient	Standardized Effect	Sum of Squares
Overall Average	24.00		
A	−5.75	−11.50	264.50
B	2.75	5.50	60.50
C	−1.50	−3.00	18.00
AB	−2.25	−4.50	40.50
AC	1.50	3.00	18.00
BC	1.00	2.00	8.00
ABC	−0.50	−1.00	2.00
Center Point	−2.25		13.50

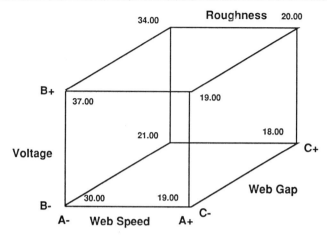

Figure 7.5 Cube plot for example.

ANOVA Result

Source	Sum of Squares	df	Mean Square	F Value	Prob > F
Model	411.50	7	58.79	35.27	0.0070
Curvature	13.50	1	13.50	8.100	0.0653
Residual	5.00	3	1.67		
Pure Error	R5.00	3	1.67		
Corr Total	430.00	11			

Root MSE = 1.291
R-Squared = 0.9880
Adjusted R-Squared = 0.9600
C.V. = 5.38

Variable	Coefficient Estimate	df	Standard Error	t for H_o Coefficient=0	Prob > |t|
Intercept	24.750	1	0.456		
A	−5.750	1	0.456	−12.60	0.0011
B	2.750	1	0.456	6.025	0.0092
C	−1.500	1	0.456	−3.286	0.0462
AB	−2.250	1	0.456	−4.930	0.0160
AC	1.500	1	0.456	3.286	0.0462
BC	1.000	1	0.456	2.191	0.1162
ABC	−0.500	1	0.456	−1.095	0.3534
Center Point	−2.250	1	0.791	−2.846	0.0653

Final equation in terms of coded variables:

$$\text{Roughness} = 24.750 - 5.750 * A + 2.750*B - 1.500*C - 2.250*A*B$$
$$+ 1.500*A*C + 1.000*B*C - 0.500*A*B*C$$

Final equation in terms of uncoded variables:

$$Roughness = 31.500 - 0.250*Webspeed + 0.900*Voltage - 1.850*Webgap$$
$$- 0.025*Webspeed*Voltage + 0.040*Webspeed*Webgap$$
$$+ 0.050*Voltage*Webgap - 0.001*Webspeed*Voltage*Webgap$$

Obs Order	Actual Value	Predicted Value	Residual	STUDENTS Lever	COOK'S Resid	Dist	t VALUE
1	30.00	30.00	−1.637E-11	1.000	0.000	0.000	0.000
2	19.00	19.00	9.095E-12	1.000	0.000	0.000	0.000
3	37.00	37.00	−1.273E-11	1.000	0.000	0.000	0.000
4	19.00	19.00	1.637E-11	1.000	0.000	0.000	0.000
5	21.00	21.00	1.819E-12	1.000	0.000	0.000	0.000
6	18.00	18.00	−1.819E-21	1.000	0.000	0.000	0.000
7	34.00	34.00	−5.547E-12	1.000	0.000	0.000	0.000
8	20.00	20.00	5.457E-12	1.000	0.000	0.000	0.000
9	24.00	22.50	1.5	0.250	1.342	0.067	1.732
10	22.00	22.50	−0.5	0.250	−0.447	0.007	−0.378
11	23.00	22.50	0.5	0.250	0.447	0.007	0.378
12	21.00	22.50	−1.5	0.250	−1.342	0.067	−1.732

Complete analysis of the example indicates that high webspeed, low voltage, and high web gap can be used to minimize surface roughness.

7.5 FRACTIONAL FACTORIAL EXPERIMENTS

For many practical situations, it may be impossible to collect all the observations required by a full factorial experiment. In such cases, fractional factorial experiments are used. In a fractional factorial experiment, only a fraction of the treatment replicates are run. The advantages of fractional factorial experiments include the following:

- lower cost of experimentation;
- reduced time for experimentation;
- efficiency of analysis.

When the number of factors, k, is greater than 5 ($k > 5$), then the number of runs required for a full factorial experiment will be impractical for most industrial applications. However, in some industries, such as the semiconductor industry, where computer simulations are used in the design phase of certain products, the number of runs will be of little concern. Whereas in most other industries, such as chemical, petrochemical, process, paper and pulp, as well as parts industries, where a large number of factors must be examined, it will often be very desirable to reduce the number of runs in an experiment by taking a fraction of the full 2^k factorial design.

In a 2^{k-p} fractional factorial design there are:

- 2 levels of each factor under consideration;
- k number of factors to be studied;
- 2^{k-p} that can be estimated including the overall mean;
- 2^{k-p} minimum number of experimental runs;
- p number of independent generators;
- 2^{k-p} number of words in defining relations (including I).

The requirement is that $2^{k-p} > k$

p = degree of fractionation

p=1 (half fraction)

p=2 (quarter fraction)

2^{k-p} = number of distinct conditions in the cube portion of a design.

For example, a one-half of a 2^3 factorial design is referred to as 2^{3-1} fractional factorial design.

The disadvantages of fractional designs involve loss of one or more of the interaction effects that can be studied in a full factorial design. Also, the design of a fractional factorial experiment can be complicated since it may be difficult to select the treatment combinations to be used. Fractional factorial designs are denoted as follows:

1/2 fractional design: one-half of complete factorial experiment;

1/4 fractional design: one-fourth of complete factorial experiment;

1/8 fractional design: one-eighth of complete factorial experiment.

7.6 A 2^4 FACTORIAL DESIGN

Conjecture

We want to investigate all combinations of two levels of each of four factors, A, B, C, and D, and obtain estimates of all effects including all interactions. We may wish to include some center points or replicate points to obtain estimate of the experimental error.

Design

The design can be setup as shown below.

The analysis of the above design will provide uncorrelated and independent estimates of the following:

- the overall average of the response;
- the main effects due to each factor, A, B, C, D;
- the estimates of six two-factor interaction effects, AB, AC, AD, BC, BD, CD;
- the estimates of four three-factor interaction effects, ABC, ABD, ACD, BCD;

Design Point	A	B	C	D	AB	AC	AD	BC	BD	CD	ABC	ABD	ACD	BCD	ABCD
1	−	−	−	−	+	+	+	+	+	+	−	−	−	−	+
2	+	−	−	−	−	−	−	+	+	+	+	+	+	−	−
3	−	+	−	−	−	+	+	−	−	+	+	+	−	+	−
4	+	+	−	−	+	−	−	−	−	+	−	−	+	+	+
5	−	−	+	−	+	−	+	−	+	−	−	−	+	+	−
6	+	−	+	−	−	+	−	−	+	−	−	+	−	+	+
7	−	+	+	−	−	−	+	+	−	−	−	+	+	−	+
8	+	+	+	−	+	+	−	+	−	−	+	−	−	−	−
9	−	−	−	+	+	+	−	+	−	−	−	+	+	+	−
10	+	−	−	+	−	−	+	+	−	−	+	−	−	+	+
11	−	+	−	+	−	+	−	−	+	−	+	−	+	−	+
12	+	+	−	+	+	−	+	−	+	−	−	+	−	−	−
13	−	−	+	+	+	−	−	−	−	+	+	+	−	−	+
14	+	−	+	+	−	+	+	−	−	+	−	−	+	−	−
15	−	+	+	+	−	−	−	+	+	+	−	−	−	+	−
16	+	+	+	+	+	+	+	+	+	+	+	+	+	+	+

- the estimate of one four-factor interaction effect, ABCD.

Full factorial designs can be generated for any number of factors, k. However, it should be noted that the number of runs needed for a full factorial design increases rapidly with increasing k and shown below.

Number of Factors k	Number of Experimental Runs
2	4
3	8
4	16
5	32
6	64
7	128
8	256
9	512
10	1024
11	2048
12	4096
13	8192
14	16364
15	32768

Conjecture

An investigator wishes to investigate the effects of four factors (k=4) using only eight runs.

Design

A 2^{4-1} fractional factorial design of eight runs can be set up as illustrated below.

Procedure

I.   Set up a full 2^3 design of eight runs as follows:

Design Point	A	B	C
1	−	−	−
2	+	−	−
3	−	+	−
4	+	+	−
5	−	−	+
6	+	−	+
7	−	+	+
8	+	+	+

II.   Assign the fourth factor D to the highest order interaction.
   D=ABC
   D=ABC is known as generator

III.   Generate the + and − column for D by multiplying columns A, B, and C together to obtain the following:

Design Point	A	B	C	D=ABC
1	−	−	−	−
2	+	−	−	+
3	−	+	−	+
4	+	+	−	−
5	−	−	+	+
6	+	−	+	−
7	−	+	+	−
8	+	+	+	+

Note that the levels of factor D are the products of the levels of factors A, B, and C.

IV. Obtain the defining relation (I) by multiplying both sides of the generator by D as:

D*D=ABC*D

I=ABCD (A resolution IV design)

The defining relation will be used to determine the resolution of a design and to generate the confounding patterns of the effects.

Design resolution

The resolution of a design is the number of letters in the smallest word of the defining relation. For example in the above design, the defining relation I=ABCD has one word which is ABCD, and the number of letters is equal to four, hence a resolution IV design. In a resolution IV design, the main effects are confounded with three-factor and higher order interactions, and two-factor interactions are confounded with each other and higher order interactions. Similarly, a resolution III design has the main effects confounded with two-factor and higher order interactions. A 2^{5-2} design of eight runs is of resolution III. An extremely useful design is a 2^{5-1} design of resolution V.

This design is used to investigate 5 factors in only 16 runs and has the power to estimate the main effects clear of any other factors and the two-factor interactions clear of any other factors as well, if three-factor and higher order interations are assumed to be negligible. Additional information on design resolution can be found in Box, Hunter, and Hunter (1978), Ayeni (1991), as well as in many other experimental design books and papers.

Defining relation

The defining relation (I) is the column of +1. Any factor multiplied by itself gives I. For example:

A*A=I, B*B=I, AB*AB=AABB=II=I, ABC*ABC=AABBCC=III=I

Other operators which are not equal to I are:

A*AB=B=IB=B, AB*BCE=AICE=ACE

V. Use the defining relation I=ABCD to generate the effects or confounding patterns as follows:

1. To obtain the confounding patterns for main effect A, multiply both sides of the defining relation by A as:

A*I=A*ABCD=BCD.

Therefore, A=BCD. This means that when we estimate the effect of factor A, we are not only estimating the effect of A but also the effect of the three-factor interaction BCD. This is known as CONFOUND-ING.

Counfounding occurs when the effects of two or more factors cannot be separated. In the above example, we are really estimating the sum of two effects A + BCD.

2. Similarly, to obtain any two factor interaction, say BC, multiply both sides of defining relation by BC as:

$$BC*I=BC*ABCD=AD.$$

Therefore, BC=AD, that is the effects of BC and AD are confounded with each other. Thus, estimating the effect of BC implies that we are really estimating the sum of BC + AD.

Confounding patterns

The complete confounding patterns are:

Effect	2^{4-1}	Confounding Patterns
A	IV	A + BCD
B		B + ACD
C		C + ABD
D		D + ABC
AB		AB + CD
AC		AC + BD
BC		BC + AD

From the above main effects, we can see that when we believe we are estimating the main effects, we are actually estimating the sum of the main effects and the three-factor interactions. However, since three factor interactions and higher order interactions are generally assumed to be negligible or nonexistent, we can obtain estimates of all the main effects clear of all other effects. Although all the two-factor interactions are confounded with each other, this is the price we pay in running 8 experiments rather than 16 experiments. Unless certain two-factor interactions are known not to exist, it will be necessary to run another half fraction if each two-factor effect is to be estimated clear of all other effects. Interested readers should refer to Hicks (1982) for further details on factorial designs and fractional factorial designs.

7.7 SATURATED DESIGNS

Saturated designs are designs that can be used to investigate n−1 factors in n number of runs. For example, one can study the effects of 15 factors using only

16 runs. In fact, it is also possible to investigate the effects of 31 factors using 32 runs. These designs are extremely useful in screening applications, as well as in situations where main effects are believed to dominate over two-factor and higher order interactions. All saturated designs are of resolution III. This means that main effects are confounded with two-factor and higher order interactions. It is, therefore, extremely important initially to screen for factors that are critical to the response of interest, since only a few of these factors exist, and later conduct a more thorough investigation of those factors identified through a full factorial design or a central composite design. Some examples of saturated designs are presented below.

Number of Factors	Number of Runs	Type of Design
3	4	2^{3-1}
7	8	2^{7-4}
15	16	2^{15-11}
31	32	2^{31-26}
63	64	2^{63-57}

Example of a saturated design

A 2^{7-4} fractional factorial design can be used to investigate k=7 factors with only eight runs. For this design, the number of fractions is p=4. In any saturated design, all possible interactions are used up in building the generators. Since p=4 in a 2^{7-4} design, there will be a total of four generators. The design set up is provided below.

Procedure

I. Set up a full 2^3 design of eight runs.

Design Point	A	B	C
1	−	−	−
2	+	−	−
3	−	+	−
4	+	+	−
5	−	−	+
6	+	−	+
7	−	+	+
8	+	+	+

II. Assign the remaining four variables (D, E, F, G) to all the interactions to obtain the four generators.

D=AB E=AC F=BC and G=ABC (these are the generators)

III. Generate the + and − columns for the generators as provided below.

Design Point	A	B	C	D=AB	E=AC	F=BC	G=ABC
1	−	−	−	+	+	+	−
2	+	−	−	−	−	+	+
3	−	+	−	−	+	−	+
4	+	+	−	+	−	−	−
5	−	−	+	+	−	−	+
6	+	−	+	−	+	−	−
7	−	+	+	−	−	+	−
8	+	+	+	+	+	+	+

IV. The defining relation (I) is given below. Notice that the smallest word has three letters, hence a resolution III design.

$$I=ABD=ACE=BCF=ABCG=BCDE=ACDF=CDG=ABEF=BEG$$
$$=AFG=DEF=ADEG=BDFG=CEFG=ABCDEFG$$

V. The confounding patterns can be generated as before by multiplying the factors on both sides of the defining relations. The confounding patterns are provided below after three-factor and higher order interactions have been deleted.

Effects	2^{7-4}	Confounding Patterns
A	III	A+BD+CE+FG
B		B+AD+CF+EG
C		C+AE+BF+DG
AB		AB+D+CG+EF
AC		AC+E+BG+DF
BC		BC+F+AG+DE
ABC		CD+BE+AF+G

7.8 RESPONSE SURFACE METHODOLOGY

Response surface methodology involves an analysis of the prediction equation or response surface fitted to a set of experimental data. Response surface strategies can be classified into two categories. These are single phase and double phase strategies.

Single phase strategy

This strategy requires running a full factorial design plus center points and star points to fit a second order response surface. This is shown graphically in Figure 7.6.

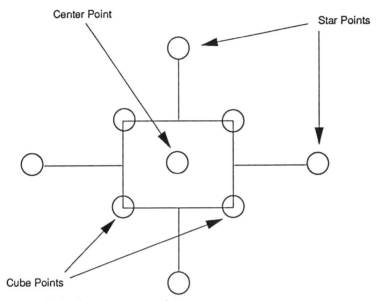

Figure 7.6 Single phase response surface strategy.

Double phase strategy

This strategy requires initial running of a full factorial design with some center points. Analyze the data by fitting a first order model, then test for lack of fit, and use the center points to test for the effects of curvature. If there is a significant lack of fit or if the quadratic effect is significant or both, then proceed further by running a second design which include the star points and additional center points. Then analyze the data from the two designs together. A double phase response surface strategy is depicted in Figure 7.7.

The selection of which design phase to consider depends on several factors which are discussed below.

The major goal of the experiment

If the major goal of the experiment is to optimize the process and one is considering only two to three factors to study, with no other problems as listed below, then one can proceed straight with single phase strategy.

The cost of running the experiment

If the cost of running the experiment is a major concern and one is required to minimize cost as much as possible, then select a double phase strategy. Fitting a

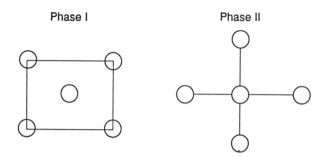

Figure 7.7 Double phase response surface strategy.

first order model first and further determining through a curvature test that a second order model is not necessary will not only save you a substantial amount of money, but will at the same time save you a fairly large amount of experimental time.

The number of variables to be studied

If the number of variables to be studied is greater than five, then select a double phase strategy and run a fractional factorial of resolution four or better first.

The time required to complete the project

If longer time is required to complete each run in the experiment, then you may select a double phase strategy. You will save a lot of time if it is determined that a second degree model is not necessary.

Type of control variables under study

If all the control variables are qualitative variables, then select double phase strategy. You only need to run a full or fractional factorial design with some replicates. No star points or center points are possible for this case.

Prior knowledge of the experimenter

If the experimenter (through prior experiment or any other means) knew in advance that within the range of study, the first order model would be adequate, then select a double phase.

Maximum number of runs possible

If there is a limitation on the number of runs possible, then consider double phase strategy.

Response surface example

A process engineer has just completed a 2^{6-2} screening design where he studied six factors on mineral penetration of a fiber. The response of interest is the fiber thickness. The screening experiment identified three key factors, Webspeed, %Solids, and Fiber weight. The engineer decided to determine the optimum operating conditions of these critical factors that can be used to achieve a minimum thickness of 0.40.

Objective

To determine control handles that will achieve a target thickness of 0.40 or better.

Design

A three-factor central composite design as shown below is selected. The ranges of interest to be studied are:

Factors	−1.633	−1	0	1	1.633
Webspeed	43.67	50	60	70	76.33
% Solids	36.83	40	45	50	53.16
Fiber weight	16.83	20	25	30	33.16

The resulting design and the response are presented in Table 7.2.

Table 7.2 Data for response surface example

Obs No.	Run Order	Block	WebSpeed X1	% Solids X2	F. Weight X3	Thickness (Response)	Design ID
1	6	1	50.000	40.000	20.000	0.320	1
2	1	1	70.000	40.000	30.000	0.336	2
3	5	1	50.000	50.000	30.000	0.361	3
4	3	1	70.000	50.000	20.000	0.399	4
5	2	1	60.000	45.000	25.000	0.404	5
6	4	1	60.000	45.000	25.000	0.380	6
7	8	2	50.000	40.000	30.000	0.321	7
8	12	2	70.000	40.000	20.000	0.356	8
9	9	2	50.000	50.000	20.000	0.350	9
10	11	2	70.000	50.000	30.000	0.404	10
11	10	2	60.000	45.000	25.000	0.353	11
12	7	2	60.000	45.000	25.000	0.375	12
13	14	3	43.670	45.000	25.000	0.353	13
14	16	3	76.330	45.000	25.000	0.373	14
15	19	3	60.000	36.835	25.000	0.342	15
16	13	3	60.000	53.165	25.000	0.441	16
17	17	3	60.000	45.000	16.835	0.361	17
18	15	3	60.000	45.000	33.165	0.348	18
19	18	3	60.000	45.000	25.000	0.378	19
20	20	3	60.000	45.000	25.000	0.374	20

Analysis

Analysis of the data in Table 7.2 yields the results below:

```
              Estimated effects for thickness – 3-factor study
                 average   =    0.348264
                 A:X1      =    0.016792
                 B:X2      =   -0.027696
                 C:X3      =    0.037718
                 AB        =    0.000206
                 AC        =    0.000134
                 BC        =    0.000350
                 AA        =   -0.000166
                 BB        =    0.000188
                 CC        =   -0.000922
                 block 1   =    0.001400
                 block 2   =   -0.012166
                 block 3   =    0.010666
      Standard error estimated from total error with 8 d.f. (t = 2.30665)
```

Table 7.3 ANOVA for Thickness – 3 factor study

Independent Variable	Coefficient Estimate	df	Standard Error	t for H0 Coeff=0	Prob > |t|
Intercept	0.3776	1	0.0066	57.6000	
Block 1	0.0007				
Block 2	-0.0061				
block 3	0.0053				
A: Web Speed	0.0132	1	0.0044	2.9930	0.0173
B: %Solids	0.0257	1	0.0044	5.8380	0.0004
C: Fiber Weight	-0.0018	1	0.0044	-0.4128	0.6906
AA	-0.0083	1	0.0044	-1.8850	0.0962
BB	0.0024	1	0.0044	0.5315	0.6095
CC	-0.0115	1	0.0044	-2.6050	0.0314
AB	0.0051	1	0.0057	0.9017	0.3935
AC	-0.0034	1	0.0057	-0.5938	0.5690
BC	0.0044	1	0.0057	0.7698	0.4635
Total error	0.00207	8			
Total (corr.)	0.01682	19			
R-squared = 0.8737					
R-squared (adj. for d.f.) =	0.7316				

 Figure 7.8 shows the Pareto chart for the response (thickness). The chart indicates the relative contributions of the effects from the three factors as well as interactions. Figure 7.9 shows the response surface with respect to Factor X2 and Factor X3. Figure 7.10 shows the response surface with respect to X1 and X3. Figure 7.11 shows the contour surface with respect to X1 and X2. Figure 7.12 shows the contour surface with respect to X1 and X3. Figure 7.13 shows the response surface with respect to X1 and Factor X2.

Regression coefficients for Thickness:3-factor response surface study

constant	=	0.050916
A:X1	=	0.008396
B:X2	=	−0.013848
C:X3	=	0.018859
AB	=	0.000103
AC	=	−0.000067
BC	=	0.000175
AA	=	−0.000083
BB	=	0.000094
CC	=	−0.000461
block 1	=	0.000700
block 2	=	−0.006083
block 3	=	0.005333

Pareto Chart for Standardized Effects on Thickness

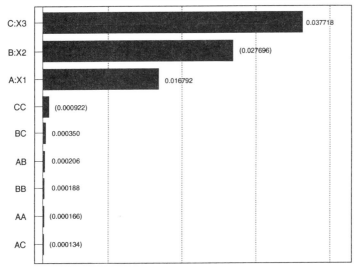

Figure 7.8 Pareto chart for the response surface analysis.

Results

The results of the analyses indicate that at $\alpha = 0.05$, we can conclude that the three factors (web speed, % solids, and fiber weight) are statistically important to fiber thickness. Based on the response surface curves, one set of optimal operating conditions to achieve 0.40 thickness or better is found to be as follows:

Factor	Optimum operating level
Web speed	58.91
% solids	49.69
Fiber weight	27.58

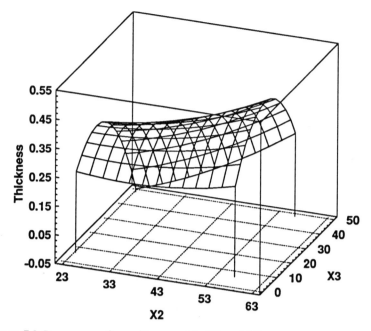

Figure 7.9 Response surface with respect to X2 and X3.

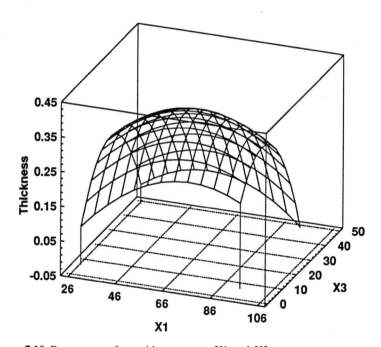

Figure 7.10 Response surface with respect to X1 and X3.

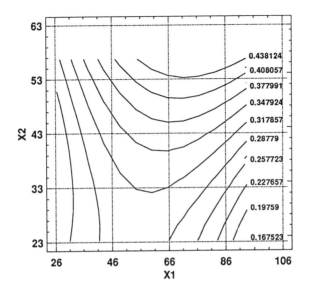

Figure 7.11 Contour surface with respect to X1 and X2.

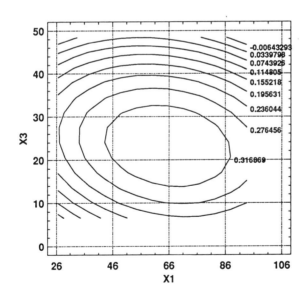

Figure 7.12 Contour surface with respect to X1 and X3.

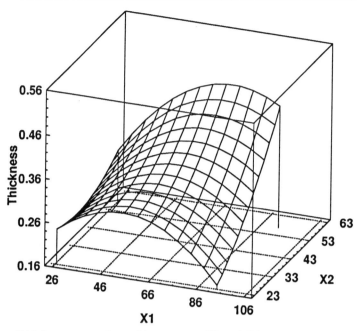

Figure 7.13 Response surface with respect to X1 and X2.

7.9 CENTRAL COMPOSITE DESIGNS

I. Two factors central composite design – design orthogonally blocked and rotatable. An example of this is shown below.

Run	A	B	
1	−1	−1	
2	1	−1	
3	−1	1	Block 1
4	1	1	
5	0	0	
6	0	0	
7	−1.414	0	
8	1.414	0	
9	0	−1.414	Block 2
10	0	1.414	
11	0	0	
12	0	0	

II. Two factors central composite design – factorial portion replicated and design orthogonally blocked and nearly rotatable as shown below.

Run	A	B	
1	−1	−1	
2	1	−1	
3	−1	1	Block 1
4	1	1	
5	0	0	
6	0	0	
7	−1	−1	
8	1	−1	
9	−1	1	Block 2
10	1	1	
11	0	0	
12	0	0	
13	−1.633	0	
14	1.633	0	
15	0	−1.633	
16	0	1.633	Block 3
17	0	0	
18	0	0	
19	0	0	
20	0	0	

III. Three factors central composite design – orthogonally blocked and nearly rotatable as seen in the layout below.

Run	A	B	C	
1	−1	−1	1	
2	1	−1	−1	
3	−1	1	−1	Block 1
4	1	1	1	
5	0	0	0	
6	0	0	0	
7	−1	−1	−1	
8	1	−1	1	
9	−1	1	1	
10	1	1	−1	Block 2
11	0	0	0	
12	0	0	0	
13	−1.633	0	0	
14	1.633	0	0	
15	0	−1.633	0	
16	0	1.633	0	
17	0	0	−1.633	Block 3
18	0	0	1.633	
19	0	0	0	
20	0	0	0	

IV. Four factors central composite design – orthogonally blocked and rotatable.

Run	A	B	C	D	
1	1	1	−1	1	
2	1	−1	−1	−1	
3	−1	1	−1	−1	
4	1	1	1	−1	
5	−1	−1	1	−1	
6	1	−1	1	1	Block 1
7	−1	1	1	1	
8	−1	−1	−1	1	
9	0	0	0	0	
10	0	0	0	0	
11	0	0	0	0	
12	1	1	−1	−1	
13	1	−1	1	−1	
14	−1	1	−1	1	
15	−1	−1	−1	−1	
16	−1	−1	1	1	
17	1	−1	−1	1	Block 2
18	−1	1	1	−1	
19	1	1	1	1	
20	0	0	0	0	
21	0	0	0	0	
22	0	0	0	0	
23	−2	0	0	0	
24	2	0	0	0	
25	0	−2	0	0	
26	0	2	0	0	
27	0	0	−2	0	
28	0	0	2	0	Block 3
29	0	0	0	−2	
30	0	0	0	2	
31	0	0	0	0	
32	0	0	0	0	
33	0	0	0	0	

7.10 TIME SERIES ANALYSIS

Statistical process control (SPC) has found widespread application in industry for monitoring and controlling manufacturing processes, as well as for implementing quality and process improvement activities. The traditional Shewhart control charts have been extensively used for this purpose. The fundamental assumption in the typical application of Shewhart control charts is that the sequence of process observations are independent and uncorrelated. This assumption has been found to be reasonable in parts manufacturing industries. However, it is often not true in chemical and process industries where process data are enormous and correlated since many kinds of sensors and in-process gauges are being used with automated machines.

The presence of autocorrelation in the data can have a major impact on the expected average run lengths (ARL) performance of control charts, causing a dramatic increase in the frequency of false alarms, and the control limits of the CUSUM procedure would have to be adjusted (see Johnson and Bagshaw, 1974). In this type of situation, Alwan and Roberts (1989), Montgomery and Mastrangelo (1991), as well as other authors, have recommended fitting a time series model to track the level of the process and then using a standard control chart on the residuals to detect unusually large shocks to the process. Montgomery and Mastrangelo (1991) also presented an alternative approach based on a straightforward application of the exponentially weighted moving average (EWMA) statistics due to the practical implementation drawback of the method proposed by Alwan and Roberts (1989).

7.10.1 Correlated observations

Correlated observations such as those experienced by continuous process industries (petroleum, chemical, mineral processing, pulp and paper, etc.), as well as those management data such as sales, profits, and so on can be monitored and controlled by fitting an appropriate time series model to the observations and then applying control charts to the stream of residuals from this model (Alwan and Roberts, 1989; Ermer 1979, 1980; Yourstone and Montgomery, 1989; Montgomery and Friedman, 1989; Montgomery and Mastrangelo, 1991). The general time series model employed is the autoregressive integrated moving average (ARIMA) model (Box and Jenkins, 1976). This model can be represented as:

$$\Phi_p(B)(1 - B)^d Y_t = \upsilon_q(B)a_t$$

where $\Phi_p(B)$ is an autoregressive polynomial of order p, $\upsilon_q(B)$ is a moving average polynomial of order q, d is the dth difference of the series, B is the backward shift operator, and a_t is a sequence of normally and independently distributed random 'shocks' with mean zero and constant variance σ_a^2.

$$\Phi_p(B) = (1 - \Phi_1 B - \Phi_2 B^2 - \ldots \Phi_p B^p)$$
$$\upsilon_q(B) = (1 - \upsilon_1 B - \upsilon_2 B^2 - \ldots \upsilon_q B^q)$$

An extensive application of this general ARIMA model can be found in the paper by Ayeni and Pilat (1992). If $\hat{Y}_t$ is the predicted value obtained from an appropriately identified and fitted ARIMA model, then the residuals given by:

$$a_t = Y_t - \hat{Y}_t$$

will behave like independent and identically distributed random variables (Box and Jenkins, 1976). Therefore, control charts can then be applied to the set of residuals. If a shift occurs in the process average, the identified model will no longer be applicable, and this effect will be detected on the control charts applied to the residuals.

As an illustration of this approach, consider Figure 7.14, which presents 150 observations collected during a study of the moisture content of a raw material. The measurements are fiber weight scan averages. Each scan takes about 25 seconds.

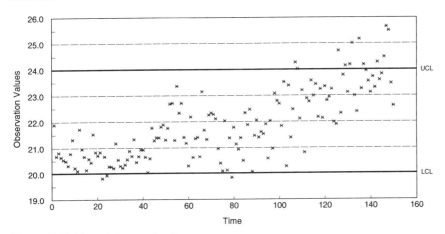

Figure 7.14 Plot of time series data.

Figure 7.14 shows a control chart for individuals with control limits based on a process standard deviation estimated from a moving range control chart. This chart shows many out-of-control signals.

Time series analysis example

MINITAB software can be used to analyze time series data. For the data in Figure 7.14, the autocorrelation and partial autocorrelation functions can be obtained as shown in Figure 7.15. The autocorrelation function of the 150 weights are shown before differencing. The inability of the autocorrelation function to die out rapidly shows that weights are highly autocorrelated and differencing of the data will be necessary. After differencing with degree of differencing $d = 1$, the autocorrelation function dies out rapidly at lag $q = 1$, indicating a moving average process IMA (1). This is shown in Figure 7.16. The partial autocorrelation function (Figure 7.17) shows some exponential decay confirming that a moving average model can represent the weight data.

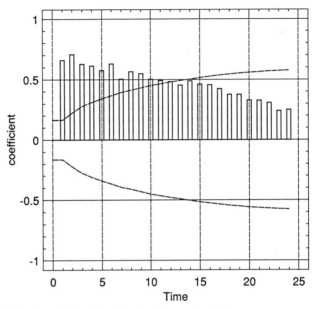

Figure 7.15 Autocorrelation function for time series data.

Estimation of parameters using an integrated moving average of order 1 yields a coefficient estimate of 0.8125. Since the observations are highly autocorrelated, we need to be very suspicious about the out-of-control signals. We are not sure if they are actually due to special causes or if they are false alarms induced by the autocorrelation structure of the data. A detailed examination of the sample autocorrelation and partial autocorrelation functions shows that the data in Figure 7.14 can be identified as an ARIMA (0,1,1), which can be represented as:

$$Y_t = Y_{t-1} - \upsilon_1 a_{t-1} + a_t$$

Thus, using all the available data, the fitted model is:

$$Y_t = Y_{t-1} - 0.8125a_{t-1} + a_t$$

The residuals from the model show that they are random (uncorrelated) indicating that the ARIMA (0,1,1) model is an adequate fit. The individual

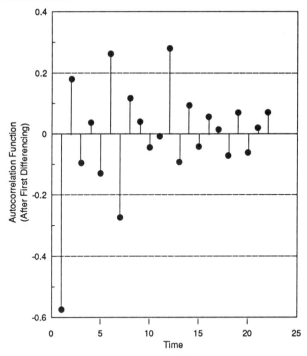

Figure 7.16 Autocorrelation function after d=1 differencing.

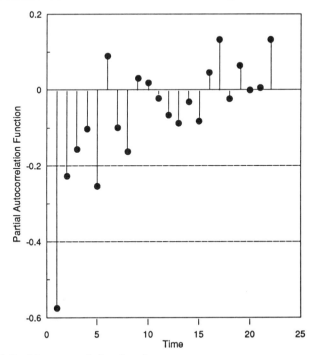

Figure 7.17 Partial autocorrelation function.

control chart shows that the process is in control and that the out-of-control signals observed previously were false alarms induced by the autocorrelation structure of the data.

7.11 EXPONENTIALLY WEIGHTED MOVING AVERAGE

The time series modeling approach illustrated in the preceding example is difficult to implement in the SPC environment. One major problem is the time that will be required to develop an ARIMA model for each quality characteristic of interest when applying control charts to several variables. Alwan (1990) extensively covered several issues regarding implementation of time series approach to SPC application. Several authors, such as Box, Jenkins, and MacGregor (1974), Hunter (1986), and most recently Montgomery and Mastrangelo (1991) have proposed the use of exponentially weighted moving average (EWMA) control chart as a possible compromise or an approximation to the general ARIMA model. The EWMA was first suggested by Roberts (1959) and can be represented as:

$$Z_t = \alpha X_t + (1 - \alpha)Z_{t-1}$$

where $0 < \alpha \leq 1$ and X_t is the observation at time t, Z_t is the EWMA at time t, and α is the smoothing constant. The value of Z_0 is either a target or a process average. The advantages of EWMA are listed below:

- applicable in certain situations where data are autocorrelated;
- useful in approximating other members of the ARIMA family;
- data need not be independent as in Shewhart charts;
- applicable to processes whose means drifts over time;
- can serve as a compromise between the Shewhart and the CUSUM charts;
- EWMA uses all data in descending weights so that the most recent data are given more weight;
- very sensitive to small shifts in the process average;
- provides the ability to make adjustments due to its predictive capability.

Below are examples of Shewhart (Figure 7.18), EWMA (Figure 7.19), and CUSUM (Figure 7.20) charts for the data in Table 7.4. If possible one can plot all the three charts together for proper protection against both large and small process shifts. Figure 7.19 contains the EWMA chart. Figure 7.20 also contains an exponential regression fit ($R^2 = 67.93\%$) for the CUSUM values. The results show a shift in the process level at sample number 10.

Cumulative sum chart

The cumulative sum (CUSUM) chart procedure was developed by Page (1954) and Bernard (1959) as a sequential likelihood ratio test for testing the hypothesis that the process average is equal to the target value. CUSUM uses

Table 7.4 Data for Plotting EWMA and CUMSUM Charts

Time	Film Quality	EWMA $\alpha = 0.2$	X–9.888	CUSUM
1	5.5	9.01	−4.38	−4.38
2	8.5	8.91	−1.38	−5.76
3	4.2	7.97	−5.68	−11.44
4	8.9	8.15	−0.98	−12.42
5	6.2	7.76	−3.68	−16.10
6	7.5	7.71	−2.38	−18.48
7	5.8	7.33	−4.08	−22.56
8	9.3	7.72	−0.58	−23.14
9	4.9	7.15	−4.98	−28.12
10	8.1	7.35	−1.78	−29.90
11	11.9	8.26	2.02	−27.88
12	9.5	8.51	−0.38	−28.26
13	12.3	9.26	2.42	−25.84
14	11.9	9.79	2.02	−23.82
15	12.4	10.31	2.52	−21.30
16	10.3	10.31	0.42	−20.88
17	11.1	10.47	1.22	−19.66
18	12.3	10.83	2.42	−17.24
19	10.8	10.83	0.92	−16.22
20	13.9	11.44	4.02	−12.30
21	11.9	11.53	2.02	−10.28
22	11.3	11.49	1.42	−8.86
23	15.0	12.19	5.12	−3.74
24	12.4	12.23	2.52	−1.22
25	11.3	12.05	1.42	+0.20

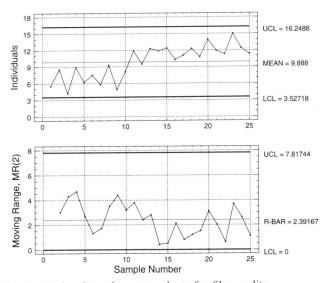

Figure 7.18 Individual and moving range charts for film quality.

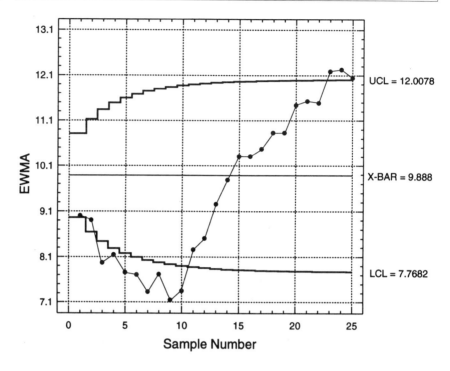

Figure 7.19 EWMA chart for film quality example.

the same assumption of independence as the Shewhart chart. The procedure requires that we plot the following sum of deviations from target:

$$\sum(Y_i - Target)$$

Any change in the process average from target will show up as a change in the slope of the CUSUM chart. This procedure has the ability to detect smaller changes in the process average more rapidly than the Shewhart chart. However, CUSUM charts are not as sensitive as Shewhart charts in detecting cycles, spikes and trends. For these reasons, it is a good practice to use CUSUM in addition to Shewhart charts. The CUSUM chart in Figure 7.20 is based on a target of 9.88. The plot shows that a shift occurs in the process average after subgroup number 10.

7.11.1 Engineering feedback control

Case history: A process engineer was monitoring a production operation in a nonfeedback control mode during normal production in order to observe the

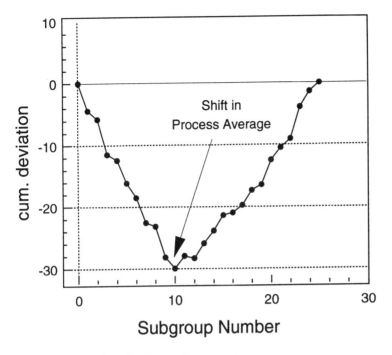

Figure 7.20 CUSUM chart for film quality example.

natural variance of the process. The following were what the engineer experienced.

- Using the feedback system, the process initially centered around the target weight of 21.5 gm.
- Then by taking off the feedback controller at the target weight of 21.5 gm, the weights displayed immediately varied slowly around the target weights of 21.5 gm.
- After a few minutes, the range had significantly increased with most of the weights falling outside the specification range. All the observed packages at this time were rejected.
- The production group at this time had no choice other than to minimize cost. They, therefore, discontinued the nonfeedback approach and the feedback system was installed again.
- The feedback system again brought the process back in control immediately after being installed.

The above situation often occurs in continuous process industries for processes which mix, react, and/or separate materials continuously. Chemical, pulp and paper, and petroleum refinery are a few of the continuous process industries. In these industries the automatic process control methods have dominated. The assumption behind the engineering process control approach is that the process is always being disturbed by causes that cannot be completely eliminated. In this situation, the process average level is not stable, but drifting continuously over time due to a myriad of causes such as wood variations in pulp and paper making, equipment ageing, ambient temperature, quality of raw materials, and so on. Under this assumption, the logical approach has been to devise a control algorithm to be used to respond continuously to all deviations from target by compensating for the disturbances with some other variables. These continuous processes are a significant part of American industry and present unique challenges to controlling and improving product quality.

An excellent example of a feedback control problem was presented by Box, Hunter, and Hunter (1978, pp. 598–602). In the example, they considered a polymer process that was colored by adding dye at the inlet of a continuous reactor. At the outlet, the color index y was checked every 15 minutes and if it has deviated from the target value of T=9, the rate of the addition of dye X at the inlet could be increased or decreased. In their approach, they used a time series model to develop a controller or optimal control equation so that the deviations e_t from the target have the smallest standard deviation.

7.11.2 SPC versus APC

Statistical process control (SPC) and automatic process control (APC) have been instrumental in quality improvement efforts in industry. Several papers have appeared in the literature, independently, on SPC and APC, but most recently, several techniques on integrating both methods have been published (MacGregor, 1987; Box and Kramer, 1990; Tucker, Faltin, Weil, and Doganaksoy, 1989; Palm, 1990). While the tactical approaches taken by these authors somewhat differ, several key practical considerations were presented. Some of the authors fully discussed some misconceptions concerning both methods, as well as a full explanation of each approach.

Statistical process control (SPC)

- Originates from manufacturing parts industry.
- Signals significant process changes from past performance.
- The philosophy is to minimize variability by finding and removing disturbances.
- Analyzes and controls infrequent or off-line measurements.
- Improves procedures, methods, and equipment.
- Monitors long-term performance.
- Expensive measurements and control actions.
- Low serial correlation.
- Monitoring may be done manually or by computer.

- The approach is to take action only when monitoring detects changes.
- Reflects Deming philosophy.

Automatic process control (APC)

- Originates from continuous process industry.
- Deals with how to adjust process to meet targets.
- The philosophy is to minimize variability by adjusting process to compensate the impact of disturbances which cannot be removed economically.
- Analyzes and controls high-speed on-line measurements.
- Accomplishes complex control strategies.
- Monitors short-term performance.
- Cheap measurements and control actions.
- High serial correlation.
- Adjustment is typically computer-based.
- The approach is continually to perform specified adjustments.
- Performs multivariate control and optimization.
- Deviates from Deming philosophy.

Criticisms of SPC and APC

There have been some aspects of controversy that sometimes arise between SPC and APC. This controversy has been fully discussed in the literature. Interested readers should refer to Box and Kramer (1990), MacGregor (1987), and Palm (1990).

SPC practitioners have sometimes criticized APC for the following:

- overcompensating disturbances;
- compensating disturbances rather than removing them;
- concealing information rather than removing it.

APC practitioners have in turn argued that Shewhart control charts are:

- inefficient for regulating a process;
- inefficient in coping well with fast system dynamics;
- misleading if sensing correlations over time.

Overcompensation, disturbance removal, and information concealing

Box and Kramer (1990) and MacGregor (1991) demonstrated that in the presence of a drifting process average, by actively implementing an active optimal control strategy, a feedback scheme can provide significant reduction in variability. In addition, Box and Kramer (1990) provided a couple of examples where some disturbances cannot be removed. For example, a temperature variation in Minnesota from winter to summer may be too extreme for some people. In this case, people who cannot withstand this severe change may either relocate to Louisiana or Florida. However, if they decide to stay in Minnesota, they will have to compensate for the cold weather by using a furnace controlled by a thermostat supplying appropriate feedback control. Although, automatic control conceals the nature of compensated disturbances, Box and Kramer (1990), and MacGregor and Harris (1990) also pointed out that this need not happen.

One can have the best of both worlds, if one uses SPC charts to monitor the control system. Provided the dynamics of the system are known, they show how the exact compensation can be computed and the original disturbance reconstructed. These qualities can then be displayed on charts and be subjected to routine examinations from the standpoint of generalized concept of common and special causes, where common causes are associated with the modelled process changeable only by management action, and special causes are associated with temporary deviations from the modelled process, as indicated by outliers. In this way, one can simultaneously minimize variability by active process control and at the same time have the ability to detect and eliminate special-cause disturbances.

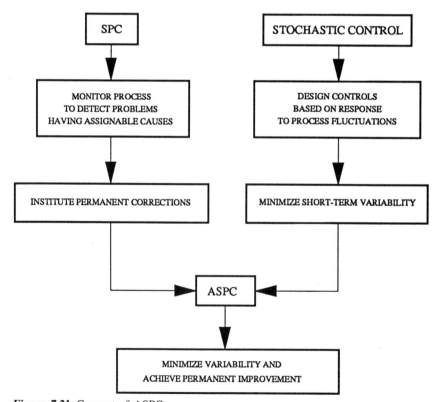

Figure 7.21 Concept of ASPC.

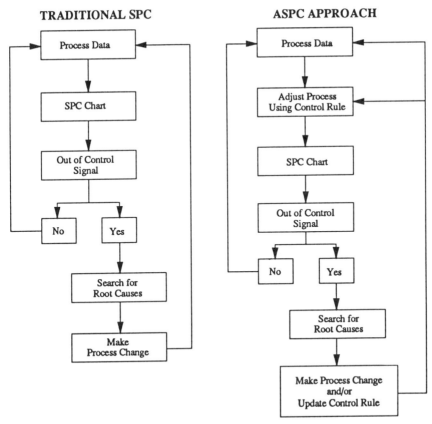

Figure 7.22 Flowchart for implementing ASPC.

Integration of SPC and APC

It is important to note that there are several approaches one can take for quality and process controls. Which approach or class of approaches one can take depends on the problem at hand and how realistic the assumptions are for the real problem under study. In deciding between SPC and APC, it is always important to distinguish between variations that can be eliminated at the source and those that cannot be eliminated at all. As can be seen from the above discussions, both SPC and APC seek to reduce variation, promoting process understanding, as well as facilitating process improvement. For these reasons, the majority of the authors mentioned above have proposed the integration of both SPC and APC whenever possible. Tucker, Faltin, Weil, and Doganaksoy (1989) provided an excellent concept of integrating both SPC and APC. Their concept is known as the algorithmic statistical process control (ASPC). The concept of ASPC is presented in Figure 7.21 while Figure 7.22 presents the flowchart for implementing ASPC.

7.12 SYSTEMS APPROACH TO PROCESS ADJUSTMENT

In many continuous process industries and, in particular, chemical and petrochemical industries, materials are produced in batches. One major goal in these industries is to reduce batch-to-batch variability that is very prevalent. For this reason, adjustments are often made to the already produced batches so as to provide a more uniform incoming material on batch-to-batch basis for the next process step. In this industry it is common to have material produced in one part of a process become the incoming material for the next process step. It is also common that the incoming material from the first process step will be adjusted in order to provide a more uniform material on a batch-to-batch basis for the next process step. Over time, this adjustment becomes an inherent part of the process. Caffrey (1990) demonstrated that when a reasonable adjustment strategy is made to a process, say process A, very little benefit may be realized by another process, say process B, which is the next process step. But by considering the process as a whole, a more optimal strategy can be employed. The goal here is to view the whole process in an integrated manner.

7.13 ARIMA MODELING OF PROCESS DATA

Let us consider the single input, single output system shown in Figure 7.23. Assume the output Y is sampled at discrete equi-spaced intervals of time, and its value at time t is represented by Y_t.

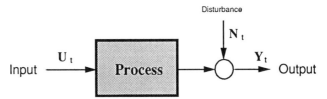

Figure 7.23 Input–output process for ARIMA example.

In Figure 7.23, N_t represents the total effect on the output Y of all disturbances occurring anywhere in the system. If the disturbance is not compensated for, it would cause the output Y to drift away from target. The input variable at time t, u_t, can be manipulated to affect changes in the output, Y. The general model that can be used to represent the process dynamics and the stochastic disturbances relies mainly on discrete transfer function models for the process and discrete autoregressive integrated moving average (ARIMA) time series models for the disturbances. This model (Box and Jenkins, 1970) can be represented as:

$$Y_t = \frac{w(B)B^b}{\delta(B)} u_t + \frac{\upsilon(B)}{\Phi(B)(1-B)^d} a_t$$

The first term is a transfer function model of the process relating the dynamic effect of u_t to the output Y_t and it is referred to as a discrete transfer model of order (r,s,b), while the second term represents the independent effect of all disturbances occurring in the system on the output Y_t and referred to as a discrete ARIMA model of order (p,d,q). B is the backward shift operator, $BY_t = Y_{t-1}$, b is the whole periods of process delay. The components $\delta(B)$ and $w(B)$ are polynomials of order r and s respectively in the operator B. This can be represented as

$$\delta(B) = 1 - \delta_1 B - \delta_2 B^2 - \ldots - \delta_r B^r$$
$$w(B) = w_0 - w_1 B - w_2 B^2 - \ldots - w_s B^s$$

Generally, if no manipulations were made in the input variable, u_t, the ARIMA model for the disturbance, N_t, would represent the behavior of the process output, Y_t. This can be represented as:

$$N_t = \frac{\upsilon(B)}{\Phi(B)(1-B)^d} a_t$$

where:

$$\Phi(B) = (1 - \Phi_1 B - \Phi_2 B^2 - \ldots - \Phi_p B^p)$$

is an autoregressive polynomial of order p,

$$\upsilon(B) = (1 - \upsilon_1 B - \upsilon_2 B^2 - \ldots - \upsilon_q B^q)$$

is a moving average polynomial of order q, $(1 - B)^d$ is the backward difference operator of order d, and a_t is a sequence of independent normally distributed random shocks with mean zero and constant variance, σ_a^2. When $d=1$, N_t gives rise to non-stationary disturbances in which the process average level is free to drift from time to time, while for $d=2$ one obtains disturbances in which both the level and trend or slope of the disturbance drift over time.

Model identification and estimation

Detailed descriptions of model identification and estimation procedures are fully covered in Box and Jenkins (1976), as well as MacGregor (1989) and, therefore, need not be covered in this book. MINITAB can be used for the identification and estimation for the ARIMA part of the combined model as described previously. SAS program can be used for the identification and estimation of both the transfer function and the ARIMA components of the model.

7.14 MINIMUM VARIANCE CONTROL (MVC)

The main idea of optimal stochastic control theory is that, given a model as described above whose combined process dynamic and disturbance model of the system has been identified, one can design a controller which will optimize some specified performance index involving the output and input variables. One case due to MacGregor (1989) is the minimum variance control (MVC). For this case, the controller is designed to compensate for the disturbances, N_t, in such a way that the variance of the difference between the output and target is minimized. Although, several disturbance models can be considered from N_t, one simple case is the integrated moving average model (IMA) since it arises frequently in SPC. This model can be represented as:

$$(1 - B)Y_t = (1 - \upsilon B)a_t$$

The minimum variance controller (MVC) for this disturbance model (Figure 7.24) is given by MacGregor (1989) as:

$$u_t = -\frac{1}{g} \cdot \frac{(1 - \upsilon)}{(1 - \upsilon B)} (Y_t - u_{t-1})$$

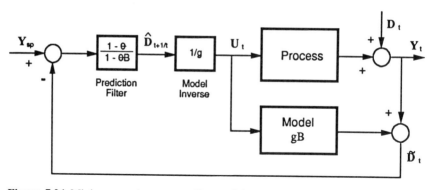

Figure 7.24 Minimum variance controller model.

Process dynamics with disturbance

For the case where process dynamics are important, usually in the continuous process industries, we consider a simple case first order process:

$$Y_t = \frac{w_0}{(1 - \delta B)} u_{t-1} + \frac{(1 - \upsilon B)}{(1 - B)} a_t$$

The minimum variance controller (MVC) is given by:

$$u_t = \frac{(1 - \upsilon)}{w_0} \cdot \frac{(1 - \delta B)}{(1 - B)} Y_t$$

The specific situations for which stochastic control theory is extremely well suited are when:

- drifting stochastic disturbances are the main disturbances in the system for which control is needed;
- there is significant sampling or measurement noise;
- the process exhibits a time delay or dead-time between the manipulated input and the output.

Appendix A
Glossary and acronyms

5S's: *Seiri, Seiton, Seiso, Seiketsu, Shitsuke* (Organization, Neatness, Cleaning, Standardization, Discipline)
AQC: Achieving Quick Changeover
AZD: Achieving Zero Defects
CFM: Continuous Flow Manufacturing
CMI: Continuous Measurable Improvement
CPI: Continuous Process Improvement
DFA: Design for Assembly
DFM: Design for Manufacture
DOE: Design of Experiments
JIT: Just In Time
MIPS: Minimum Inventory Production System
QA: Quality Assurance
QC: Quality Control
QFD: Quality Function Deployment
SPC: Statistical Process Control
TBP: Team-based Performance
TEI: Total Employee Involvement
TPM: Total Preventive Maintenance
TQC: Total Quality Control
TQM: Total Quality Management
ZIPS: Zero Inventory Production System
ZUD: Zero Unplanned Downtime

100% inspection Inspection of all the units in a lot or batch. Also called screening inspection.

Accuracy A description of how closely the measurements of an instrument match the true values of the parameters being measured.

Analysis of variance (ANOVA) A statistical technique by which the total variation of a set of data is subdivided into component parts, each of which is associated with a specific source of variation. The purpose of ANOVA is to test some hypothesis on the parameters of the model or to estimate variance components.

Assignable cause   A detectable factor that contributes to variations in a process.

Attribute   A characteristic that is classified in terms of whether or not it meets a given requirement (e.g. go, no go).

Batch (or lot)   A collection of units of a product manufactured by one supplier under manufacturing conditions that are presumed to be uniform and consistent.

c chart (count chart)   A control chart for evaluating the stability of a process in terms of the number (count) of occurrences of a particular event in a sample.

Calibration (based on analysis)   The process of establishing the accuracy of a measuring instrument based on an analysis within the operating environment.

Calibration (based on comparison)   The process of comparing the accuracy of one measuring instrument against another measuring instrument (standard or gauge) for the purpose of adjusting the accuracy of the subject instrument.

Central line   A line on a control chart representing the long-term central tendency of a parameter being studied.

Certainty   The degree of assurance with which some quantity may be estimated.

Certification (supplier certification)   The process by which products are obtained from a supplier and tested for the purpose of documenting the units from the supplier as qualified or certified products. It is alternately referred to as qualification.

Chance causes (random causes)   Random and undetectable factors which contribute to variations in a process.

Change in mean   A measure of the deviation in long-term central tendency of a process from a reference point.

Characteristic   A distinguishing property of the units of a product.

Class boundaries   The end points of the possible values of a parameter that is classified into classes.

Class interval   The width of each bar in a frequency histogram.

Class limits   The upper and lower bounds of the class into which items are classified.

Component   A single, identifiable part of an assembled product.

Confidence interval   A statistical interval that has a certain level of chance of containing the representative value of a parameter.

Confidence level   The probability (or level of confidence) associated with a confidence interval.

Confidence limits   The end points of a confidence interval.

Conformance   The affirmation that a product meets certain requirements.

Conformity   The state of meeting specified requirements by a product.

Consumer's risk   The probability of accepting a bad batch from a producer's production lot.

Contingency table   A tabulation of rows and columns to display relationships between various factors.

Control   The corrective actions by which some desired result is ensured.

Control chart   A chart on which limits are drawn and on which are plotted values of a statistic obtained from sequential samples of a product.

Control chart factor   A factor, usually varying with sample size, to convert specified statistics or parameters into a central measure or control limits relevant to the control chart.

Control charts for individual observations   A control chart in which individual observations are evaluated in order to assess the stability of a process.

Control limits   Limits on a control chart that are used as criteria for indicating the state of statistical control of a process.

Control system   The system of controls by which control of some desired result is achieved.

Correction factor   An adjustment associated with the measurement of parameter values from an origin other than their mean.

Corrective action   Steps taken to correct adverse conditions affecting a process.

Cumulative count control chart (CCC chart)   A graphical method used for monitoring a process by plotting the cumulative count of conforming units instead of nonconforming units.

Cumulative frequency   The total frequency of parameter values that are located below or at a class boundary.

Customer feedback and corrective action   A program of feedback and corrective action based upon customer-supplied data.

Cycle   A single performance of a complete set of operating conditions.

Cycle time   The elapsed time between the commencement and completion of a cycle.

Data   Statistics obtained from measurements and observations in a process.

Defect   A deficiency associated with the failure to meet requirements imposed on a product with respect to a single quality characteristic.

Defective   The state of exceeding the maximum number of allowable defects in a product.

Degrees of freedom   An integer number representing the result of subtracting the number of independent parameters computed in a statistical test from the sample size. It is used for entering statistical tables.

Dependant variable   A characteristic or variable whose value is directly influenced by the values of some other variables.

Design   The representation of ideas, concepts, or plans in a written form.

Destructive testing   Diagnostic tests that stress the characteristics of a product or process to the point of destruction.

Deviation   Any departure from the specified range of a characteristic.

Dispersion   The degree of spread present in a set of observations.

Distribution curve   The line enveloping a frequency distribution.

Drift   The change over time in a characteristic of a product.

Effect of a factor   The change in a response variable based on a change in the level of a factor.

Estimated process average   Expected average yield of a process based on a sample from the process.

Evolutionary operation (EVOP)   An experimental procedure for collecting information to improve a process without disturbing production.

Experimental design   The planning of experiments to collect statistically valid data and generate statistically valid analysis by varying factor levels under controlled conditions.

Factor   A variable that affects the response or output of a process.

Factor level   A specific setting of the value of a factor in an experimental study.

Factorial experiment   An experiment designed to determine the presence or absence of interactions and assess the effects of one or more factors when each factor is studied at a minimum of two levels. In a full factorial experiment all combinations of all factor levels are investigated.

Feedback loop   A sequence of forward and backward communication on process performance used as an input to perpetrate or improve process stability.

Fraction defective   The total number of defective units divided by the total number of items.

Frequency   The number of occurrences of a given type of event or the number of members of a population falling into a specified class.

Frequency distribution   A measure of the frequency of occurrence of the respective values of a process parameter.

Frequency polygon   The line enveloping a frequency histogram and passing through the midpoint of each class interval.

Gantt chart   A chart that shows the task schedule in a process. It may also display the status of various tasks, personnel assignments, and costs.

Gauge (noun)   A measuring device used to measure the physical dimensions of a product.

Histogram   A graphical representation of the class distribution of the values of a process parameter.

Homogeneous   The state of having characteristics that are uniformly distributed throughout a process or a sample from the process.

Independent variable   A variable characteristic of an item whose value is independent of the values of other characteristics of the item.

Inherent process variability   The variability that is inherent in a process when operating in a state of statistical control.

Inner noise   Internal factors, such as wear and tear, that influence the functionality and variability of a product.

Inspection   The process of checking the characteristics of a product for conformity.

Inspection by attributes An inspection in which the item is classified as either defective or nondefective (conforming or nonconforming) or the number of defects with respect to a given requirement.

Inspection by variables Inspection in which certain quality characteristics of the item are evaluated with respect to a scale of measurements and expressed as divisions along the scale.

Inspection system The established program by which the inspection of a product is carried out. The inspection system encompasses personnel, equipment, and procedures.

Interaction effect The effect produced by the interaction between two or more factors that affect the characteristics of a product.

Kurtosis coefficient The degree to which a distribution is flattened or peaked.

Loss function A continuous cost function that measures the cost impact of the variability of a product.

Lot *See* Batch

Lower control limit (LCL) The lower of the two control limits governing the conformity of an item on a control chart.

Main effect The effect of a factor acting on its own from one level to another to affect the outcome in a factorial experiment.

Measurement error Error in a recorded observation due to measurement inaccuracies.

Measurement standard A standard against which the output of a measuring instrument is compared.

Measuring system The collection of physical elements used to obtain a measurement of the characteristics of an object.

Median The value within a distribution above and below which an equal number of parameter values fall.

Metrology The field or function associated with the processes of measurement.

Mode The value within a statistical distribution that has the greatest frequency of occurrence.

Modified control chart A control chart with modified limits based on subgroup average.

Moving range control chart A control chart in which the range of the latest *n* observations is used for evaluating the stability of the variability in a process.

Multivariate control chart A control chart for evaluating the stability of a process in terms of the levels of two or more process parameters.

Nested experiment An experiment in which the level of one factor is chosen within the levels of another factor.

Noise factor An extraneous factor that disturbs the function of a product.

Nominal value The desired value of a process parameter from which variations are measured in terms of tolerance limits.

Nonconforming unit A unit of product or service containing at least one nonconformity.

Nonconformity A departure of a quality characteristic from its intended level in such a way that the departure adversely affects the overall quality of a product.

Normal cost The minimum activity cost associated with the performance of an activity at the minimum feasible resource level.

Normal time The minimum time in which an activity can be performed at the normal cost.

np chart A control chart for evaluating the stability of a process in terms of the total number of units in a sample that meet a certain classification.

Optimistic activity time The expected activity duration which would occur if every aspect of the performance of the activity goes as well as it possibly could.

Orthogonal matrix (array) A fractional matrix that assures a balanced and fair comparison of the levels of a factor in an experimental study such that the columns in the matrix can be evaluated independent of one another.

Out of control The condition describing a process from which all special causes of variation have not been eliminated. This condition is evident on a control chart by nonrandom patterns within the control limits.

Outer noise Ambient noise factors (e.g. temperature, humidity, etc.) that affect variation within a process.

p (proportion) A ratio indicating the number of units of a product that meet a certain classification in a sample of the product.

p chart A control chart for evaluating the stability of the process in terms of the proportion of a sample meeting a certain classification.

Pareto chart A graphical tool for percentage classification of the potential problem areas in a process according to their contribution to a specified criterion of measure such as cost or number of defects.

Percent defective The fraction defective multiplied by 100.

Percent nonconforming The fraction nonconforming multiplied by 100.

Pilot line A production line set up to collect information on a proposed production system.

Pilot lot A small batch of a product sampled from a pilot line for the purpose of studying the characteristics of a product or process.

Pooling The combination of the sum of squares and the degrees of freedom of factors in an analysis of variance to obtain a better estimate of experimental error.

Population The universal collection of similar items from which samples are drawn for measurement and statistical analysis.

Process One event or a collection of events within which people, tools, and materials interact to perform operation(s) which cause one or more characteristics of a raw material to be altered or generated.

Process average The average value of a process in terms of the percentage or proportion of variant units.

Process capability A standardized evaluation of the inherent ability of a process to perform specified operations after significant causes of variation have been eliminated. Process capability usually is set equal to six standard deviations of the variability.

Process capability study A controlled collection of statistics from a process for the purpose of statistically determining the capability of the process to produce acceptable products under specified conditions.

Process quality A statistical measure for the quality of product from a given process.

Process spread The total variability that exists in items produced by the process.

Process tolerance The range over which the values of a characteristic of the product from a process are allowed to vary. Process tolerance is distinguished from design tolerance.

Process under control A process in which the various factors affecting variability are maintained within defined control limits.

Producer's risk The probability rejecting a good batch from a producer's production lot.

Qualification (supplier qualification) The process by which products are obtained from a supplier and tested for the purpose of documenting the units from the supplier as qualified or certified products. It is alternately referred to as certification.

Quality The combined features and characteristics of a product that influence its ability to satisfy specified needs.

Quality assurance The process which sets the standards for product quality.

Quality audit A systematic and independent examination to determine whether quality activities and results comply with planned arrangements, and whether these arrangements are effectively implemented and are suitable to achieve objectives.

Quality characteristic An aspect of an item that can be measured or observed with respect to how it contributes to the acceptability and/or functioning of the item.

Quality control The operational techniques and activities that are used to satisfy quality requirements.

Quality potential The probability that the values of the characteristics of a product will lie within specified limits.

R chart (range chart) A control chart in which the subgroup range R is used for evaluating the stability of the variability of a process.

Random sampling The process of selecting sample units in such a manner that all units under consideration have an equal chance of being selected as the sample.

Range The difference between the smallest and largest values in a set of observations.

Range chart The part of a quality control chart on which are plotted the values of the ranges of samples to provide a measure of the variability of the product and/or process.

Rational subgroup One of the small groups within which it is believed that assignable causes are constant and into which observations can be subdivided in carrying out statistical analysis.

Rejects The items of product that are not accepted because they fail to meet specific quality criteria.

Relative frequency The ratio of the number of times a particular value (or a value falling within a given class) is observed to the total number of observations.

Repeatability An indication of the closeness of the agreement between the results of successive measurements of the same value of the same physical quantity carried out under identical conditions.

Replication The performance of an experiment or part of an experiment more than once. Each performance, including the first one, is called a replicate.

Response The result obtained when an experiment is run under a specific set of conditions.

Rework Any process whereby defective material is altered in an effort to make it acceptable.

Run The process of producing a quantity of a product in a continuing sequence of operations within one production cycle.

Run chart A graph of a characteristic versus sampling sequence used to detect trends.

s chart (sample standard deviation chart) A control in which the subgroup standard deviation is used for evaluating the stability of the variability of a process.

Sample One or more units of a product drawn from a specific lot for the purpose of inspection.

Sample size The number of units contained in a sample drawn from a production batch.

Sampling frequency The ratio of the number of units of a product randomly selected for inspection at an inspection station to the number of units of the product going through the inspection station.

Sampling interval The fixed interval of time or units of output between samples.

Sampling plan A plan according to which one or more samples are drawn from a population.

Sampling procedure The specific steps through which a sampling plan is carried out.

Scatter diagram A plot of one variable against another that displays their relationship.

Scrap A nonconforming unit of a product that is not usable and cannot be economically reworked.

Significance test A statistical procedure to determine whether some quantity that is subject to a random variation differs from a hypothesized value by an amount greater than that attributable to random variation alone.

Skewed distribution An asymmetric curve of a distribution having a longer tail to the right (skewed to the right) or to the left (skewed to the left).

Specification A specification of the requirements to be met by the characteristics of a product for the product to be acceptable.

Standard deviation A measure of the dispersion of a set of values around its average value. When standard deviation is denoted by 's', it represents the sample standard deviation. When denoted by 'σ' it represents the population or universe standard deviation.

Standard error The standard deviation of a sampling distribution.

Standardization The reduction of the number of characteristics or features of a system or the reduction of the number of ways these may vary or interact.

Statistic A quantity calculated from a sample of observations used to establish an estimate of some population parameter.

Statistical control The condition describing a process from which all assignable causes of variation have been eliminated and only chance causes remain. This is identified on a control chart by the absence of points beyond the control limits and by the absence of nonrandom patterns or trend within the control limits.

Statistical process control The use of statistical tools such as histograms, control charts, and other variation analysis techniques to analyze a process or its output so as to take appropriate action to achieve and maintain a state of statistical control.

Statistical tolerance limits A set of limits calculated from the results of sample observations and between which a stated fraction of the population will lie with a given probability.

Stratification The physical or conceptual division of a population into separate parts called strata.

Subgroup A set of elements having one or more characteristics in common.

System A group of elements having dependent and independent effects which act together to achieve a specific function.

Test An examination of one or more characteristics of a product.

Test procedure A measurement instruction describing the method by which one or more quality characteristics are to be assessed.

Tolerance The total allowable variation around a level or state (upper limit minus lower limit).

Tolerance limits Limits that define the conformance boundaries for an individual unit of a product.

Total process variability The inherent process variability plus variations due to factors that have been allowed to change, such as operator errors, equipment adjustments, and so on.

Treatment A given combination of the levels of all factors to be included in an experimental study.

Triple C A management concept that emphasizes the integration of communication, cooperation, and coordination functions for the purpose of improving process performance.

***u* chart (count per unit chart)**   A control chart for evaluating the stability of a process in terms of the average count of a given classification event occurring within a sample.

Upper control limit (UCL)   An upper limit of a range of values in a control chart used for determining when corrective actions may be needed.

Variable   A quantity that may take any one of a specified range of values.

Variance (population)   A measure of dispersion of a population.

Variance (sample)   An estimate of the measure of dispersion of a finite population based on a sample drawn from the population.

Verification   The act of reviewing, inspecting, testing, checking, auditing, or establishing whether items meet specified requirements.

X-bar chart (average chart)   A control chart in which the subgroup average is used for evaluating the stability of the process level.

Appendix B
Process conversion factors

NUMBER PREFIXES

Prefix	SI Symbol	Multiplication Factors	Example
tera	T	$1\ 000\ 000\ 000\ 000 = 10^{12}$	tera fortune
giga	G	$1\ 000\ 000\ 000 = 10^9$	giga byte
mega	M	$1\ 000\ 000 = 10^6$	mega bucks
kilo	k	$1\ 000 = 10^3$	kilo byte
hecto	h	$100 = 10^2$	hectogram
deca	da	$10 = 10^1$	decade
deci	d	$0.1 = 10^{-1}$	decimal
centi	c	$0.01 = 10^{-2}$	centimeter
milli	m	$0.001 = 10^{-3}$	millimicron
micro	μ	$0.000\ 001 = 10^{-6}$	microcomputer
nano	n	$0.000\ 000\ 001 = 10^{-9}$	nanosecond
pico	p	$0.000\ 000\ 000\ 001 = 10^{-12}$	picosecond
femto	f	$0.000\ 000\ 000\ 000\ 001 = 10^{-15}$	femto chance
atto	a	$0.000\ 000\ 000\ 000\ 000\ 001 = 10^{-18}$	atto likelihood

AREA

Multiply	by	to obtain
acres	43 560	sq feet
	4 047	sq meters
	4 840	sq yards
	0.405	hectare
sq cm	0.155	sq inches
sq feet	144	sq inches
	0.09290	sq meters
	0.1111	sq yards
sq inches	645.16	sq millimeters
sq kilometers	0.3861	sq miles
sq meters	10.764	sq feet
	1.196	sq yards
hectare	10000	sq meters
sq miles	640	acres
	2.590	sq kilometers

VOLUME

Multiply	by	to obtain
acre-foot	1233.5	cubic meters
cubic cm	0.06102	cubic inches
cubic feet	1728	cubic inches
	7.480	gallons (US)
	0.02832	cubic meters
	0.03704	cubic yards
liter	1.057	liquid quarts
	0.908	dry quart
	61.024	cubic inches
gallons (US)	231	cubic inches
	3.7854	liters
	4	quarts
	0.833	British gallons
	128	US fluid ounces
barrel	40 gallons	
quarts (US)	0.9463	liters

MASS

Multiply	by	to obtain
carat	0.200	cubic grams
grams	0.03527	ounces
kilograms	2.2046	pounds
ounces	28.350	grams
pound	16	ounces
	453.6	grams
stone (UK)	6.35	kilograms
	14	pounds
ton (net)	907.2	kilograms
	2000	pounds
	0.893	gross ton
	0.907	metric ton
ton (gross)	2240	pounds
	1.12	net tons
	1.016	metric tons
tonne (metric)	2,204.623	pounds
	0.984	gross ton
	1000	kilograms

TEMPERATURE

Conversion formulas

Celsius to kelvin	K = C + 273.15
Celsius to Fahrenheit	F = (9/5)C + 32
Fahrenheit to Celsius	C = (5/9)(F − 32)
Fahrenheit to kelvin	K = (5/9)(F + 459.67)
Fahrenheit to Rankin	R = F + 459.67
Rankin to kelvin	K = (5/9)R

ENERGY, HEAT, POWER

Multiply	*by*	*to obtain*
BTU	1055.9	joules
	0.2520	kg-calories
watt-hour	3600	joules
	3.409	BTU
HP (electric)	746	watts
BTU/second	1055.9	watts
watt-second	1.00	joules

VELOCITY

Multiply	*by*	*to obtain*
feet/minute	5.080	mm/second
feet/second	0.3048	meters/second
inches/second	0.0254	meters/second
km/hour	0.6214	miles/hour
meters/second	3.2808	feet/second
	2.237	miles/hour
miles/hour	88.0	feet/minute
	0.44704	meters/second
	1.6093	km/hour
	0.8684	knots
knot	1.151	miles/hour

PRESSURE

Multiply	by	to obtain
atmospheres	1.01325	bars
	33.90	feet of water
	29.92	inches of mercury
	760.0	mm of mercury
bar	75.01	cm of mercury
	14.50	pounds/sq inch
dyne/sq cm	0.1	N/sq meter
dyne	0.00001	newton
newtons/sq cm	1.450	pounds/sq inch
pounds/sq inch	0.06805	atmospheres
	2.036	inches of mercury
	27.708	inches of water
	68.948	millibars
	51.72	mm of mercury

LENGTH

Multiply	by	to obtain
angstrom	10^{-10}	meters
feet	0.30480	meters
	12	inches
inches	25.40	millimeters
	0.02540	meters
	0.08333	feet
kilometers	3280.8	feet
	0.6214	miles
	1094	yards
meters	39.370	inches
	3.2808	feet
	1.094	yards
miles	5280	feet
	1.6093	kilometers
	0.8694	nautical miles
millimeters	0.03937	inches
nautical miles	6076	feet
	1.852	kilometers
yards	0.9144	meters
	3	feet
	36	inches

CONSTANTS

speed of light	2.997,925 x 10^{10} cm/sec
	983.6 × 10^6 ft/sec
	186,284 miles/sec
velocity of sound	340.3 meters/sec
	1116 ft/sec
gravity	9.80665 m/sec square
(acceleration)	32.174 ft/sec square
	386.089 inches/sec square

Appendix C
Statistical tables

NORMAL DISTRIBUTION

z	.00	.01	.02	.03	.04	.05	.06	.07	.08	.09
.0	.5000	.5040	.5080	.5120	.5160	.5199	.5239	.5279	.5319	.5359
.1	.5398	.5438	.5478	.5517	.5557	.5596	.5636	.5675	.5714	.5753
.2	.5793	.5832	.5871	.5910	.5948	.5987	.6026	.6064	.6103	.6141
.3	.6179	.6217	.6255	.6293	.6331	.6368	.6406	.6443	.6480	.6517
.4	.6554	.6591	.6628	.6664	.6700	.6736	.6772	.6808	.6844	.6879
.5	.6915	.6950	.6985	.7019	.7054	.7088	.7123	.7157	.7190	.7224
.6	.7257	.7291	.7324	.7357	.7389	.7422	.7454	.7486	.7517	.7549
.7	.7580	.7611	.7642	.7673	.7704	.7734	.7764	.7794	.7823	.7852
.8	.7881	.7910	.7939	.7967	.7995	.8023	.8051	.8078	.8106	.8133
.9	.8159	.8186	.8212	.8238	.8264	.8289	.8315	.8340	.8365	.8389
1.0	.8413	.8438	.8461	.8485	.8508	.8531	.8554	.8577	.8599	.8621
1.1	.8643	.8665	.8686	.8708	.8729	.8749	.8770	.8790	.8810	.8830
1.2	.8849	.8869	.8888	.8907	.8925	.8944	.8962	.8980	.8997	.9015
1.3	.9032	.9049	.9066	.9082	.9099	.9115	.9131	.9147	.9162	.9177
1.4	.9192	.9207	.9222	.9236	.9251	.9265	.9279	.9292	.9306	.9319
1.5	.9332	.9345	.9357	.9370	.9382	.9394	.9406	.9418	.9429	.9441
1.6	.9452	.9463	.9474	.9484	.9495	.9505	.9515	.9525	.9535	.9545
1.7	.9554	.9564	.9573	.9582	.9591	.9599	.9608	.9616	.9625	.9633
1.8	.9641	.9649	.9656	.9664	.9671	.9678	.9686	.9693	.9699	.9706
1.9	.9713	.9719	.9726	.9732	.9738	.9744	.9750	.9756	.9761	.9767
2.0	.9772	.9778	.9783	.9788	.9793	.9798	.9803	.9808	.9812	.9817
2.1	.9821	.9826	.9830	.9834	.9838	.9842	.9846	.9850	.9854	.9857
2.2	.9861	.9864	.9868	.9871	.9875	.9878	.9881	.9884	.9887	.9890
2.3	.9893	.9896	.9898	.9901	.9904	.9906	.9909	.9911	.9913	.9916
2.4	.9918	.9920	.9922	.9925	.9927	.9929	.9931	.9932	.9934	.9936
2.5	.9938	.9940	.9941	.9943	.9945	.9946	.9948	.9949	.9951	.9952
2.6	.9953	.9955	.9956	.9957	.9959	.9960	.9961	.9962	.9963	.9964
2.7	.9965	.9966	.9967	.9968	.9969	.9970	.9971	.9972	.9973	.9974
2.8	.9974	.9975	.9976	.9977	.9977	.9978	.9979	.9979	.9980	.9981
2.9	.9981	.9982	.9982	.9983	.9984	.9984	.9985	.9985	.9986	.9986
3.0	.9987	.9987	.9987	.9988	.9988	.9989	.9989	.9989	.9990	.9990
3.1	.9990	.9991	.9991	.9991	.9992	.9992	.9992	.9992	.9993	.9993
3.2	.9993	.9993	.9994	.9994	.9994	.9994	.9994	.9995	.9995	.9995
3.3	.9995	.9995	.9995	.9996	.9996	.9996	.9996	.9996	.9996	.9997
3.4	.9997	.9997	.9997	.9997	.9997	.9997	.9997	.9997	.9997	.9998

CRITICAL VALUES OF THE t-DISTRIBUTION

v	$t_{0.10}$	$t_{0.05}$	$t_{0.025}$	$t_{0.01}$	$t_{0.005}$
1	3.078	6.314	12.706	31.821	63.657
2	1.886	2.920	4.303	6.965	9.925
3	1.638	2.353	3.182	4.541	5.841
4	1.533	2.132	2.776	3.747	4.604
5	1.476	2.015	2.571	3.365	4.032
6	1.440	1.943	2.447	3.143	3.707
7	1.415	1.895	2.365	2.998	3.499
8	1.397	1.860	2.306	2.896	3.355
9	1.383	1.833	2.262	2.821	3.250
10	1.372	1.812	2.228	2.764	3.169
11	1.363	1.796	2.201	2.718	3.106
12	1.356	1.782	2.179	2.681	3.055
13	1.350	1.771	2.160	2.650	3.012
14	1.345	1.761	2.145	2.624	2.977
15	1.341	1.753	2.131	2.602	2.947
16	1.337	1.746	2.120	2.583	2.921
17	1.333	1.740	2.110	2.567	2.898
18	1.330	1.734	2.101	2.552	2.878
19	1.328	1.729	2.093	2.539	2.861
20	1.325	1.725	2.086	2.528	2.845
21	1.323	1.721	2.080	2.518	2.831
22	1.321	1.717	2.074	2.508	2.819
23	1.319	1.714	2.069	2.500	2.807
24	1.318	1.711	2.064	2.492	2.797
25	1.316	1.708	2.060	2.485	2.787
26	1.315	1.706	2.056	2.479	2.779
27	1.314	1.703	2.052	2.473	2.771
28	1.313	1.701	2.048	2.467	2.763
29	1.311	1.699	2.045	2.462	2.756
30	1.310	1.697	2.042	2.457	2.750
40	1.303	1.684	2.021	2.423	2.704
60	1.296	1.671	2.000	2.390	2.660
120	1.289	1.658	1.980	2.358	2.617
∞	1.282	1.645	1.960	2.326	2.576

CRITICAL VALUES OF THE CHI SQUARE DISTRIBUTION

v	$\xi^2_{0.995}$	$\xi^2_{0.99}$	$\xi^2_{0.975}$	$\xi^2_{0.95}$	$\xi^2_{0.05}$	$\xi^2_{0.025}$	$\xi^2_{0.01}$	$\xi^2_{0.005}$
1	0.0000393	0.000157	0.000982	0.00393	3.841	5.024	6.635	7.879
2	0.0100	0.0201	0.0506	0.103	5.991	7.378	9.210	10.597
3	0.0717	0.115	0.216	0.352	7.815	9.348	11.345	12.838
4	0.207	0.297	0.484	0.711	9.488	11.143	13.277	14.860
5	0.412	0.554	0.831	1.145	11.070	12.832	15.086	16.750
6	0.676	0.872	1.237	1.635	12.592	14.449	16.812	18.548
7	0.989	1.239	1.690	2.167	14.067	16.013	18.475	20.278
8	1.344	1.646	2.180	2.733	15.507	17.535	20.090	21.955
9	1.735	2.088	2.700	3.325	16.919	19.023	21.666	23.589
10	2.156	2.558	3.247	3.940	18.307	20.483	23.209	25.188
11	2.603	3.053	3.816	4.575	19.675	21.920	24.725	26.757
12	3.074	3.571	4.404	5.226	21.026	23.337	26.217	28.300
13	3.565	4.107	5.009	5.892	22.362	24.736	27.688	29.819
14	4.075	4.660	5.629	6.571	23.685	26.119	29.141	31.319
15	4.601	5.229	6.262	7.261	24.996	27.488	30.578	32.801
16	5.142	5.812	6.908	7.962	26.296	28.845	32.000	34.267
17	5.697	6.408	7.564	8.672	27.587	30.191	33.409	35.718
18	6.265	7.015	8.231	9.390	28.869	31.526	34.805	37.156
19	6.844	7.633	8.907	10.117	30.144	32.852	36.191	38.582
20	7.434	8.260	9.591	10.851	31.410	34.170	37.566	39.997
21	8.034	8.897	10.283	11.591	32.671	35.479	38.932	41.401
22	8.643	9.542	10.982	12.338	33.924	36.781	40.289	42.796
23	9.260	10.196	11.689	13.091	35.172	38.076	41.638	44.181
24	9.886	10.856	12.401	13.848	36.415	39.364	42.980	45.558
25	10.520	11.524	13.120	14.611	37.652	40.646	44.314	46.928
26	11.160	12.198	13.844	15.379	38.885	41.923	45.642	48.290
27	11.808	12.879	14.573	16.151	40.113	43.194	46.963	49.645
28	12.461	13.565	15.308	16.928	41.337	44.461	48.278	50.993
29	13.121	14.256	16.047	17.708	42.557	45.722	49.588	52.336
30	13.787	14.953	16.791	18.493	43.773	46.979	50.892	53.672

CONTROL CHART CONSTANTS (PART I)

n	A_2	A_3	A_6	B_3	B_4	c_4	d_2
2	1.880	2.659		0.000	3.267	0.7979	1.128
3	1.023	1.954	1.187	0.000	2.568	0.8862	1.693
4	0.729	1.628		0.000	2.266	0.9213	2.059
5	0.577	1.427	0.691	0.000	2.089	0.9400	2.326
6	0.483	1.287		0.030	1.970	0.9515	2.534
7	0.419	1.182	0.509	0.118	1.882	0.9594	2.704
8	0.373	1.099		0.185	1.815	0.9650	2.847
9	0.337	1.032	0.412	0.239	1.761	0.9693	2.970
10	0.308	0.975		0.284	1.716	0.9727	3.078
11	0.285	0.927	0.350	0.321	1.679	0.9754	3.173
12	0.266	0.886		0.354	1.646	0.9776	3.258
13	0.249	0.850		0.382	1.618	0.9794	3.336
14	0.235	0.817		0.406	1.594	0.9810	3.407
15	0.223	0.789		0.428	1.572	0.9823	3.472
16	0.212	0.763		0.448	1.552	0.9835	3.532
17	0.203	0.739		0.466	1.534	0.9845	3.588
18	0.194	0.718		0.482	1.518	0.9854	3.640
19	0.187	0.698		0.497	1.503	0.9862	3.689
20	0.180	0.680		0.510	1.490	0.9869	3.735
21	0.173	0.663		0.523	1.477	0.9876	3.778
22	0.167	0.647		0.534	1.466	0.9882	3.819
23	0.162	0.633		0.545	1.455	0.9887	3.858
24	0.157	0.619		0.555	1.445	0.9892	3.895
25	0.153	0.606		0.565	1.435	0.9896	3.931
> 25	$3/\sqrt{n}$			$1 - 3/\sqrt{2n}$	$1 + 3/\sqrt{2n}$		

CONTROL CHART CONSTANTS (PART II)

n	d_3	d_4	D_3	D_4	D_5	D_6	E_2
2	0.853	0.954	0.000	3.267	0.000	3.865	2.660
3	0.888	1.588	0.000	2.574	0.000	2.745	1.772
4	0.880	1.978	0.000	2.282	0.000	2.375	1.457
5	0.864	2.257	0.000	2.114	0.000	2.179	1.290
6	0.848	2.472	0.000	2.004	0.000	2.055	1.184
7	0.833	2.645	0.076	1.924	0.078	1.967	1.109
8	0.820	2.791	0.136	1.864	0.139	1.901	1.054
9	0.808	2.915	0.184	1.816	0.187	1.850	1.010
10	0.797	3.024	0.223	1.777	0.227	1.809	0.975
11	0.787	3.121	0.256	1.744			
12	0.778	3.207	0.283	1.717			
13	0.770	3.285	0.307	1.693			
14	0.762	3.356	0.328	1.672			
15	0.755	3.422	0.347	1.653			
16	0.749	3.482	0.363	1.637			
17	0.743	3.538	0.378	1.622			
18	0.738	3.591	0.391	1.608			
19	0.733	3.640	0.403	1.597			
20	0.729	3.686	0.415	1.585			
21	0.724	3.730	0.425	1.575			
22	0.720	3.771	0.434	1.566			
23	0.716	3.811	0.443	1.557			
24	0.712	3.847	0.451	1.548			
25	0.709	3.883	0.459	1.541			

Bibliography

Abdelnour, G., Chang, C. and Cheung, J. Y. (1991) A tuning approach for fuzzy logic controllers. *Proceedings of the Fifth Oklahoma Symposium on Artificial Intelligence*, Norman, OK, November, pp. 215–24.

Abernathy, W. J. and Wayne, K. (1974) Limits of the learning curve. *Harvard Business Review*, **52**, Sept.–Oct., pp. 109–19.

Akao, Y. and Asaka, T. (eds), *Quality Function Deployment*, Productivity Press Inc., Cambridge, MA.

Alchian, A. (1963) Reliability of progress curves in airframe production. *Econometrica*, **31**(4), pp. 679–93.

Alexander, D. C. and Mustafa Pulat, B. (1985) *Industrial Ergonomics: A Practitioner's Guide*, Industrial Engineering and Management Press, Norcross, GA.

Alwan, L. C. and Roberts, H. V. (1989) Time series modeling for statistical process control, in *Statistical Process Control in Automated Manufacturing*, (eds J. B. Keats and N. F. Hubele), Marcel Dekker, New York, pp. 87–95.

Amsden, R. T., Butler, H. E., and Amsden, D. M. (1989) *SPC Simplified: Practical Steps to Quality*, Quality Resources, White Plains, New York.

Amsden, D. M., Butler, H. E. and Amsden, R. T. (1990) *SPC Simplified Workbook: Practical Steps to Quality*, Quality Resources, White Plains, New York.

Asher, H. (1956) Cost–quantity relationships in the airframe industry. *Report No. R–291, The Rand Corporation*, Santa Monica, CA, July 1, 1956.

Ayeni, B. J. (1989) Parameter estimation for hyperbolic decline curve. *Journal of Energy Resources Technology*, **111**, December, pp. 279–283.

Ayeni, B. J. (1991) Design Resolution. *Statistically Speaking*, Internal Publication, 3M IS&DP Statistical Consulting, August, p. 4.

Ayeni, B. J. (1991) Multivariate process control, paper presented to 3M Technical Staff, June.

Ayeni, B. J. and Ayeni, F. O. (1993) Bayesian estimation procedure for petroleum discoveries of an exploratory well, paper accepted by *Journal of Petroleum Science and Engineering*.

Ayeni, B. J. and Boullion, T. L. (1984) Application of time series model to oil production forecasting, paper presented at the 58th Annual Meeting of the Louisiana Academy of Sciences, Feb. 6–8, p. 68.

Ayeni, B. J. and Boullion, T. L. (1985) Estimation in a mixture of two normal distributions, in the *Proceedings of the 59th Annual Meeting of the Louisiana Academy of Sciences*, **58**, Feb. 7–9, p. 146.

Ayeni, B. J. and Boullion, T. L. (1986) Oil production forecasting for a West Cameron block 33 field in South Louisiana, in the *Proceedings of the 60th Annual Meeting of the Louisiana Academy of Sciences*, **59**, Feb. 6–8, p. 64.

Ayeni, B. J. and Pilat, R. (1992) Crude oil reserve estimation: An application of the autoregressive integrated moving average (ARIMA) model. *Journal of Petroleum Science and Engineering*, **8**(1), pp. 13–28.

Badiru, A. B. (1985) Process capability analysis on a microcomputer, *Softcover Software*, Industrial Engineering and Management Press, Norcross, Georgia, pp. 7–14.

Badiru, A. B. (1987) Communication, cooperation, coordination: the Triple C of project management, in *Proceedings of 1987 IIE Spring Conference*, Washington, DC, May, pp. 401–404.

Badiru, A. B. (1988a) *Project Management in Manufacturing And High Technology Operations*, John Wiley and Sons, New York.

Badiru, A. B. (1988b) Cost-integrated network planning using expert systems. *Project Management Journal*, **19**(2), April, pp. 59–62.

Badiru, A. B. (1990a) A management guide to automation cost justification. *Industrial Engineering*, **22**(3), Feb., pp. 26–30.

Badiru, A. B. (1990b) A systems approach to total quality management. *Industrial Engineering*, **22**(3), March, pp. 33–36.

Badiru, A. B. (1990c) Systems integration for total quality management. *Engineering Management Journal*, **2**(3), Sept., pp. 23–28.

Badiru, A. B. (1991a) *Project Management Tools for Engineering and Management Professionals*, Industrial Engineering and Management Press, Norcross, GA.

Badiru, A. B. (1991b) Manufacturing cost estimation: a multivariate learning curve approach. *Journal of Manufacturing Systems*, **10**(6), pp. 431–441.

Badiru, A. B. (1991c) A simulation approach to PERT network analysis. *Simulation*, **57**(4), October, pp. 245–255.

Badiru, A. B. (1991d) Total quality management: a project management approach. *Proceedings of Project Management Institute Annual Symposium*, Dallas, Texas, September, pp. 62–67.

Badiru, A. B. (1992) Computational survey of univariate and bivariate learning curves. *IEEE Transactions on Engineering Management*, **39**(2), May, pp. 176–188.

Badiru, A. B. (1992) *Expert Systems Applications in Engineering and Manufacturing*, Prentice-Hall, New Jersey.

Badiru, A. B. and Jen–Gwo Chen, J. (1992) IEs help transform industrial productivity and quality in Taiwan. *Industrial Engineering*, **24**(6), June, pp. 53–55.

Badiru, A. B. and Smith, J. R. (1982) Setting tolerances by computer simulation. *Proceedings of IIE Fall Conference*, Cincinnati, Ohio, November, pp. 284–288.

Baloff, N. (1971) Extension of the learning curve: some empirical results. *Operations Research Quarterly*, **22**(4), pp. 329–340.

Belkaoui, A. (1976) Costing through learning. *Cost and Management*, **50**(3), pp. 36–40.

Belkaoui, A. (1986) *The Learning Curve*, Quorum Books, Westport, Conn.

Bellini, E. V., Paulovich, D. A., Garrett, N. H. and Joachim, D. R. Plat automation improves product quality and efficiency. *Industrial Engineering*, **24**(6), pp. 49–51.

Bemis, J. C. (1981) A model for examining the cost implications of production rate. *Concepts: The Journal of Defense Systems Acquisition Management*, **4**(2), pp. 84–94.

Bernard, G. A. (1959) Control charts on stochastic processes. *Journal of the Royal Statistical Society*, **B21**, pp. 239–271.

Beyer, W. H. (ed.) (1991) *CRC Standard Probability and Statistics Tables and Formulae*, CRC Press, Boca Raton, FL.

Box, G. E. P. (1957) Evolutionary operation: a method for increasing industrial productivity. *Journal of the Royal Statistical Society*, Series C (Applied Statistics), **6**, pp. 2–23.

Box, G. E. P. and Draper, N. R. (1969) *Evolutionary Operation: A Statistical Method for Process Improvement*, John Wiley and Sons, New York.

Box, G. E. P. and Draper, N. R. (1987) *Empirical Model-Building and Response Surfaces*, John Wiley, New York.

Box, G. E. P. and Jenkins, G. M. (1970) *Time Series Analysis: Forecasting and Control*, Holden-Day, San Francisco.

Box, G. E. P. and Jenkins, G. M. (1976) *Time Series Analysis: Forecasting and Control*, Holden-Day, San Francisco.

Box, G. E. P. and Kramer, T. (1990) Industrial process control: a multifaceted problem. *ASQC Quality Congress Transactions*, San Francisco, pp. 86–95.

Box, G. and Kramer, T. (1992) Statistical process monitoring and feedback adjustment: a discussion. *Technometrics*, **34**(3), Aug., pp. 251–267.

Box, G. E.P. and Wilson, K. B. (1951) On the experimental attainment of optimum conditions. *Journal of the Royal Statistical Society*, Series B, **13**, pp. 1–45.

Box, G. E. P., Hunter, W. G. and Hunter, J. S. (1978) *Statistics for Experimenters*, John Wiley, New York.

Box, G. E. P., Jenkins, G. M. and MacGregor, J. F. (1974) Some recent advances in forecasting and control. *Applied Statistics*, **23**, pp. 158–179.

Bussey, L. E. and Eschenbach, T. G. (1992) *The Economic Analysis of Industrial Projects*, 2nd edn, Prentice-Hall, Englewood Cliffs, NJ.

Caffray, S. J. (1990) Chemical batch adjustment strategy. *ASQC Quality Congress Transactions*, San Francisco, pp. 368–373.

Camm, J. D., Evans, J. R. and Womer, N. K. (1987) The unit learning curve approximation of total cost. *Computers and Industrial Engineering*, **12**(3), pp. 205–213.

Camm, J. D., Gulledge, Jun., T. R. and Womer, N. K. (1987) Production rate and contractor behavior. *The Journal of Cost Analysis*, **5**(1), pp. 27–38.

Carlson, J. G. H. (1973) Cubic learning curves: precision tool for labor estimating. *Manufacturing Engineering and Management*, **71**(5), pp. 22–25.

Carlson, J. G. H. and Rowe A. J. (1976) How much does forgetting cost? *Industrial Engineering*, **8**, September, pp. 40–47.

Carr, G. W. (1946) Peacetime cost estimating requires new learning curves. *Aviation*, **45**, April.

Chen, J. T. (1983) Modeling learning curve and learning complementarity for resource allocation and production scheduling. *Decision Sciences*, **14**, pp. 170–186.

Chen, Y. and Tang, K. (1992) A pictorial approach to poor-quality cost management. *IEEE Transactions on Engineering Management*, **39**(2), May, pp. 149–157.

Clements, R. (1991) *Handbook of Statistical Methods in Manufacturing*, Prentice-Hall, Englewood Cliff, NJ.

Conley, P. (1970) Experience curves as a planning tool. *IEEE Spectrum*, **7**(6), pp. 63–68.

Conway, R. W. and Schultz, A., Jun. (1959) The manufacturing progress function. *Journal of Industrial Engineering*, **1**, pp. 39–53.

Cooper, J. D. and Fisher, M. J. (1979) *Software Quality Management*, Petrocelli Book, New York.

Cox, C. A. (1992) Keys to success in quality function deployment. *APICS*, April, pp. 25–28.

Cox, L. W. and Gansler, J. S. (1981) Evaluating the impact of quantity, rate, and competition. *Concepts: The Journal of Defense Systems Acquisition Management*, **4**(4), pp. 29–53.

Crosby, P. B. (1979) *Quality is Free: The Art of Making Quality Certain*, McGraw-Hill, New York.

Crosby, P. B. (1984) *Quality Without Tears: The Art of Hassle-free Management*, McGraw-Hill, New York.

Crow, D. A. (1992) Process industries need a new generation of system solutions. *APICS*, April, pp. 29–32.

Dada, M. and Srikanth, K. N. (1990) Monopolistic pricing and the learning curve: an algorithmic approach. *Operations Research*, **38**(4), pp. 656–666.

DeJong, J. R. (1957) The effects of increasing skill on cycle time and its consequences for time standards. *Ergonomics*, November, pp. 51–60.

Deming, W. E. (1982) *Out of the Crisis*, Cambridge University Press.

Deming, W. E. (1982) *Quality, Productivity and Competitive Position*, MIT, Center for Advanced Engineering Study, Cambridge, MA.

Dingus, V. and Golomski, W. (eds) (1991) *A Quality Revolution in Manufacturing*, Industrial Engineering and Management Press, Norcross, GA.

DOE (1981) *Cost and Schedule Control Systems: Criteria for Contract Performance Measurement: Work Breakdown Structure Guide*, US Department of Energy, Office of Project and Facilities Management, Washington, DC 20585.

Donath, N., Globerson, S. and Zang, I. (1981) A learning curve model for multiple batch production process. *International Journal of Production Research*, **19**(2), pp. 165–175.

Dougherty, E. R. (1990) *Probability and Statistics for the Engineering, Computing, and Physical Sciences*, Prentice-Hall, Englewood Cliffs, NJ.

Duncan, A. J. (1974) *Quality Control and Industrial Statistics*, 4th edn, Irwin, Inc., Homewood, IL.

Ebert, R. J. (1976) Aggregate planning with learning curve productivity. *Management Science*, **23**, pp. 171–182.

Ebrahimpour, M. and Withers, B. E. (1992) Employee involvement in quality improvement: a comparison of American and Japanese manufacturing firms operating in the U.S. *IEEE Transactions on Engineering Management*, **39**(2), May, pp. 142–148.

Enrick, N. L. (1985) *Quality, Reliability, and Process Improvement*, 8th edn, Industrial Press, Inc., New York.

Ermer, D. S. (1979) Metal surface characterization by dynamic data systems methodology. *ASQC Technical Conference Transactions*, Houston, TX.

Ermer, D. S. (1980) A control chart for dependent data. *ASQC Technical Conference Transactions*, Atlanta, GA.

Ewan, W. D. (1963) When and how to use CUSUM charts. *Technometrics*, **5**, pp. 1–22.

Fabrycky, W. J. and Blanchard, B. S. (1991) *Life-Cycle Cost and Economic Analysis*, Prentice-Hall, Englewood Cliffs, NJ.

Fasser, Y. and Brettner, D. (1992) *Process Improvement in the Electronics Industry*, John Wiley and Sons, New York.

Feigenbaum, A. V. (1983) *Total Quality Control*, McGraw-Hill, New York.

Fisk, J. C. and Ballou, D. P. (1982) Production lot sizing under a learning effect. *IIE Transactions*, **14**(4), pp. 257–264.

Fleischer, G. A. (1984) *Engineering Economy: Capital Allocation Theory*, Brooks/Cole Engineering Division, Monterey, CA.

Forman, E. H., Saaty, T. L., Selly, M. A. and Waldom, R. (1983) *Expert Choice, Decision Support Software*, McLean, VA.

Frank, S. and Halle, S. (1992) Is your total quality effort doomed to fail. *APICS*, April, pp. 22–24.

Gibson, J. E. (1990) *Modern Management of the High-Technology Enterprise*, Prentice-Hall, Englewood Cliffs, NJ.

Gilbreath, R. D. (1986) *Winning At Project Management: What Works, What Fails, and Why*, John Wiley, New York.

Gitlow, H., Gitlow, S., Oppenheim, A. and Oppenheim, R. (1989) *Tools and Methods for the Improvement of Quality*, Irwin, Homewood, IL.

Globerson, S. and Shtub, A. (1984) The impact of learning curves on the design of long cycle time lines. *Industrial Management*, **26**(3), May/June, pp. 5–10.

Glover, J. H. (1966) Manufacturing progress functions: an alternative model and its comparison with existing functions. *International Journal of Production Research*, **4**(4), pp. 279–300.

Gold, B. (1981) Changing perspectives on size, scale, and returns. *Journal of Economic Literature*, **19**(1), pp. 5–33.

Goldberger, A. S. (1968) The interpretation and estimation of Cobb-Douglas functions. *Econometrica*, **35**(3–4), pp. 464–472.

Golden, B. L., Wasil, E. A. and Harker, P. T. (eds) (1989) *The Analytic Hierarchy Process: Applications and Studies*, Springer-Verlag, New York.

Graver, C. A. and Boren, H. E., Jun. (1967) Multivariate logarithmic and exponential regression models. RM-4879-PR, The RAND Corporation, Santa Monica, CA.

Gulezian, R. C. (1979) *Statistics for Decision Making*, W. B. Saunders Company, Philadelphia.

Gulledge, T. R. and Khoshnevis, B. (1987) Production rate, learning, and program costs: survey and bibliography. *Engineering Costs and Production Economics*, **11**, pp. 223–236.

Gulledge, T. R., Jun. and Litteral, L. A. (eds) (1989) *Cost Analysis Applications of Economics and Operations Research*, Springer-Verlag, New York.

Gulledge, T. R. and Womer, N. K. (1986) *The Economics of Made-to-Order Production*, Springer-Verlag, Berlin.

Gulledge, T. R., Jun., Womer, N. K. and Dorroh, J. R. (1984) Learning and costs in airframe production: a multiple output production function approach. *Naval Research Logistics Quarterly*, **31**, pp. 67–85.

Gulledge, T. R., Jun., Womer, N. K. and Murat Tarimcilar, M. (1985) A discrete dynamic optimization model for made-to-order cost analysis. *Decision Sciences*, **16**, pp. 73–90.

Gutierrez, G. J. and Kouvelis, P. (1991) Parkinson's law and its implications for project management. *Management Science*, **37**(8), pp. 990–1001.

Hacquebord, H. (1989) *Statistical Thinking for Leaders*, Training Manual.

Hahn, G. (1989) Statistics-aided manufacturing: a look into the future. *The American Statistician*, **43**, pp. 74–79.

Hahn, G. J. and Boardman, T. (1985) Statistical concepts for quality improvement: a new perspective. *Quality Progress*, **18**(10), pp. 30–36.

Hahn, G. J. and Cockrum, M. B. (1987) Adapting control charts to meet practical needs: a chemical processing application. *Journal of Applied Statistics*, **14**, pp. 33–50.

Harker, P. T. and Vargas, L. G. (1987) The theory of ratio scale estimation: Saaty's analytic hierarchy process. *Management Science*, **33**(11), pp. 1383–1403.

Harris, T. J. and MacGregor, J. F. (1987) Design of multivariate LQ controllers using transfer functions. *American Institute of Chemical Engineers Journal*, **33**, Oct.

Herzberg, F. (1968) One more time: how do you motivate employees? *Harvard Business Review*, **45**(1), pp. 53–62.

Hicks, C. R. (1982) *Fundamental Concepts in the Design of Experiments*, 3rd edn, Holt, Reinhart, and Winston, New York.

Hill, W. J. and Hunter, W. G. (1966) A review of response surface methodology. *Technometrics*, **8**, pp. 571–582.

Hirano, H. (1991) *JIT Implementation Manual: The Complete Guide to Just-in-Time Manufacturing*, Productivity Press, Inc., Cambridge, MA.

Hirchmann, W. B. (1964) Learning curve. *Chemical Engineering*, **71**(7), pp. 95–100.

Hoffman, F. S. (1950) Comments on the modified form of the air craft progress functions. *Report No. RN-464, The Rand Corporation*, Santa Monica, CA.

Hogg, R. V. and Ledolter, J. (1992) *Applied Statistics for Engineers and Physical Scientists*, MacMillan Publishing Co., New York.

Hordes, M. D. (1992) 10 burning questions concerning quality improvement. *Industrial Engineering*, **24**(9), pp. 56–57.

Howell, S. D. (1980) Learning curves for new products. *Industrial Marketing Management*, **9**(2), pp. 97–99.

Hradesky, J. L. (1988) *Productivity and Quality Improvements*, McGraw-Hill, New York.

Humphreys, K. K. (ed) (1984) *Project and Cost Engineer's Handbook*, 2nd edn, Marcel Dekkar, Inc.

Hunter, J. S. (1986) The exponentially weighted moving average. *Journal of Quality Technology*, **18**(4), pp. 203–210.

Imai, M. (1986) *Kaizen: The Key to Japan's Competitive Success*, Random House, New York.

Imhoff, E. A., Jun. (1978) The learning curve and its applications. *Management Accounting*, **59**(8), pp. 44–46.

Ishikawa, K. (1986) *Guide to Quality Control*, 2nd rev. edn, Quality Resources, White Plains, New York.

Ishikawa, K. (1990) *Introduction to Quality Control*, Quality Resources, White Plains, New York.

Jackson, J. E. (1977) Evaluate control procedures by examining errors in process adjustment. *Journal of Quality Technology*, **9**, pp. 47–55.

Jelen, F. C. and Black, J. H. (1983) *Cost and Optimization Engineering*, McGraw-Hill, NY.

Jewell, W. S. (1984) A generalized framework for learning curve reliability growth models. *Operations Research*, **32**(3), May–June, pp. 547–558.

Jobson, J. D. (1991) *Applied Multivariate Data Analysis, Volume I: Regression and Experimental Design*, Springer-Verlag, New York.

Johnson, R. A. and Bagshaw, M. (1974) The effect of serial correlation on the performance of CUSUM tests. *Technometrics*, **16**, pp. 103–112.

Joiner, B. (1985) The key role of statisticians in the transformation of North American industry. *The American Statistician*, **19**, pp. 229–234.

Juran, J. M. (1988) *Juran on Leadership for Quality*, The Free Press, New York.

Juran, J. M. (1989) *Juran on Planning for Quality*, The Free Press, New York.

Juran, J. M. and Gryna, F. M. Jun. (1980) *Quality Planning and Analysis*, 2nd edn, McGraw-Hill, New York.

Juran, J. M. and Gryna, F. M. (1988) *Juran's Quality Handbook*, 4th edn, McGraw-Hill, New York.

Kanagawa, A. and Ohta, H. (1990) Fuzzy design for fixed-number life tests. *IEEE Transactions on Reliability*, **39**(3), August, pp. 394–398.

Kane, V. (1989) *Defect Prevention Systems: Use of Simple Statistical Tools*, Marcel Decker, New York.

Kane, V. E. (1986) Process capability indices. *Journal of Quality Technology*, **18**(1), pp. 41–52.

Kaufman, A. and Gupta, M. M. (1987) *Fuzzy Mathematical Models in Engineering and Management Science*, North-Holland, New York.

Keats, J. B. and Hubele, N. F. (eds) (1989) *Statistical Process Control in Automated Manufacturing*, Marcel Dekker, New York.

Keeney, R. L. and Raiffa, H. (1976) *Decisions with Multiple Objectives; Preferences and Value Tradeoffs*, John Wiley, New York.

Kelly, M. R. (1991) *Everyone's Problem Solving Handbook: Step-by-Step Solutions for Quality Improvement*, Quality Resources, White Plains, New York.

Kenarangui, R. (1991) Event-tree analysis by fuzzy probability. *IEEE Transactions on Reliability*, **40**(1), April, pp. 120–124.

Knecht, G. R. (1974) Costing, technological growth and generalized learning curves. *Operations Research Quarterly*, **25**(3), Sept., pp. 487–491.

Kokoska, S. and Nevison, C. (1989) *Statistical Tables and Formulae*, Springer-Verlag, New York.

Koontz, H. and O'Donnel, C. (1959) *Principles of Management*, 2nd edn, McGraw-Hill, New York.

Kopcso, D. P. and Nemitz, W. C. (1983) Learning curves and lot sizing for independent and dependent demand. *Journal of Operations Management*, **4**(1), Nov., pp. 73–83.

Koulamas, C. (1992) Quality improvement through product redesign and the learning curve. *Omega*, **20**(2), pp. 161–168.

Kume, H. (1989) *Statistical Methods for Quality Improvement*, AOTS, Tokyo, Japan.

Lehr, L. (1989) Quality is a measure of company success. *IE Financial Services News*, Institute of Industrial Engineers, Norcross, Georgia, **XXIII**(2), Winter, p. 1.

Lester, R. H., Enrick, N. L. and Mottley, H. E. (1992) *Quality Control for Profit: Gaining the Competitive Edge*, 3rd edn, Marcel Dekker, Inc., New York.

Levy, F. K. (1965) Adaptation in the production process. *Management Science*, **11**(6), April, pp. B136–B154.

Liao, W. M. (1979) Effects of learning on resource allocation decisions. *Decision Sciences*, **10**, pp. 116–125.

Liepins, G. E. and Uppuluri, V. R. R. (eds) (1990) *Data Quality Control*, Marcel Dekker, Inc., New York.

Lighthall, F. F. (1991) Launching the space shuttle Challenger: disciplinary deficiencies in the analysis of engineering data. *IEEE Transactions on Engineering Management*, **38**(1), pp. 63–74.

Lillrank, P. and Kano,N. (1989) *Continuous Improvement: Quality Control Circles in Japanese Industry*, Center for Japanese Studies, The University of Michigan, Ann Arbor, MI.

Lochner, R. H. and Mater, J. E. (1990) *Designing for Quality: An Introduction to the Best of Taguchi and Western Methods of Statistical Experimental Design*, Quality Resources, White Plains, New York.

MacGregor, J. F. (1976) Optimal choice of the sampling interval for discrete process control. *Technometrics*, **18**(2), pp. 151–160.

MacGregor, J. F. (1987) Interfaces between process control and online statistical process control. *Computing and Systems Technology Division Communications*, **10**, pp. 9–20.

MacGregor, J. F. (1988) Statistical process control. *Chemical Engineering Progress*, **84**, pp. 21–31.

MacGregor, J. F. (1990) A different view of the funnel experiment. *Journal of Quality Technology*, **22**(4), Oct., pp. 255–259.

MacGregor, J. F. and Harris, J. H. (1990) Discussion of EWMA control schemes properties and enhancements. *Technometrics*, **32**(1), Feb., pp. 23–26.

MacGregor, J. F., Harris, T. J. and Wright, J. D. (1984) Duality between control of processes subject to randomly occurring deterministic disturbances and ARIMA stochastic disturbances. *Technometrics*, **26**, pp. 389–397.

Mallampati, D. and Shenoi, S. (1991) Accelerating learning in fuzzy logic controllers. *Proceedings of the Fifth Oklahoma Symposium on Artificial Intelligence*, Norman, OK, November, pp. 207–214.

Maslow, A. H. (1943) A theory of human motivation. *Psychological Review*, **1**, pp. 370–396.

McGregor, D. (1960) *The Human Side of Enterprise*, McGraw-Hill, New York.

McIntyre, E. V. (1977) Cost–volume–profit analysis adjusted for learning. *Management Science*, **24**(2), pp. 149–160.

Merli, G. (1990) *Total Manufacturing Management: Production Organization for the 1990s*, Productivity Press, Inc., Cambridge, MA.

Michaels, J. V. and Wood, W. P. (1989) *Design to Cost*, John Wiley, New York.

Mishne, P. P. (1988) A new attitude toward quality. *Manufacturing Engineering*, October, pp. 50–55.

Mizuno, S. (1988) *Company-wide Total Quality Control*, Asian Productivity Organization, Tokyo.

Mizuno, S. (ed.) (1988) *Management for Quality Improvement*, Quality Resources, White Plains, NY.

Montgomery, D. C. (1990) *Introduction to Statistical Quality Control*, 2nd edn, John Wiley, New York.

Montgomery, D. C. and Friedman, D. J. (1989) Statistical process control in a computer-integrated manufacturing environment, in *Statistical Process Control in Automated Manufacturing*, (eds J. B. Keats and N. F. Hubele), Marcel Dekker, New York, pp. 67–87.

Montgomery, D. C. and Mastrangelo, C. M. (1991) Some statistical process control methods for autocorrelated data. *Journal of Quality Technology*, **23**(3), July, pp. 179–193.

Myers, R. H. (1976) *Response Surface Methodology*, Virginia Polytechnic Institute, Blackburg, VA.

Myers, R. H., Khuri, A. I. and Vining, G. (1992) Response surface alternatives to the Taguchi robust parameter design approach. *The American Statistician*, May, **46**(2).

Naderi, B. and Baggerman, M. (1992) The result of ergonomics at the forefront in manufacturing quality. *Industrial Engineering*, **24**(4), April, pp. 42–46.

Nanda, R. (1979) Using learning curves in integration of production resources. *Proceedings of 1979 IIE Fall Conference*, pp. 376–380.

Negoita, C. V. and Ralescu, D. (1987) *Simulation, Knowledge-Based Computing, and Fuzzy Statistics*, Van Nostrand Reinhold, New York.

Nelson, C. R. (1973) *Applied Times Series Analysis for Mangerial Forecasting*, Holden-Day, Inc., San Francisco, CA.

Nelson, L. S. (1984) The Shewhart control chart – tests for special causes. *Journal of Quality Technology*, **16**(4), October, pp. 237–239.

Nelson, L. S. (1992) Control charts for individual measurements. *Journal of Quality Technology*, **14**(3), July.

Newman, W. H., Warren, E. K. and McGill, A. R. (1987) *The Process of Management: Strategy, Action, Results*, Prentice-Hall, Englewood Cliffs, NJ.

Noori, H. (1990) *Managing The Dynamics of New Technology: Issues in Manufacturing Management*, Prentice-Hall, Englewood Cliffs, NJ.

Obradovitch, M. M. and Stephanou, S. E. (1990) *Project Management: Risks and Productivity*, Daniel Spencer Publishers, Malibu, California.

Oi, W. Y. (1967) The neoclassical foundations of progress functions. *Economic Journal*, **77**, pp. 579–594.

Omachonu, V. K. (1991) *Total Quality and Productivity Management in Health Care Organizations*, Industrial Engineering and Management Press, Norcross, GA.

Osada, T. (1991) *The 5S's: Five Keys to a Total Quality Environment*, Asian Productivity Organization, Tokyo.

Ott, E. R. (1975) *Process Quality Control*, McGraw-Hill, New York.

Ott, E. R. and Schilling, E. G. (1990) *Process Quality Control: Troubleshooting and Interpretation of Data*, 2nd edn, McGraw-Hill, New York.

Page, E. S. (1954) *Continuous Inspection Schemes*, Biometrika, **41**, pp. 100–114.

Palm, A. C. (1990) SPC versus automatic process control. *ASQC Quality Congress Transactions*, San Francisco, pp. 694–699.

Park, K. S. and Kim, J. S. (1990) Fuzzy weighted checklist with linguistic variables. *IEEE Transactions on Reliability*, **39**(3), August, pp. 389–393.

Pegels, C. C. (1969) On startup or learning curves: an expanded view. *AIIE Transactions*, **1**(3), September, pp. 216–222.

Pegels, C. C. (1976) Start up or learning curves – some new approaches. *Decision Sciences*, **7**(4), Oct., pp. 705–713.

Pelphrey, M. W. (1992) Revolutionary changes are needed in manufacturing systems. *APICS*, April, pp. 33–36.

Persico, J., Jun. (ed.) (1992) *The TQM Transformation: A Model for Organizational Change*, Quality Resources, White Plains, New York.

Peterka, P. B. and Stephenson, W. R. (1990) Nested designs: a tool for process engineers. *Chemical Engineering Press*, April, pp. 12–15.

Plossi, G. W. (1992) Flexibility is now the key to survival for manufacturing. *APICS*, April, pp. 37–41.

Preston, L. E. and Keachie, E. C. (1964) Cost functions and progress functions: an integration. *American Economic Review*, **54**, pp. 100–106.

Quinn, J. B. (1985) Managing innovation: controlled chaos. *Harvard Business Review*, May–June, pp. 73–84.

Richardson, W. J. (1978) Use of learning curves to set goals and monitor progress in cost reduction programs. *Proceedings of 1978 IIE Spring Conference*, pp. 235–239.

Roberts, S. W. (1959) Control charts based on geometric moving averages. *Technometrics*, **1**, pp. 239–250.

Ross, P. J. (1988) *Taguchi Techniques for Quality Engineering*, McGraw-Hill, New York.

Russell, J. P. (1991) *Quality Management Benchmark Assessment*, Quality Resources, White Plains, New York.

Ryan, T. P. (1989) *Statistical Methods for Quality Improvement*, John Wiley and Sons, New York.

Saaty, T. L. (1977) A scaling method for priorities in hierarchical structures. *Journal of Mathematical Psychology*, **15**, June, pp. 235–281.

Saaty, T. L. (1980) *The Analytic Hierarchy Process*, McGraw-Hill, New York.

Saaty, T. L. and Vargas, L. G. (1984) Inconsistency and rank preservation. *Journal of Mathematical Psychology*, **18**, pp. 205–214.

Saaty, T. L., Vargas, L. G. and Wendell, R. (1983) Assessing attribute weights by ratios. *Omega*, **11**(1), pp. 9–13.

Scheer, A. W. (1989) *Enterprise-Wide Data Modelling: Information Systems in Industry*, Springer-Verlag, New York.

Scherkenback, W. W. (1990) *The Deming Route to Quality and Productivity: Roadmaps and Roadblocks*, Mercury Press/Fairchild Publications, New York.

Schonberger, R. J. (1984) *Just In Time: A Comparison of Japanese and American Manufacturing Techniques*, Industrial Engineering and Management Press, Norcross, GA.

Schultz, R. L., Slevin, D. P. and Pinto, J. K. (1987) Strategy and tactics in a process model of project implementation. *Interfaces*, May–June.

Scripps, T. A. (1991) Design of experiments. *3M Internal Publication*, Corporate Quality and Manufacturing Services, SPC Training Manual, St. Paul, MN.

Scripps, T. A. (1991) Process capability. *3M Internal Publication*, Corporate Quality and Manufacturing Services, SPC Training Manual, St. Paul, MN.

Scripps, T. A. (1991) Statistical process control. *3M Internal Publication*, Corporate Quality and Manufacturing Services, SPC Training Manual, St. Paul, MN.

Shewhart, W. A. (1931) *Economic Control of Quality*, Van Nostrand, New York.

Shewhart, W. A. (1931) *Statistical Method from the Viewpoint of Quality Control*, Dover, New York.

Smith, J. (1989) *Learning Curve for Cost Control*, Industrial Engineering and Management Press, Norcross, GA.

Smunt, T. L. (1986) A comparison of learning curve analysis and moving average ratio analysis for detailed operational planning. *Decision Sciences*, **17**(4), pp. 475–495.

Smunt, T. L. (1987) The impact of worker forgetting on production scheduling. *International Journal of Production Research*, **25**(5), pp. 689–701.

Snee, R. D. (1983) Graphical analysis of process variation studies. *Journal of Quality Technology*, **15**(2), April, pp. 76–88.

Somasundaram, S. and Badiru, A. B. (1992) Project management for successful implementation of continous quality improvement. *International Journal of Project Management*, **10**(2), May, pp. 89–101.

Son, Y. K. and Park, C. S. (1987) Economic measure of productivity, quality, and flexibility in advanced manufacturing systems. *Journal of Manufacturing Systems*, **6**, pp. 193–206.

Spradlin, B. C. and Pierce, D. A. (1967) Production scheduling under a learning effect by dynamic programming. *Journal of Industrial Engineering*, **18**(3), pp. 219–222.

Steeples, M. (1992) *The Corporate Guide to the Malcolm Baldrige National Quality Award*, Business-One Irwin, Homewood, IL.

Sule, D. R. (1978) The effect of alternate periods of learning and forgetting on economic manufacturing quantity. *AIIE Transactions*, **10**(3), pp. 338–343.

Taguchi, G. (1990) *Introduction to Quality Engineering: Designing Quality into Products and Processes*, Asian Productivity Organization, Tokyo.

Tanaka, H., Fan, L. T., Lai, F. S. and Toguchi, K. (1983) Fault-tree analysis by fuzzy probability. *IEEE Transactions on Reliability*, **32**(5), December, pp. 453–457.

Tapiero, C. S. (1987) Production learning and quality control. *IIE Transactions*, **19**(4), pp. 362–369.

Taylor, F. W. (1911) *Scientific Management*, Harper and Row Publishers, Inc., New York.

The InSetter (1992) What Does 'Quality' Mean to You in Performing Your Job. *The InSetter*, **4**(1), p. 7.

Thomas, P. R. (1990) *Competitiveness Through Total Cycle Time*, McGraw-Hill, New York.

Towill, D. R. and Kaloo, U. (1978) Productivity drift in extended learning curves. *Omega*, **6**(4), pp. 295–304.

Tucker, B. *et al.* (1989) Algorithmic statistical process control: experiences and challenges in integrating statistical process monitoring and engineering control, paper presented at the 1989 Quality and Productivity Research Conference, June 5–7, University of Waterloo, Ontario, Canada.

Tushman, M. L. and Moore, W. L. (eds) (1988) *Readings in the Management of Innovation*, Ballinger Publishing Co., Cambridge, MA.

Vargas, L. G. (1990) An overview of the analytic hierarchy process and its applications. *European Journal of Operational Research*, **48**, pp. 2–8.

Wadsworth, H. M., Stephens, K. S. and Godfrey, A. B. (1986) *Modern Methods for Quality Control and Improvement*, John Wiley, New York.

Waller, E. W. and Dwyer, T. J. (1981) Alternative techniques for use in parametric cost analysis. *Concepts – Journal of Defense Systems Acquisition Management*, **4**(2), Spring, pp. 48–59.

Walton, M. (1986) *The Deming Management Method*, Perigee Books/Putnam Publishing Group, New York.

Washburn, A. R. (1972) The effects of discounting profits in the presence of learning in the optimization of production rates. *AIIE Transactions*, **4**, pp. 205–213.

Wheeler, D. J. and Lyday, R. W. (1984) *Evaluating the Measurement Process*, 2nd edn, SPC Press Inc., New York.

Willborn, W. (1989) *Quality Management System: A Planning and Auditing Guide*, Industrial Press, Inc., New York.

Winchell, B. (1991) *Continuous Quality Improvement: A Manufacturing Professional's Guide*, Society of Manufacturing Engineers, Dearborn, Michigan.

Winchell, B. (ed.) (1992) *TQM: Getting Started and Achieving Results with Total Quality Management*, Society of Manufacturing Engineers, Dearborn, Michigan.

Wittry, E. J. (1987) *Managing Information Systems: An Integrated Approach*, Society of Manufacturing Engineers, Dearborn, MI.

Womer, N. K. (1979) Learning curves, production rate, and program costs. *Management Science*, **25**(4), pp. 312–19.

Womer, N. K. (1981) Some propositions on cost functions. *Southern Economic Journal*, **47**, pp. 1111–19.

Womer, N. K. (1984) Estimating learning curves from aggregate monthly data. *Management Science*, **30**(8), pp. 982–992.

Womer, N. K. and Gulledge, T. R., Jun. (1983) A dynamic cost function for an airframe production program. *Engineering Costs and Production Economics*, **7**, pp. 213–227.

Wright, T. P. (1936) Factors affecting the cost of airplanes. *Journal of Aeronautical Science*, **3**(2), February, pp. 122–128.

Yelle, L. E. (1976) Estimating learning curves for potential products. *Industrial Marketing Management*, **5**(2/3), June, pp. 147–154.

Yelle, L. E. (1979) The learning curve: historical review and comprehensive survey. *Decision Sciences*, **10**(2), April, pp. 302–328.

Yelle, L. E. (1980) Industrial life cycles and learning curves: interaction of marketing and production. *Industrial Marketing Management*, **9**(4), Oct. pp. 311–318.

Yelle, L. E. (1983) Adding life cycles to learning curves. *Long Range Planning*, **16**(6), Dec., pp. 82–87.

Yourstone, S. A. and Montgomery, D. C. (1989) Development of a real-time statistical process control algorithm. *Quality and Reliability Engineering International*, **5**, pp. 309–317.

Zadeh, L. A. (1965) Fuzzy Sets. *Information and Control*, **8**, pp. 338–353.

Zahedi, F. (1986) The analytic hierarchy process: a survey of the method and its applications. *Interfaces*, **16**, pp. 96–108.

Index

AHP, *see* Analytic hierarchy process
Algorithmic statistical process control
  (ASPC) 313
Analytic hierarchy process (AHP) 74
  flowchart 76
APC, *see* Automatic process control
ARIMA, *see* Autoregressive integrated
  moving average
  modeling 314
ARL, *see* Average run length
ASPC, *see* Algorithmic statistical process
  control
Automatic process control (APC) 310
Automation 34
Autoregressive integrated moving average
  (ARIMA) 303, 304
Average run length (ARL) 302

Benchmark–feedback model 60
Benchmarking 52
Brainstorming 65
Breakeven analysis 92
Business–customer integration loop 38

Capability index 240
Capable process 239
Central composite designs 295
Certification 39
Change
  to quality improvement 50
  resistance to 87
Check sheets 213
China productivity center 30
CMI, *see* Continuous measurable
  improvement
Commitment, of employee 87

Communication 61
Competitive edge 28
Competitive quality 29
Complexity, of product 43
Confidence intervals 261
Conflicts, resolving 173
Continuous measurable improvement
  (CMI) 72
Continuous process improvement (CPI) 69
Control
  charts 222
    plotting 229
  limits, calculation 228
  of project network 151
Conversion, of process 118
Cooperation 62
Coordination 62
Correction 51
Correlated observations 302
Cost control 170
CPI, *see* Continuous process improvement
CPM, *see* Critical path method
Critical activities 156
Critical path method (CPM) 150
Crosby
  contributions 26
  14 steps 27
CTD, *see* Cumulative trauma disorder
Cumulative sum (CUSUM) 302, 306
Cumulative trauma disease/disorder
  (CTD) 100
Customer-oriented, fuzzy reliability
  modeling 128
Customer-producer 3
Customer involvement 37
Customer surveys 73
CUSUM, *see* Cumulative sum

Data
  analysis 186
  collection 184, 224
Decision model 171
Delphi method 66
Deming
  contributions 18
  14 points 18
  PDCA cycle 19
  philosophy 18
  prize 21
Design, of experiments 256
Detection 51
Diagnosing a process 184, 210

EFTA, *see* European Free Trade
  Association
Employee
  involvement 41
  motivation 45
Ergonomics 99
European community 9
European Free Trade Association (EFTA)
  9
European influence, on quality 9
EWMA, *see* Exponentially weighted
  moving average
Experimental design 243, 256
Experimental run 271
Exponentially weighted moving average
  (EWMA) 302, 306

Factorial designs 268
Feasibility
  managerial 90
  technical 90
Feedback
  control 308
  loop 3
  model 60
Feigenbaum, contributions 26
Fishbone diagram 211
Flow charts 210
Flow diagram 177
Formal organization 141
Fractional factorial experiments 283
Frequency sampling 225
Functional organization 141
Fuzzy quality model 123
Fuzzy set 120
  membership grid 124

Gantt charts 158

Globalization 7
GNP (gross national product) 10
Group meetings 64

Hierarchy
  of needs 46
  of project components 132
Histogram 213
Human aspects 89
Hygiene factors 47
Hypothesis testing 263

IMA, *see* Integrated moving average
Implementation model, of project 136
Improvement strategies 181, 183
Industrial engineers 32
Informal organization 141
Integrated moving average (IMA) 304
International standard, for quality 10
Involvement 37, 39, 41
Ishikawa, contributions 25
ISO 10
  9000 10

Japanese Industrial Standards 25
Japanese influence, on quality 8
JIT, *see* Just-in-time
Juran
  contributions 24
  ten steps 24
Just-in-time (JIT) 6

Key quality characteristics 176

Leadership 32, 140
Learn–forget models 110
Learning curves 101
Loss function 22

Malcolm Baldrige Award 12
Management
  by exception (MBE) 48
  by objective (MBO) 48
  support 49
Managerial feasibility 90
Matrix organization 143
MBE, *see* Management by exception
MBO, *see* Management by objective
Means, comparison of 258
Measurement scales 184

Minimum inventory production system (MIPS) 6
Minimum variance control (MVC) 316
Minnesota quality award 14
MIPS, *see* Minimum inventory production system
Mixed organization 145
Monitoring, of a process 178
Motivation, of employee 45
Motivators 47
Motorola, six sigma approach 28
Multivoting 68
MVC, *see* Minimum variance control

Needs, hierarchy of 46
Nested design 243
Nominal group technique 67
Normal probability distribution 206

Objectives, consolidaiton of 144
Opportunity flowchart 177
Organization
    matrix model 143
    of product 142
    of project 141
Orthogonality 274
Out-of-control patterns 225

Pareto diagram 211
PDCA cycle, *see* Plan–Do–Check–Act
Performance control 170
Phase-out, of project 135
Plan–Do–Check–Act (PDCA) 19–20
Planning
    levels of 50
    for quality 50
Polar plots 52
Policy 21
    for quality 139
Politics, organizational 88
Precedence constraints 151
Prevention 51
Priority, lack of 87
Problem identification 133
Process
    adjustment 314
    capability 85, 235
    conversion 118
    data
        analysis 186
        ARIMA modeling 314
    definition 84
    flow diagram 177

formulation 174
improvement
    barriers 87
    managerial aspects 128
management 174
monitoring 178
performance 84
technology transfer 116
transition 86
variation 179
Product
    complexity 43
    organization 142
    planning 43
    redesign 90
Profit ratio 96
Project
    control 135, 166
    definition 133
    implementation model 136
    leadership 140
    management 130
        steps 132
    manager, selection of 145
    organization 141
    organizing 134
    phase-out 135
    planning 133, 147
    plan, selling of 138
    reporting 135
    scheduling 134, 148
    specifications 138
    tracking 135, 147

QFD, *see* Quality function deployment
Quality
    assurance 29
    barriers 87
    business definitions 38
    characteristics 176
    circles 64
    control 29
    customer definition 38
    definition 2
    degradation 70
    function deployment (QFD) 72
    functions 4
    impact of forgetting 116
    improvement 36
        flowchart 37
        group meetings 64
        hypothesis testing 263
    manual 139

of manufactured goods 42
movement 8
policy 139
–productivity, relationship 73
of service 44
survey of meaning 45
–time–resource, tradeoff 167
–value analysis 92

Randomization 258, 274
Rationalization 34
Redesign, of product 90
Reliability 91
Replication 274
Resource
  allocation 134
  consideration 160
  leveling graph 165
  loading graph 164
Response surface methodology 290
Responsibility
  clear 88
  matrix 62
Run chart 178

Sample size 185, 224
Saturated designs 288–9
Scatter plots 212
Schedule control 168
SEA, see Single Europe Act
Service, quality of 44
Single Europe Act (SEA) 9
Six sigma 28
Slippage, of project 160
SPC, see Statistical process control
Specifications, of project 138
Stable process 182, 225
Statement of work 138
Statistical process control (SPC) 85, 222, 310
  for short runs 252
Statistics 198
Steering committee 70
Strategic planning 50
Subgroup sample size 224
Systems 2
  integration 4, 38

Taguchi
  contributions 22
  loss function 22
Taiwan 30
Technical feasibility 90
Technology
  obsolescence 88
  transfer 116
TEI, see Total employee involvement
Theory X 45, 46
Theory Y 45, 46
Time series analysis 302
Total customer satisfaction 128
Total employee involvement (TEI) 42
Total quality control 26
Total Quality Management (TQM) 4–6
  benefits 5
  characteristics 5
  justification 5
Trade-off relationships 168
Trend analysis 334
Triple C model 60, 173
Type I error 264
Type II error 264
Types of data 223

Unstable process 182
User training 39

Vendor
  certification 39
  involvement 39
  rating system 40
  selection 214

WBS, see Work breakdown structure
Work breakdown structure (WBS) 146
World class manufacturing 128

Zero defect 128
Zero inventory production system (ZIPS) 6
ZIPS, see Zero inventory production system